THE BELLE OF BEDFORD AVENUE

TRUE CRIME HISTORY

THE BELLE OF BEDFORD AVENUE

The Sensational Brooks-Burns Murder in

Turn-of-the-Century New York

Virginia A. McConnell

THE KENT STATE UNIVERSITY PRESS

Kent, Ohio

© 2019 by The Kent State University Press, Kent, Ohio 44242
All rights reserved
ISBN 978-1-60635-366-0
Manufactured in the United States of America

Cataloging information for this title is available at the Library of Congress.

23 22 21 20 19   5 4 3 2 1

This book is dedicated to my wonderful cousin, David J. Thompson, and his partner of forty-two years, John P. Elliott, who were extremely obliging and indulgent of me during my 2016 trip to New York City in search of remnants of the first decade of the twentieth century, especially those touching upon the events in this book. What good sports they were to traipse all around Brooklyn and The Evergreens Cemetery with me!

Sadly, David passed away somewhat suddenly on July 7, 2017. Nobody loved and knew New York City, past and present, more than he.

CONTENTS

ACKNOWLEDGMENTS

Apart from my cousin David and my other "cousin" John, I owe a debt of gratitude to the Wildrick family for sharing the memories of their "Uncle Tad" and for the wonderful picture of him as a young man.

Thanks, as always, to the Walla Walla Community College librarian, Jackson Vance Matthews, for ordering the microfilm for this project and for following up with the lending libraries to insure prompt delivery.

The personnel at The Evergreens Cemetery in Brooklyn could not have been nicer or more helpful. A caretaker named Tony, who has been at Evergreens since the 1970s and knows it like the back of his hand, drove us to the Burns and Brooks sites, regaling us with colorful stories the whole time. As those sites have no memorial markers, we would never have found them, despite knowing the area where they were located. Tony brought the cemetery maps that indicated the names of all the "inhabitants" of each plot and the special code for finding them.

A big thanks to the John Jay College of Law (although they did not do it solely for my benefit!) for their archived microfilm collection of old New York City trial transcripts. The trial transcript for *People v. Brooks and Wildrick* provided much valuable insight and background into Florence and Eddie, which otherwise would not have been available because of the press's silence on this case.

My friend and neighbor Harriet Aiken gave me the insight into why Mrs. Burns might not have provided directly for her daughter Gladys in her will. Harriet was also the captive audience for all my queries, theories, setbacks, discoveries, and triumphs during our long hikes over the scope of this project.

Frances Luka, who is collaterally related to "Handsome Harry" Casey, provided me with much genealogical information on the Casey family.

INTRODUCTION

Those who think of the beginning years of the twentieth century as a time when children were obedient, disciplined, and never troublesome will quickly be disabused of that notion with the behavior of the young people encountered in this book. The notion of "the teenager" as a social construct with its own culture is usually thought to have begun in the post–World War II era, but the turn-of-the-century teens in this book were way ahead of their time in creating theirs.

Probably the young people of every era have rebelled against previous generations, but those coming of age in the early 1900s were almost catapulted into making a break from their parents and grandparents because of the great advances in technology: the invention of the automobile, along with cheaper public transportation going to more and more places, rendering chaperonage of young people impractical, plus an increase in venues for entertainment, such as Coney Island, walking contests, and vaudeville. Rebellion was shown in alcohol consumption at roadhouses and saloons that seemed to have no restrictions on whom to serve, in cigarette smoking by both sexes, and in patronizing dodgy dance halls and listening to ragtime music.

Yet, for all of that, these particular teenagers and young adults of Brooklyn and Manhattan were rebels without a cause, as they wanted for nothing: They were first- and second-generation offspring of immigrants from Ireland, Germany, and the British Isles, immigrants who had been incredibly successful in their New World ventures. Some of these youngsters had access to yachts, automobiles, summer homes, and secret hideaway apartments. They were able to stay away from home for days and sometimes weeks at a time, leaving their beleaguered parents, with their old-world ways, at a loss as to what to do to control them.

The Brooks-Burns murder case uncovered for public consumption the existence of a subculture of teenagers and young adults with a driven, relentless, almost creative dedication to actions that would shock, to a commitment to going off the rails, and to a determination to thumb their noses at convention. This early Brat Pack seemed to have had as its motto, "You're not the boss of us. We make the rules now." The more they were allowed to skate on the consequences of their behavior, the more they were convinced that it was true: They *were* in charge of their lives. Until they tragically were not.

This attitude evokes the heady hedonism of being young and in rebellion against something or nothing, in mutual self-affirmation with one's peers. I was a young adult in the 1960s and so much about these turn-of-the-century kids reminded me of that era, when "the times they were a-changin'" and the worst sin was to trust anyone over thirty. We had our own music, our own language, our own clothing styles, and that same sense of being beyond the command of what we thought were clueless adults.

The Belle of Bedford Avenue focuses on one such young woman, the arc of her life, and her deep fall from grace before she—as most of us eventually do—found herself, albeit after a very long time. The trouble in which she found herself in 1902 provides us with a window into the world of her peers, the influence of a new century, and mostly the changing ethical culture, symbolized by places like her beloved Coney Island, her generation's fantastical Disneyland, which provided an escape from the dreary expectations and watchful eyes of their parents. It is this woman and the other young people, most of whom never reached old age, who form the center of this book.

We also come up against the Unwritten Law in its application to what were considered to be helpless women who had no men in their lives who could or would avenge their honor, and so they had to do it for themselves. Before this, the Unwritten Law was primarily the "privilege" of men. And the age-old con of the Badger Game, still used today, is encountered here in a highly entertaining Grand Guignolesque farce that ultimately ended in sadly tragic consequences.

If you were a sentient being in the first decade of the twentieth century, you would be listening/singing/dancing to Scott Joplin's music (primarily "The Entertainer"), "In the Good Old Summer Time," "Bill Bailey, Won't You Please Come Home," "Tell Me Pretty Maiden (Are There Any More at Home Like You)," "School Days," "You're a Grand Old Flag," "Sweet Adeline," and "My Gal Sal" (written by the brother of author Theodore Dreiser)—songs, for the most part, familiar to twenty-first-century people as well. The energetic Theodore Roosevelt was your president. You probably went to the circus or to a vaudeville presentation or to an early silent-picture show or to one of the many hotels that held regular dances. If you were a child, you read dime novels and collected baseball cards. Yes, it was an "electric" (literally and figuratively) time to be alive!

The Brooks-Burns case presented many research difficulties. There was never an actual trial, so there was no transcript. The number of people who testified under oath at the hearing was only a very small percentage of those who were interviewed by the district attorney's office. (The importance of a cross-examination at trial cannot be overstated.) As a result, there was a lot of rumor and innuendo, some of which was undoubtedly false. Sometimes it was possible to determine which rumors were accurate and which were not, but the primary method I used was to see if they appeared in more than one newspaper as a kind of checks-and-balances system. Reported statements against the speaker's interest by someone involved in the case were usually taken as true, especially if there were no objections made to them by the authors of those statements.

Although William Randolph Hearst's *New York Journal* was a "yellow" newspaper and therefore not 100 percent reliable, I was sorry not to have access to it for a more complete picture of the people involved in the Brooks-Burns hearings. Alas, the *Journal* is not available digitally or through interlibrary loan of the microfilm. The newspapers I primarily relied on were the *New York Times*, the *Brooklyn Daily Eagle* (most of the people involved were from Brooklyn, so it was thoroughly covered by this newspaper), and Joseph Pulitzer's *New York World* (also considered a "yellow" newspaper).

Those who would like to compare yesterday's dollar figures with today's, for a more complete picture of the times, should consult Samuel H. Williamson's *Purchasing Power of Money in the United States from 1774 to the Present* (MeasuringWorth, 2018). It is available at www.measuringworth.com/ppowerus and is an invaluable tool for an economic perspective on the past. What to us would be weekend pocket money could very likely represent a significant sum to people back at the turn of the century. Here are some dollar equivalents for several of the years treated in this book:

1894–1902: $28.80
1908: $26.90
1910: $26.10
1922: $14.30
1937: $16.70

Once again, I am amazed at how successful those early journalists were in depicting "you-are-there" scenes for their readers. Without the benefit of our modern-day visual media in that era, consumers of newspapers could rely on knowing exactly what people involved in a court case wore, as well as their facial expressions, their reactions, the contents of the lunches spectators brought to make sure they did not risk losing their seats, and even the sounds and smells. Hemingway's quote about good books could equally apply to what those journalists did back then, enabling today's readers to "feel that all that happened to you and afterwards it all belongs to you: the good and the bad, the ecstasy, the remorse and sorrow, the people and the places and how the weather was."

DRAMATIS PERSONAE

The Glen Island Hotel

JOHN EARL: Night clerk at the Glen Island who signed in Walter Brooks and his female companion under an assumed name; he delayed calling an ambulance for the victim because he did not want to "cause a fuss" and bring bad publicity to the hotel

JOHN C. HAGENAH: The hotel's day clerk who was the only one who thought to go through the victim's pockets for identification

DR. JOHN V. SWEENEY: The neighborhood physician usually called in by the Glen Island for emergencies; he tended to the victim, Walter Brooks, although in the poor lighting, did not notice the bullet wound in the back of the head until daylight

GEORGE WASHINGTON: African American bellhop, temporarily taking over for his sick brother; he ushered Walter Brooks and the woman with him to their room and was later able to identify the woman as Florence Burns

The Brooks Family

MARY WILLIAMS BROOKS: Walter's mother

THOMAS W. BROOKS: Walter's father; found a woman's comb in the Glen Island hotel room and turned it over to a police officer at his home; he informed the police that Florence Burns had made threats against his son

WALTER S. BROOKS: Age twenty, the victim

The Burns Family

FLORENCE WALLACE BURNS: Age nineteen in 1902, accused of shooting Walter Brooks

FREDERICK BURNS: Florence's father, an insurance broker and nationally recognized announcer of amateur athletic events

GLADYS (GLADYSS) BURNS: Florence's sister, three years younger; although she was home the night of the shooting at the Glen Island, she claimed that she had been in bed when her sister allegedly returned home at 7:00 P.M.; Gladys, along with her parents, fled the state to avoid being subpoenaed to testify at Florence's hearing

HENRIETTA BURNS (sometimes known as Anna): Florence's mother; Henrietta's father had been an engineer in the construction of the Brooklyn Bridge

HARRY WEST METTAIS: Gladys's first husband; the marriage lasted only a couple of years

OSCAR VON DERBOSCH: Florence's uncle; financed her legal costs and provided her with a "hideaway" to avoid a subpoena during the inquest

WILLIAM O. VON DERBOSCH: Oscar's son; lived in Brooklyn with the Burnses and possibly knew exactly when Florence arrived home after the shooting at the Glen Island

The Brooks and Wells Commission Merchants Office

WALTER S. BROOKS: Partner; they dealt in sales to grocery stores

HENRY L. "HARRY" COHEN: Silent partner; Harry was notified of the shooting at the Glen Island because of the business card found in Walter's pocket; was also an important witness to meetings between Florence and Walter and to Walter's fear of being shot by either Florence or her father

JOSEPH "JOE" CRIBBINS: Age fifteen, office boy; was a witness to the times Florence came to the Brooks and Wells office each day during the week Walter was killed

THOMAS C. "T. C." WELLS: Partner

The Bedford Avenue Gang

THEODORE BURRIS: Close friend of Walter Brooks and Harry Casey; an inveterate scam artist, bully, and seducer of women

HARRY "HANDSOME HARRY" CASEY: The leader of the gang; had dated Florence and introduced her to Walter

WILLIAM MAXWELL "MAX" FINCK: Testified at the inquest that he had seen Florence carry a pistol in her muff and witnessed her point it at Ed Watson in a rage

GEORGE F. JACKSON: Was sentenced to Elmira with Max Finck for forgery

SAMUEL T. MADDOX JR.: Close friend of Harry Casey's and a frequent guest at the Caseys' summer home in the Catskills

EDWARD COLE "HANDSOME ED" WATSON JR.: Dated Florence and took her virginity

JOSEPH "JOE" WILSON: Dated Florence and also testified that he had seen her pistol inside her muff; she had told him that Walter would "suffer for it" if the rumors were true that he was seeing another girl

Young People Affiliated with Florence Burns and/or the Bedford Gang

MABEL COOPER: Confidante of Florence, who hinted to Mabel that she was pregnant and had been evicted from her home by her parents

RUTH M. DUNNE: Age seventeen in 1902, was Walter's last girlfriend; he spent nearly every day with her the last week of his life, and on the night of the shooting, he broke a date with her so he could give Florence a "big blowout" before she left for Detroit

CHARLOTTE "LOTTIE" EATON: Was engaged at one time to Walter Brooks but broke it off over his affiliation with the Bedford Gang and other "moral lapses"

HARRY GIMPEL: Dated Florence in the months before the shooting of Walter Brooks; they may have even been engaged, but Florence broke it off

HAROLD LEON "HARRY" THEALL: Florence's first "beau"; when she began stalking him after he broke up with her, his family sent him away to prep school

Other Residents of Brooklyn and Manhattan

GEORGE BADER: German-born entrepreneur, the owner of the prestigious Bader's Road House near Coney Island, a popular "watering place" for Florence and her young friends

MRS. HARRIET BIRDSALL: Another landlady; advised Florence to make up with her parents and go home

MRS. ELLA B. HITCHCOCK: Landlady of a boardinghouse where Florence stayed; Florence moved out when Mrs. Hitchcock scolded her for her "loose morals"

REV. ROBERT ROGERS: The minister who refused to marry Walter and Florence; he preached the sermon at Walter's funeral

HELEN SOUTHGATE: A young woman whose murder-suicide story was eerily similar to what Florence may have told her family and her lawyer; Helen wrote a letter of encouragement to Florence

Attorneys and Officers of the Court (Hearing and Inquest)

DETECTIVE COLBY PARKER, DETECTIVE RIORDAN, DETECTIVE SCHULTZ: Investigating officers who questioned Florence at her home and at the police station; their testimony as to what she said was thrown out by the judge at the hearing

FOSTER L. BACKUS: Florence's defense attorney; he fought long and hard for her, never giving quarter; it was such a strain on him that he suffered a nervous breakdown

NICHOLAS T. BROWN: Coroner who presided at the inquest

REBECCA SALOME FOSTER: The "Tombs Angel" who supported and encouraged Florence; she may also have received permission for Florence to have extra exercise, a privilege reserved for pregnant women

WILLIAM TRAVERS JEROME: District attorney and prosecutor; Walter Brooks's murder was one of his first cases after his election

JUSTICE JULIUS MAYER: Presiding judge at the preliminary hearing whose controversial decision to exclude Florence's damaging admissions was a crushing blow to the prosecution

GEORGE SCHURMAN: Assistant district attorney; much of the responsibility of the hearing fell on his shoulders

Witnesses (Not Encountered Elsewhere)

WILLIAM ARMIT "FATTY" EYRE: A young man who claimed to have been a friend of Walter Brooks's; he may have witnessed a spat between Walter and Florence.

DR. PHILIP JOHNSON: Assisted the coroner in the autopsy of Walter Brooks

JULIA MCCARTHY: A maid at one of the boardinghouses where Florence stayed; she found a hair comb in Florence's room that closely matched the description of the one found at the Glen Island

THOMAS SMITH: A newspaper stand operator at the Brooklyn end of the Beverley Street trolley; he, too, knew Florence by sight and name and witnessed her getting on the 11:15 P.M. car

DR. ALBERT T. WESTON: The coroner who inexplicably came up with a verdict of suicide in the death of Walter Brooks, although Justice Mayer threw that out and declared that it was, in fact, murder

ARTHUR CLEVELAND WIBLE: Age nineteen, the trolley conductor who saw Florence on his train the night of the shooting at the Glen Island; he knew her by sight and often nodded to her

POSTHEARING LIFE, 1902–9

REV. JOHN H. ELLIOTT: The minister who married Florence and Tad Wildrick

HYDE & BEHMAN: A famous Brooklyn Vaudeville theater, where Florence began her career

IRVING PINOVER: Florence's theatrical agent

MABEL STRONG: Tad Wildrick's fiancée (prior to Florence) whose tragic death was fodder for sensational newspaper articles

CHARLES WHITE "TAD" WILDRICK: Florence's first husband

The 1910 Badger Game Incident

PAUL ADAMSON: The taxi driver

ELDRIDGE HILDRETH "EDDIE" BROOKS: Florence's live-in lover and Badger Game partner

GRACE BROOKS: Eddie's mother

MIRIAM BROOKS: Eddie's sister

HON. THOMAS C. CRAIN: Presiding judge

FRANK FANELLI: The clerk at the Surprise Dept. Store, where Hurlburt took refuge

F. WAYLAND FOSTER: Charles Hurlburt's maternal uncle who was a friend and confidant in the Manhattan area

CELESTINE GRYGIEL: The landlady where Florence and Eddie were renting a room; she was shocked to find out that Eddie was not Florence's husband, although Florence had told her that he was

MARTIN HELD (probably not his real name): Eddie Brooks's partner in the attack on Charles Hurlburt

PATROLMAN JOHN HEWITT: Advised Hurlburt and later arrested Eddie Brooks

CHARLES WAYLAND HURLBURT: A lawyer and Florence's occasional lover; the victim in the Badger Game who turned the tables on his tormenters by pressing charges

LYMAN HURLBURT: Charles's deceased father

CLARK L. JORDAN: Eddie's defense attorney

MRS. MARY KAVANAUGH: Landlady at the boardinghouse where Charles Hurlburt took his meals

CHARLES C. NOTT: Prosecutor in the trial of *The People v. Wildrick and Brooks*

ROBERT H. ROY: Florence's defense attorney

AUBURN PRISON AND INTERIM YEARS, 1910–24

EDNA MABEL ATWATER: Eddie Brooks's wife

CARYL BENSEL: Tad Wildrick's second wife

GERTRUDE HARRISON CASEY: Harry Casey's second wife

MR. FINLAY (first name unknown): Florence's second husband

COL. EDWARD S. JENNINGS: Warden at Auburn Prison for Florence's second stint there

ETHEL KAHL: Friend and protegeé of Ruth Dunne, who was a bad influence on Ethel

JOHN WILLIAM MURPHY: Ruth Dunne's husband

ALONZO FREDERICK RUTLEDGE: Florence's third husband

JOHN VINCENT STANKEVICH: Florence's fourth husband

WILLIAM WASHINGTON: African American musician with whom Florence was arrested for being drunk and disorderly

MURDER AT GROUND ZERO

For George Washington, the patriotically named African American bellboy at the Glen Island Hotel in Manhattan, there was truth to the adage that "no good deed goes unpunished." He was actually employed at the Everett House Hotel, but his brother was sick and had asked him to fill in at the Glen Island for the night shift. What happened there on Valentine's Day in 1902 would turn young Washington's life upside down.[1]

Built on land that was originally owned by Robert Fulton of steamboat fame, the Glen Island Hotel was designated as a "Raines Law" hotel, one that sprang up as a way of circumventing the restrictions of New York's 1896 attack on Sunday alcohol consumption by the lower classes. The term "Raines Law hotel" became a euphemism for a "seedy" and "sleazy" establishment, one frequented by prostitutes and couples with no luggage. The Glen Island, at 88–92 Cortlandt Street, was such a place, a "hotel where no questions were asked," and was almost never mentioned without the tag line "a Raines Law hotel," with all that the term implied.[2] With its convenient access to the Brooklyn Bridge, the Glen Island was popular with young people "with no luggage" from both Brooklyn and Manhattan. Almost one hundred years later, this location would be the site of the World Trade Center and Ground Zero.

At 9:00 that Friday night, three young couples arrived within several minutes of each other. None had luggage. None indicated any kind of connection with the others. The women went into a little parlor up a set of stairs to wait for their men to register. The first man to approach the desk signed in as "H. Johnson and wife" and was given Room 32. The second man, before signing the book, asked for the cheapest room they had, then handed over $2 (the equivalent of $56.80 today), as well as $60 for the hotel safe, and registered as "J. Wilson and wife, Brooklyn, N.Y." He and his "wife" were assigned to

The Glen Island Hotel, to the left of the photo, 1908. In 2001, it would be the site of the World Trade Center and Ground Zero. (Library of Congress, det1994020530/PP/)

Room 12. The third man and his companion, "F. Dean and wife," were sent to Room 33.[3]

John Earl, the night clerk at the Glen Island, was fat, fifty, six feet tall, and described by the newspapers as not very bright.[4] He had adopted the admonition of the Three Monkeys to "see no evil, hear no evil, speak no evil" and, as much as possible, avoided calling any negative attention to doings inside the hotel. He was not alone in this approach, which undoubtedly reflected the philosophy of the owner, August Quick. One Glen Island chambermaid, Kate Doyle, declared that she was "paid to see nothing and she always earned her money."[5] The hotel also had a local doctor, John Vincent Sweeney, on twenty-four-hour call for emergencies, which frequently avoided the necessity of having to summon police and unfamiliar medical responders.

George Washington was directed to escort the second couple (J. Wilson and wife) to Room 12, which was in the old section of the building. Unlike John Earl, Washington was perceptive and astute. The woman was wearing a big black picture hat with a dark veil that hid her face and her hair color, and

George Washington, the bellhop at the Glen Island Hotel. (*New York World*)

he was curious to see what she really looked like. As they went up the stairs, the bellboy turned at the landing to make sure they were still following him. At that very moment, the woman was lifting her veil above her eyebrows and he got a good look at her. He noticed how well she was dressed too: She wore a tight-fitting, black waist-length Eton jacket and a black dress. Because of the low lighting and the black veil, Washington had the impression that her complexion and her hair were both dark.[6]

In Room 12, Washington lit both gas jets, then turned to ask if they needed anything else. He addressed his question to the woman and looked directly at her. He would not forget her strikingly beautiful face.

Around 10:30, there was a room service call from Room 12, which George Washington responded to. The woman opened the door only four or five inches but did not reveal herself other than her hand on the door. The room was dark and the bellboy could not see into it, but he got the impression that she was not completely dressed. She requested a lemon soda and some matches. When he brought them, she once again opened the door only partially, stuck out her bare arm to take the drink and the matches, then gave him 15¢: 10¢ for the soda and a 5¢ tip.

An hour later, on his way back down the hallway from delivering drinks to the couple in Room 32, Washington smelled gas. He traced it to Room 12, opened the unlocked door, lit a match (probably not the wisest choice, given the gas smell), and saw the man lying on the bed. The woman was not in the room. Frightened, Washington did not want to enter but instead went to find John Earl, who was finally able to sit down and eat his dinner in the hotel restaurant. Earl was reluctant to leave his dinner and hoped this was not turning into a medical emergency requiring outside intervention. He told Washington to go back up there and find out what was going on in Room 12. The bellboy balked at going alone, so twenty-seven-year-old waiter John Anema was sent with him.

Washington refused to go into the room and, in fact, never entered it again in his short stint with the Glen Island. He stood in the doorway while John Anema went in to turn off one of the gas jets and light the other. "Is he dead?" Washington asked. That's how bad "J. Wilson" looked. "I don't know," Anema responded, but he did not touch the man on the bed. They stayed there for a few minutes, discussing what they should do, and eventually went back to report to Earl, who resignedly abandoned his dinner and went up to check on the patron.

John Earl did not see any wound on the unconscious guest on the bed in Room 12, but there was some blood on the pillowcase, and he could see that the man had vomited. He spoke to him but got no response. At this point, he should have sent for an ambulance, but he did not. Instead, he went to the cashier, William Piper, to ask what should be done. Piper advised calling the doctor. Dr. John V. Sweeney arrived at 1:15 A.M., nearly two hours after George Washington first reported the smell of gas to John Earl.[7]

Dr. Sweeney found the young man shivering and shaking, with signs of asphyxiation, as well as a slight smell of chloral hydrate (a prescription knock-out drug most commonly used as a sleep aid) around his mouth. The wound on the man's head was attributed to his possibly falling after passing out from the gas. The doctor washed the wound, administered strychnine and nitroglyc-erine to combat the effects of the gas and chloral, and advised Earl to call an ambulance. Earl, however, did not want to "cause a fuss," so did nothing. He was hoping that the problem would resolve itself by morning, and he downplayed the whole thing, later claiming the smell of gas was not very strong, whereas the bellboy had said it nearly knocked him over when he opened the door. Dr. Sweeney left around 2:30 A.M.[8]

Nothing else was done with the possibly dying guest until the next morning at 7:00, when someone was sent to check on him. Not only was he still unconscious but now there was quite a bit of blood on the sheets and pillow. Dr. Sweeney was sent for again, arrived at 7:30, and then in the better light realized that the victim had a bullet wound, not a wound from a fall. The bullet had entered the back of his head from a point approximately two inches to the left of his right ear and on a line with the top of the ear, then had traveled downward to the chin. Dr. Sweeney, thinking that he had been called to examine a different man from the one the night before, had not brought his instruments and had to go back to his home to get them, returning at 8:30. He attempted to probe for the bullet but could not find it. Nor could anyone find a gun in the room.

The wound had a burn mark around it but no powder marks, indicating that the gun had been placed right up against the victim's head, and the downward angle meant that the shooter had stood over him to do it.

Once again, Dr. Sweeney advised Earl and the staff to call an ambulance, which was finally done at about 9:00 A.M. By this time, the day clerk, John C. Hagenah, had arrived and immediately went up to Room 12. The man on the bed was naked and his clothes were strewn about the room. Of all the hotel staff, Hagenah was the only one who thought to look through the victim's coat and pants pockets. There, he found thirty-two dollars in bills, a few coins, a note signed by a girl named Ruth, and business cards indicating his real name: Walter S. Brooks, a commission merchant with Brooks and Wells at 17 Jay Street in Manhattan. He was twenty years old.[9]

Instead of calling the police, however, someone from the hotel phoned the number on the business card and spoke with one of Brooks's partners, twenty-six-year-old Henry L. "Harry" Cohen. Cohen, in turn, called the Brooks home and spoke with Walter's father, Thomas W. Brooks. The elder Brooks hurried to the hotel, where he found his son still alive but unconscious. John Hagenah gave him the money from the billfold ($32) and the safe ($60), a watch, and other items belonging to his son.[10]

As they waited for the ambulance to arrive (curiously, it did not do so for almost two hours), Thomas Brooks did two things: He picked up a woman's celluloid hair comb from the dresser and put it in his pocket. Then he made an astonishing statement to the two policemen (summoned to the scene by Dr. Sweeney and not by anyone at the Glen Island) regarding his son's condition: "Officers, I am not surprised. I have expected this for a long time. My boy has been in scrapes with girls before this and I expected this would happen. A girl named Florence Burns has made threats against my son."[11]

THE BEDFORD AVENUE GANG

The generation coming of age in New York in the new century, many of them children and grandchildren of immigrants, were rebelling against what they saw as a restrictive code of behavior. Much like the baby boomers who grew up in the 1960s, the turn-of-the-century sons and daughters of the prosperous middle class, children of privilege, wanted to do things a different way from the generations before them. They had their own music (ragtime), their own clothing styles (colored vests for the boys, "rainy-day" dresses that revealed girls' ankles, and automobile coats for both).[1] They frequented forbidden dance halls; hung out at Coney Island; drank beer, gin rickeys, and martini cocktails at roadhouses; and had sex—all while still in their teens.

FLORENCE BURNS

Even by her own admission, Florence Wallace Burns was out of control from an early age. Born on Easter Sunday, April 9, 1882, to the daughter of strict German immigrants and the son of strict Scottish immigrants, Florence early on adopted the code of her peers: to do what she wanted when she wanted and with whom she wanted. Her parents were at a loss as to what to do with her.[2]

Frederick Burns, Florence's father, was a successful insurance broker in Manhattan, but his real claim to fame was as an announcer of athletic events—track, field, walking contests, bicycle racing, and just about anything under the auspices of the Amateur Athletic Union. He was widely known and respected as "the silver-tongued Fred Burns" and kept a .32-caliber starter's pistol in the home for those occasions when he was responsible for signaling the beginning of an event as well as announcing it. (Both Florence and

Florence Burns (*New York World,* from a portrait)

her mother were excellent markswomen with this pistol and had even won prizes for target shooting.)[3]

Mrs. Burns was the former Henrietta Von derBosch. Her father, Wilhelm Friedrich Von derBosch, had been one of John Roebling's chief engineers in the construction of the Brooklyn Bridge, completed in 1883 when Florence was one year old.[4]

Florence did not do well in school. For one thing, she was lazy. For another, she was more interested in boys than in her studies. Finally, although she was very beautiful and desirable, the many young men she dated declared her ultimately boring and a dullard when the physical attraction wore off. Consequently, although most of her friends, both male and female, attended the local high schools—primarily Erasmus and the Brooklyn Boys' High School—Florence did not go beyond the eighth grade, although she once made a brief attempt at a business school.[5]

Florence's first serious "beau" was Harold Leon "Harry" Theall, son of a wealthy Brooklyn druggist. While he was at Erasmus High School, they dated when she was sixteen and Harry was a year older, but then when he broke it off with her—coming to the same conclusion as all Flo's boyfriends eventually did, that she was dull—she alarmed him and his family with behavior that today would qualify as stalking. There were rumors that she had threatened to kill him if he did not marry her, but these may have been only rumors. However, when an interviewer asked Harry's father about it, he never denied it. Nevertheless, the Thealls solved the problem by sending their son to a prep school "out West" (Wisconsin!), after which Harry enrolled in the Yale Law School as a special student two years later.[6]

Florence chafed against what she saw as her parents' and teachers' old-fashioned rules and restrictions. "My mother should have been born a century ago," she complained. Her father once got so frustrated with her that he pulled her across a room by her hair. As well as wanting their two daughters (Gladys was born in 1885) to be well-behaved, genteel girls, Mr. and Mrs. Burns were also keenly aware of the opinions of their neighbors in Flatbush. Florence had gotten kicked out of the Sheepshead Bay Race Track at Coney Island for smoking in public and may have also gotten kicked out of school. She was hanging out with what was considered a wild crowd and was the subject of unflattering gossip. One time, Fred Burns got a private detective, John Walsh, to look for his errant daughter. Walsh found her at Coney Island at a dancing pavilion and persuaded her to go to an aunt's house in Manhattan, from which she was taken to her home in Brooklyn.[7]

In an effort to stop the gossip and get Florence away from the bad influence of her friends, Fred Burns took her to Montreal and enrolled her in a convent school. She was not happy there and claimed the other girls made fun of her (she did not say why), so she ran away, somehow making her way back to Brooklyn on her own. After that, she was sent to a farm in New Jersey, possibly owned by a relative, as both Burnses had family in that state. However, she horsewhipped the farmer and ran away from there too.[8]

Often confined by her parents to her bedroom, Florence told a friend that she could not bear it anymore and had attempted to end her life by blowing out the pilot light on the gas fixtures.[9]

By the age of seventeen, Florence was heavily involved with the Bedford Avenue Gang, sometimes referred to as the Bedford Avenue Hounds, running with them nearly every day and most nights.[10] If the boys did not come calling for her on a given night, she was just wild with restlessness and anxiety. From then on, the Bedford Gang was her new family, the place where she felt most comfortable, living the kind of life she had always wanted, unfettered by the tired old ethics of the Victorian-era middle class. It was a new century, and it called for a new set of standards.[11]

THE BEDFORD AVENUE GANG

Although the neighborhood of Bedford and Stuyvesant Avenues would achieve infamy much later in the century for its racial violence, it was an entirely different kind of gang that preyed on people in the early 1900s. The neighborhood at that time was comprised of gorgeously ornate row houses and stand-alones owned by upper-middle-class professionals and business owners, predominantly German and Irish immigrants who had been successful in the New World. To their great dismay, the marauding gang was made up of their own sons, with their daughters following the gang as adoring and complicit groupies.

The Bedford Avenue Gang's main goal was to get money from unsuspecting citizens, primarily shopkeepers. It did not matter that most of these young men had plenty of spending money from their parents. It was more for the thrill of the con, as well as to finance their love of fine and fancy clothing.

Gang members were identifiable by their "uniforms" and hairstyles: their hair was parted very low on the left side; they wore diamonds and corsets(!), brightly colored (usually red, while the still-too-young gang aspirants adopted pink) vests, and long spike-tailed overcoats that resembled those worn by a circus ringmaster. Most of them carried canes as thick as baseball bats, which could also be used as cudgels. Theodore Burris, Walter Brooks's best friend, walked about with an intimidating Great Dane to go with his Great Cane.

One of their favorite scams was for one of them to go into a haberdashery, pass himself off as the son of a prominent customer, and, using a forged order, commission a suit or an overcoat to be delivered to the customer's address. Then, when the item was being delivered, the young man would waylay the delivery boy and take possession of the garment. Walter Brooks, the shooting victim, was one of the gang members who had done this at least once.

Another favorite trick was to represent themselves as advertising men for newspapers, magazines, and programs to be sold at sporting events, then approach businesses to procure ads for these publications, some of which were nonexistent, and take the payment for them. Needless to say, neither the ad appeared nor the money delivered to the publication.

Several members of the Bedford Gang would invite a "sucker" to have dinner with them at a fancy restaurant, order expensive food and drinks, then quietly slip away one by one on various pretexts until only the hapless mark was left to pay the bill. When Walter Brooks and his friends pulled this scam on an unsuspecting young man at Brooklyn's prestigious Hotel St. George, the maître d' luckily was able to identify most of the gang members. He called

From an ad for men's corsets, 1893 (University of Virginia Historical Collections at the Claude Moore Health Sciences Library)

their fathers and told them that, if the bill were not paid, he would have their sons arrested. The bill got paid.

Another version of this scam, pulled twice on the same ice cream shop in the summer of 1901, was for the gang to go in and order ice cream, eat it on the premises, then drift out as one of them approached the counter to pay. Naturally, the clerk assumed that this young man was paying for the group he had been with, but he paid only for his own ice cream, claiming no responsibility for his friends. When the store manager later came across some of these scoundrels on a street corner, he gave them a few black eyes.

Gang members passed bad checks, forged others, cheated at cards, stole cars for joyriding, started fights, and shoplifted. Theodore Burris, Walter Brooks's aforementioned best friend, could well serve as the role model for the Bedford Avenue Gang.[12] He was a one-man crime wave. Tall and muscular at just over six feet, Burris did not hesitate to take on either policemen or civilians. He once punched a physician he saw on the street, a perfect stranger to him, because he didn't like his looks: the man was small and had a turned-up nose. The only son of a millionaire stockbroker, Ted seemed to have gone somewhat berserk after he graduated from high school in about 1898 and went on a ten-year crime spree. A veritable Peter Pan, he refused to do any kind of honest labor. Instead, he used his generous allowance—much of it provided by his adoring mother over the wishes of his fed-up father—to frequent racetracks and nightclubs and to indulge in affairs with married women. His father was so disgusted and so frustrated that he had Ted arrested for vagrancy, a charge young Burris smoothly talked his way out of, as he did every other charge against him.

Burris stole money, rings, cars, and once even a prize French bulldog worth $1,000. He impersonated other society men and passed bad checks using their names. He hit a hotel detective over the head with a blackjack, or maybe his "cane," then robbed him. When a police officer arrested him for larceny, Ted assaulted him and hurt him quite badly. It took five other officers to subdue him, whereupon he boasted that he had been a tackle on the Cornell football team before leaving college in his freshman year, which is why he could fight so well. But it was just another one of his made-up stories: neither Cornell nor Harvard, which another newspaper reported as the school he had briefly gone to, had ever enrolled him.[13]

The adjectives most frequently used to describe Theodore Burris were "urbane," "jaunty," and "imperturbable." He had a sort of ebullient "kangaroo walk," a fad practiced mostly by young women, which required thrusting the upper body forward with the head held high and proceeding forward in a "hoppy, springing stride and swinging arms."[14] This arrogant insouciance so enraged one judge that he yelled at Ted to "walk straight," a command the latter completely ignored. He was constantly defended and bailed out by his sisters, his mother, his brother-in-law, his friends, and even some of his victims, who refused to press charges. The prominence of his family made prosecutors reluctant to charge him and judges reluctant to sentence him. In short, Theodore Burris was the very epitome of what his fellow Bedford Gang members aspired to be.

Yet, despite Burris's recklessness, he confessed that he made a conscious decision to stay away from Florence Burns because he knew she would cause him trouble.

Probably the most egregious activity of the Bedford Avenue Gang was "ruining" as many young women as possible, either through seduction, date rape after putting chloral hydrate in drinks, or gang rape, then bragging about their exploits. In many instances, the girls themselves were willing accomplices because these boys belonged to prominent, wealthy families. Gang members took the girls to Coney Island or met them in so-called "houses of assignation,"

FADS.

These Fads Have Been Denounced by the Irving Park Woman's Club.

Yellow Journalism.　　The Athletic Girl.　　Authors with long names.　　The kangaroo walk.

Cartoon showing the "kangaroo walk" fad (*Chicago Tribune*, reprinted in www.news-papers.com and used with permission from www.Ancestry.com)

which they rented in Brooklyn. Harry Casey had his own yacht, which the gang used for sexual purposes. Neither the boys nor the girls had learned a lesson from the death of Jennie Bosschieter in nearby Paterson, New Jersey.[15]

THE MURDER OF JENNIE BOSSCHIETER

Seventeen-year-old Jennie Bosschieter, a millworker's daughter, enjoyed dating and hanging out with the sons of Paterson's upper-class families. An immigrant from the Netherlands and a member of the laboring class, Jennie was very aware of the advantage to herself and her family that such a marriage would bring. She flirted with the young men, as did the other mill girls, and accepted their invitations to join them at restaurants and saloons. Although not a gang in the sense of the Bedford Avenue Hounds, four of Paterson's scions—Andy Campbell, Billy Death (pronounced "Deeth"), George Kerr, and Walter McAlister—spent a lot of time together in these establishments and targeted the mill girls as their prey.

One night in October 1900, they persuaded Jennie Bosschieter to join them for drinks and slipped some chloral hydrate into her absinthe, using more of the drug than usual. They hailed a cab and carried the unconscious teenager out a side door, then instructed the cab driver to take them to a remote location. There, they all took turns raping her. Back in the cab, they could not rouse her, so they had the driver take them to a doctor's house. The doctor informed them that the girl was dead, whereupon they got back in the cab and dumped the body by the side of the road. The cab driver turned them in and directed police to the doctor as well. The quartet had the typical mindset of the upper classes that servants and laborers were deaf, dumb, and blind.

What killed Jennie Bosschieter was an overdose of chloral hydrate. The citizens of Paterson were divided as to whether these sons of upstanding, prominent families should go to prison, and the victim was painted in the media and in local gossip as "a girl no better than she should be" in the parlance of the day. All four were found guilty after one of them ultimately confessed the whole thing, and all served fifteen years. The judge was sorry he could not have imposed the death sentence on them even though the jury had recommended mercy, but he made it plain that he thought they deserved it.

CONEY ISLAND AND BADER'S ROAD HOUSE

Eighteen-year-old Florence Burns willingly succumbed to seduction in February 1901 by a twenty-five-year-old divorced man, Edward Cole Watson Jr. Watson was known as "the handsomest man in Brooklyn," a title Florence said he would rather have than president of the United States. He was a gang member whose own father had testified against him in the 1899 divorce hearing because he knew that "Handsome Ed" had cheated on his wife of two years. Word of Florence's fall from grace got out to her parents, and, horrified by both their daughter's behavior and the resultant neighborhood gossip, they threw her out of the house. For a while, that was fine with Florence.[16]

For Florence and the Bedford Avenue Gang, their base of operations was Coney Island and, by extension, nearby Bader's Road House. Although Coney Island had been in existence for many years, it was not until its rebirth in 1895 that it was able to overcome its bad reputation as a dangerous and criminal place with the establishment of a series of family-friendly amusement parks. Moreover, the growing number of affordable transportation options brought a diverse crowd of patrons from the other boroughs besides Brooklyn. In 1895, a nickel trolley carried them to the gates, and an express train from the Brooklyn Bridge could get there in a little over a half hour. For all classes and all ages, Coney Island was eminently accessible and affordable for a quick trip after a hard workday or a more extended visit on a weekend.

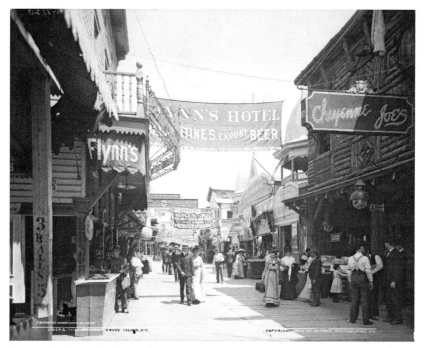

Coney Island, 1903 (Library of Congress, det1994005602/PP/)

Coney Island was attractive because it invited its patrons to relax the strict standards of interaction, courtship, decorum, and clothing. Strangers mingled with each other on the beaches in "bathing costumes" and struck up conversations without having been introduced. For young men and women especially, Coney Island was a place to escape adult supervision, and its rides provided opportunities for close physical contact with each other. Just to join the exuberant crowds on the promenades and boardwalks was a powerful attraction even for those who had no money to spend. Florence Burns's friends commented that it was a rare day when she was not seen on the boardwalk in the summer of 1901. And when she and her friends were not at Coney Island, they were at Bader's Road House.[17]

The proprietor of Bader's Road House was George D. Bader, born in Germany in 1855. Bader had positioned his hotel/bar/restaurant in an extremely advantageous location: on Ocean Parkway at the juncture of the Coney Island concourse, near a railroad station. The boulevard was a popular one with cyclists, horsemen, and carriages, and Bader made sure to accommodate them

BROOKLYN EAGLE POST CARD, SERIES 17, No. 100.
BADER'S FAMOUS ROAD HOUSE—OCEAN PARKWAY AND KING'S HIGHWAY.

Bader's Road House, early 1900s postcard (Author's collection)

with racks for bicycles and sheds for horses. The elegantly appealing hotel could house fifty guests, and often did, but it also did a booming business in serving Coney Island day visitors stopping by for a meal or a drink.

Although Bader's Road House was strategically located and would have been successful in any event, George Bader's larger personality and his eye for promotion were probably what put him over the top. Bader's was a stopping point along the way for bicycle tours and also for a contest as to which would be the first sleigh to arrive at each roadhouse in winter. The prize was a magnum of champagne.

George Bader greeted his guests with hearty enthusiasm and often insisted on their ordering a dish he wanted them to try. Few could resist him. One time, a wealthy thirty-eight-year-old customer arrived in his automobile "runabout" (an early version of the roadster) with his twenty-four-year-old fiancée. They had been engaged for some time and the fiancée must have been wondering when a date would be set. George Bader took care of that for her. He asked, "Why not get married here and now?" Then he got in the customer's runabout, dragged a minister out of a nearby formal dinner to perform the ceremony, whisked him back to the dinner afterward, and sent the newlyweds on their way to Niagara Falls for their honeymoon. The bride had just enough time to send her family a telegram announcing the marriage.[18]

Bader's was not the only hangout for the Bedford Avenue Gang and their groupies—among them Harry Casey, Samuel Maddox (the son of a judge and himself a law student), Bud Kennahan, Joe Wilson, Florence Burns, George Williams, Ed Watson, Mabel Cooper, Ruth Dunne, William "Max" Finck, Grace von Brocklin, Theodore Burris, George Jackson, and Walter Brooks—but it was probably their favorite. There does not seem to have been any kind of age restriction on alcohol, as these seventeen- and eighteen-year-olds were able to order beer, wine, gin rickeys and fizzes, martini cocktails, and whatever else they wanted. Florence's alcohol of choice was always gin, with an occasional beer on a hot day.

Harry Casey, wearing the fancy "swallowtail" coat preferred by the Bedford Gang (*New York World*)

Florence had moved on from "Handsome Ed" Watson to Joe Wilson, and, by August 1901, her current beau was Bedford Gang leader Harry Casey, the charming nineteen-year-old ne'er-do-well son of a millionaire Irish immigrant named Richard Casey. Harry Casey, like his friend Theodore Burris, had charisma in abundance and used it to his advantage. The Caseys had a summer home in the Catskills, where Harry entertained many of his city friends and charmed the locals with his comedy routines and exaggerated accounts of derring-do. He was also well on his way to being an alcoholic.[19]

Like the father of Theodore Burris, Mr. Casey was fed up with his son's lifestyle. Harry liked fine clothes and charged his frequent purchases to his father's account, causing the elder Casey to publish a notice in the newspaper that he would no longer be responsible for his son's debts.[20]

Before there was such a crime as joyriding, Harry stole cars for a wild ride, then would leave them in the approximate vicinity from where he had taken them. Despite being arrested, he served no time, as the owners had suffered no permanent loss of their vehicles and did not wish to press charges against the son of the well-known and well-to-do president of the Whiskey Trust.[21]

Early one morning, after a night of revelry, Harry Casey and several of his male friends were whooping it up in the Bedford area. Harry had a pistol and drunkenly shot out some street lights. While wrestling with a friend for possession of the gun, he pulled the trigger and shot the other man in the hand. Harry was charged with felonious assault, but the wound was not serious and the friend refused to prosecute.[22]

By the summer of 1901, Harry was getting tired of Florence and looking for a way to end the relationship without a lot of hysterics on her part, which she was prone to when she did not get her way. He found his opportunity one day at Bader's when he introduced her to fellow gang member Walter Brooks.

FLORENCE BURNS AND
WALTER BROOKS

If Florence Burns's parents were overly strict with their fractious daughter, Walter Brooks's were prime enablers. Certainly, there was a double standard in play in societal expectations of the behavior of girls and that of boys, but an undoubted influence had to be Thomas and Mary Brooks's loss of their first child, two-year-old Gertrude, who died of bronchitis in 1876.[1] They focused all their energies on their only living child, Walter, bailing him out of those "scrapes" Mr. Brooks had referred to when his son was dying in the Glen Island Hotel. Both parents denied any wrongdoing or less than model behavior on the part of their son and canonized him as the perfect and ideal young gentleman: he was a successful businessman; he was basically a stay-at-home young man, preferring the company of his parents and rarely going out at night; he had no serious love affairs and, in fact, wasn't really very fond of girls; he preferred hanging out with other young men; he didn't drink alcohol and was never drunk in his life until he met Florence Burns; he adored his parents. This last one was actually true.[2]

Walter S. Brooks was born in Brooklyn, New York, on August 17, 1881, where his parents had moved from their native Virginia. His father was a compositor (typesetter) with one of the New York daily newspapers. Walter grew into a handsome, strapping young man a little over six feet tall and weighing 170 pounds. At Brooklyn Boys' High School, he played football and hockey. With his outgoing personality and charm, on top of his good looks, he was an absolute magnet for young women. Unfortunately, Walter's moral compass was not always pointed in the right direction.[3]

Walter's affiliation with the Bedford Avenue Gang caused him to participate in its illegal activities. He was known in his neighborhood as something of a wild young man, "rather fast," addicted to fine clothes, alcohol, and pretty women.

Walter S. Brooks (*New York World,* from a portrait)

Instead of going on to college, as many of his classmates did, he chose instead to go into business with two other young men: Thomas C. Wells and Henry L. "Harry" Cohen. They were commission merchants, acting as middlemen in purchasing wholesale goods for sale to small grocers.[4]

Walter Brooks had earlier gotten into trouble with the Department of Agriculture when he and some previous partners had made a large purchase of spoiled condensed milk at a very low price, took off the old labels, put on new ones falsely stating that the milk was the product of the New Jersey Milk Company, and sold them at the regular price. When they got caught, Walter saved himself from a prison sentence by turning state's evidence against the others. Spoiled condensed milk could have caused illness or death to young infants.[5]

Another time, he had a consignment of sour vinegar, valued at $500–$600, condemned by the Board of Health before he could sell it. At the time of his death, he owed money for five hundred pounds of raisins that he had received and neglected to pay for, despite several requests from the seller.[6]

Although Brooks enjoyed the company of young women, he was not as fond of making a commitment to them. His main goal at age twenty was to bed women but not to marry any of them. The year before he met Flo Burns, he had gotten himself engaged to a Brooklyn girl named Lottie Eaton, but she broke it off because of his Bedford Gang affiliation and for "moral lapses," which she declined to enumerate. "The most charitable thing is to report that it was a mutual decision," she said, although clearly it was not. Then, of course, there are those "several scrapes with women" that indicate he had taken their virginity, maybe even got them pregnant or otherwise ruined their reputations, then refused to marry them. Neighbors of the Brookses asserted that Walter's "attractive physical personality fascinated several girls who afterward had good reason to regret their acquaintance with him."[7]

It is unclear exactly how much and in what way Walter's parents bailed him out of all these problems. We do know that Mr. Brooks's lawyer represented gang member Joseph Wilson at his forgery trial, so the elder Brooks must have been well aware of his son's connection to this gang.[8] And it may be that the Brookses paid for abortions or made payoffs to get Walter out of his "scrapes with women."

So, when Walter fell in love with the equally self-indulgent and entitled Florence Burns, it was a disaster waiting to happen. When "Handsome" Harry Casey (like Ed Watson, he, too, used the descriptive title) introduced Florence and Walter at Bader's Road House in August 1901, they were immediately attracted to each other and from then on were very nearly inseparable. It is interesting to note that, of the six known boyfriends Florence had dated by 1902, three of them—Watson, Casey, and Brooks—had the reputation of being "lady-killers" who bragged about their ability to lead young women to their ruin.

To an impetuous and reckless boy like Walter Brooks, the nineteen-year-old Florence Burns was absolutely irresistible. At five feet seven, with blue eyes and blonde hair (the latter with a little help from a bottle), the daring and rebellious Florence was not only stop-men-in-their-tracks beautiful but athletic as well. She was good at rowing and swimming—she was the first girl to swim across the Hudson from the Bowery[9]—and pistol shooting. Walter Brooks fell fast and hard for her. For her own part, Florence claimed she loved him "even more than my mother and father"[10]—although, for her, that was not exactly a high bar to get over. There is no doubt that they were infatuated with each other. Unlike many other girls, Flo was not put off by Walter's reputation and his membership in the Bedford Avenue Gang. In fact, his "bad boy" image may have been part of what appealed to her.

Given the propensities of both of them, there is no doubt that Florence and Walter's relationship became physically intimate very quickly. Just as quickly, though, things began to change between them. First of all, there was Walter's wandering eye. By October, gossip was getting back to Florence that he was chasing another girl. When she saw her former boyfriend, Joe Wilson, at Bader's, she told him that, if it were true, Walter would "suffer for it."[11] Second, Flo's parents discovered that she was having sexual relations with Brooks and subsequently evicted her from their house—once again, their fallback position with her—and forbade her to return until she married him. Possibly, there was a pregnancy involved as it seems to have been a drastic action on their part and they had not taken the same marry-or-else stance over her relationship with Ed Watson. Or it might have been that the neighbors—whose negative comments, Florence asserted, were more to be dreaded by her mother than the bubonic plague—had gotten wind of it. The Burnses might have needed to demonstrate that they did not condone this behavior. Because of this, Florence began to agitate Walter about getting married. Walter, of course, was not in the least interested in this plan. Nor were his parents or those of his friends who knew of her reputation, which they said would destroy Walter's own, and they all discouraged him from marrying her. Given Walter's personal behavior, this is ironic in the extreme but illustrative of the double standard for men and for women.

FLORENCE FRIGHTENS THE BROOKSES

It wasn't until Friday, November 1, 1901, that Walter got around to introducing Florence to his mother.[12] The three of them met for lunch at Walter's favorite and most frequented restaurant, the Cosmopolitan Hotel on Chambers Street in Manhattan. That Sunday, November 3, she went to the Brookses' home at 258 Decatur Street in Brooklyn, where she accompanied Walter and his mother to church. The following Sunday, November 10, Florence went to church with them again and then stayed to eat Sunday dinner with the family. She stopped in two or three times that week and accompanied them to church again on Sunday, November 17. She next visited on the evening of Wednesday, November 20. During this time, Florence was living in a boardinghouse on Ralph Avenue, the rent for which was being paid by Walter.

November 21 marked the beginning of a three-week saga that would later prompt a magistrate to remark, "It is enough to say that the situation in that house is a peculiar and doubtful one." On that day, Walter brought a very sick Florence to the Brooks home and begged his parents to allow her to stay with them. He felt responsible for her illness, he said, which was later explained to mean that he had kept her out in bad weather and she had subsequently caught a cold. Her own parents would not let her back into their home, but she clearly needed medical attention.

Florence would remain ill for two weeks with what was variably presented as pneumonia, typhoid, malaria, or a cold, and the Brookses' family doctor was called in to attend her. Her mother visited her only once in that time, her father not at all. In fact, Fred Burns had harsh words to say about Walter's father—that he ought to be put in jail because of Thomas's objection to a marriage that would save the reputations of Fred's daughter and the Burns family.

At no time did Thomas Brooks attempt to get Fred Burns to pay for Florence's medical attention or any other of their expenditures on her behalf during her three-week stay with them, which gives rise to the suspicion that the Brookses recognized that she had a "moral claim" on them. Was the illness really due to the effects of an abortion that Florence had had performed on herself? Or did the Brookses arrange for one? Since Walter and his mother also came down with something that sounds very much like a flu virus, that is likely the source of Flo's illness as well.

However, it is still possible that Florence was pregnant. In September, after only a month of dating Walter, she told her friend Mabel Cooper, as well as Mabel's mother, that she was in "serious trouble" and that her father had found out and threw her out of the house. Walter was responsible for her predicament, and if she did not "regain her health" (this probably means through abortion or miscarriage), she would force him to marry her or she would "revenge herself against him."[13]

After Florence had fully recovered from the flu or whatever else was ailing her, she continued to stay in the Brooks house and went on a campaign to force Walter to marry her, one that smacked more of desperation than affection. Thinking she could achieve this goal through his mother, she told Mrs. Brooks that, if Walter did not marry her, she would shoot him with her father's pistol. Mrs. Brooks, stooping to trade taunts with a child, asked her why she did not shoot herself instead, to which Florence replied, "Because I love Walter too much." Another time, the elder's response to this oft-repeated threat was, "If you do, then I will shoot you." "You will not have to," Florence retorted. "I will kill myself."

The Brookses took to eavesdropping on the two young people having conversations on the subject of marriage. The best place for this was in the dining room right beneath the parlor, where the ceiling was low and a heat register made it easy to hear. What Thomas Brooks heard on Sunday, December 8, sums up the gist of all these "discussions" between Flo and Walter:

FLO: What do you intend to do about marrying me? I think it is time to come to some understanding about this.

WALTER: Where do you intend to live if we marry? In the street?

FLO: Well, we must get married.

WALTER: The best thing you can do is to get employment. I will speak to a friend and try to get you a position as a cloak model.

FLO [*angrily stamping her foot on the floor*]: I won't do any such thing. I don't intend to ruin myself by going to work.

During one of these confrontations, Flo became so distraught that she passed out, although there was a strong suspicion that she might have faked it. When Walter said he could not bear to leave his mother and father, she called him a "big kid" for wanting to stay in the family nest.

Thomas Brooks asked Florence why she kept trying to get his son to marry her (as if he didn't know!), especially since Walter could not afford to support a wife. He told her to go to her parents and ask them to take her back, but Florence insisted that she and Walter would get married and that her parents would not allow her to go home before then.

Without telling Florence, Thomas Brooks paid a visit to Fred Burns and practically begged him to take back his daughter, who was disrupting his household. But Fred was adamant: she was not welcome in their house until she became Mrs. Walter Brooks. Thomas told him he and his wife would never consent to this marriage. Florence must leave their house.

On Wednesday, December 11, before he went to work, Thomas Brooks went to Flo's room and told her that she had to leave and that he had told her parents this. He had allowed her to stay with them while she was sick, but now she was well. "This must be your last day in my house," he said, and gave her some money for streetcar fares. "I'm not going to leave," was her reply.

Nevertheless, she did leave, only to return that night. And they let her in! It was, indeed, a "peculiar and doubtful" situation, especially when Florence claimed she had gone home to get her father's pistol to shoot Walter but was unable to find it. The Brookses must have felt that they would never be rid of her, but it is also obvious that they felt some obligation toward her because of their son's relations with her. Possibly they feared that this temperamental, occasionally reckless, and not terribly smart girl would cause a scandal for their family—even though it would for her as well.

Somewhere around this time, between December 13, when she—mercifully—left the Brooks home and December 23, when she moved to yet another boardinghouse, Florence convinced her parents to take her back in. She lied to them that she and Walter would be getting married after all. When no wedding was in the offing, the Burnses threatened eviction once again. Desperate, Florence sent an urgent note to Walter at his Jay Street office that she *must* see him. She instructed him to phone Speh's Drug Store, two blocks away, to send someone to the Burns home to say that someone wanted to speak to Florence on the phone. (Unlike the Brookses, the Burnses had no telephone.)[14]

Thos W Brooks

Thomas W. Brooks, Walter's father (*New York World*)

They subsequently met, and Florence's arguments must have taken hold and caused Walter to relent. Or it may be that, if they got married, Walter felt he could deliver her back to the Burnses on a "temporary" basis until he could afford to support both of them, which would rid him of her at least for a while. If he never made arrangements for her to join him, well, it would be her parents' responsibility to take care of her.

Whatever the reason, Flo and Walter presented themselves to the current minister at the Brookses' church, the Church of the Good Shepherd on McDonough Street in Brooklyn, and asked to be married right away. The Reverend Robert Rogers thought it was odd that they were in such a hurry and had no witnesses with them. He would later state different reasons for refusing to marry them, such as Walter's parents had not given their consent or they were too young. Once, he simply declined to state his reason unless called to do so in a court of law, but it was most likely because he could sense that the prospective bridegroom was reluctant. It's also possible that he was aware that his parishioners, Mr. and Mrs. Brooks, objected to Florence Burns.[15] Whatever the reason, there was no wedding and, consequently, Florence was once again ordered out of her parents' home and needed a place to live.

The Brookses breathed a sigh of relief when a friend of Walter's, who was not a gang member, suggested a reputable boardinghouse, run by Mrs. Ella B. Hitchcock on West 144th Street, and Florence moved in there on December

23. The agreement was for Florence to pay ten dollars a week, but she paid none of it during her monthlong stay, and by this time Walter had stopped supporting her.[16]

However, Walter frequently visited Flo at Mrs. Hitchcock's, and Flo told the landlady they were engaged. Given the supposed engagement and the mores of that era, Mrs. Hitchcock felt that Florence was "indiscreet [in her] conduct in receiving men friends," sometimes at "unseemly hours." She did not hesitate to share her feelings with Flo, who resented the landlady's interference and promptly packed up and left. She rewarded Mrs. Hitchcock's monthlong sufferance of her nonpaying tenancy by stealing some clothing and a silver bag. Mrs. Hitchcock did not report the theft.[17]

After Florence left Mrs. Hitchcock's, she moved into yet another boardinghouse, this one run by Mrs. Harriet Birdsall, and began dating Harry Gimpel, a twenty-three-year-old sales clerk who had escorted her to the Old Guard Ball, put on every January at the Hotel St. George. Mrs. Birdsall must have been a much more sympathetic landlady than the judgmental Mrs. Hitchcock because Flo confided in her quite a bit. She told her she was earning money by selling advertising subscriptions. This was one of the scams run by the Bedford Gang but was probably done legitimately by Florence, albeit with her customary indolence. And she gave Mrs. Birdsall the exact date when she lost her virginity (when she "went wrong") to Ed Watson—February 15, 1901—exactly one year before the death of Walter Brooks. After that, she said, her family "treated her shamefully" because her disgrace was known to everyone in the neighborhood. Her parents would not even let her look out the windows for fear the neighbors would see her.[18]

For a while, Florence wore a ring given to her by Harry Gimpel, and some of her friends thought she was more in love with him than with Walter, but she told Mrs. Birdsall that she broke off her engagement to Harry for Walter. If this engagement was real and not something that existed only in her mind, it would seem that Flo's problems—impending baby or not—could have been solved with a marriage to Harry Gimpel, who was not a gang member and who had a steady job.

Florence was not ready to let Walter Brooks go completely, however. She asked Mrs. Birdsall's advice as to whether she should try to get her parents to take her back in, and Mrs. Birdsall told her it was the best place for her. Besides, Flo had yet to pay even a dime of rent for her ten-day stay and ultimately left without doing so. On February 5, 1902, Flo got permission to move back in with her parents, mainly because Walter talked with Fred Burns and dangled the possibility of an impending marriage. According to Harry Cohen, Walter was relieved to have her under the care of her father, so that she no longer relied on Walter or made him feel guilty about not supporting her. He felt this was the best way to be rid of her.[19]

Walter was somewhat in fear of Flo's hot temper and her father's righteous anger over the situation. Both of them were crack pistol shots. In the days leading up to his murder, Walter would joke with Harry Cohen that he was going over to the Burnses' "to get shot." About a week before the incident in the Glen Island Hotel, Walter told Harry that, if he didn't come to work the next day by 9:30, he should go over to the Burns house and demand to know what they had done with him. Both Flo and Fred were constantly badgering him about the marriage. Fred told him, "If you don't marry her, young man, I'm going to hell!" This could have meant that Fred would be condemned for having a fallen daughter or that Fred would be forced to kill Walter to avenge her honor.[20]

Florence and her father's desperation—and, presumably, Mrs. Burns's as well—is another hint that there must have been a baby on the way. If Flo was in "serious trouble" in September and hoping to either "regain her health" or get married, as she told Mabel Cooper, then February would be the time when a pregnancy would begin to show. There would be no more need for speculation among the neighbors; the truth would be plainly visible to all.

All their pleading fell on Walter's very deaf ears. While he still felt physically attracted to Florence, he had no intention of tying himself to her for the rest of his life. In marrying her, he would be going against the wishes of his parents, the warnings of his friends, and the self-indulgent lifestyle he had created for himself.

WALTER BROOKS'S LAST WEEK

Now that Florence was back at home and not in Walter's own home or a nearby boardinghouse, he could feel well and truly done with her. He had made the good-faith gesture of going to Reverend Rogers, and he had done what he could to support her financially. Besides, he had been dating another girl for about a month, seventeen-year-old Ruth Dunne[1]—tall, thin, and blonde— who adored him but who was reluctant to go out with him while he was still involved with Flo. He assured Ruth that he was doing his best to break away, but Flo was difficult and the whole thing was complicated. He feared Flo's bad temper and her vindictive nature, so he wanted to proceed with caution.[2]

Let us, then, examine the final week of Walter's life:[3]

FRIDAY, FEBRUARY 7

With a girl who was neither Florence Burns nor Ruth Dunne, Walter Brooks tried to book a room for the night at the Hotel Lincoln in Manhattan. He registered them as "H. Wilson and wife, Brooklyn, N.Y." Since the couple had no luggage, they were turned away.[4]

SATURDAY, FEBRUARY 8

This was most likely the day that Walter sent a letter to Flo in an attempt to break it off with her.

The Burns home in Flatbush. It is still there, recognizable because of the turret. (*New York World*)

SUNDAY, FEBRUARY 9

Walter, along with his friends Harry Casey, Harry Cohen, and Tom Sharkey, went to Madison Square Garden for the first day of the six-day walking contest. At that time, he told them that he was breaking it off completely with Flo and they assured him that it was a good move on his part.

It's difficult for us to understand this today, but the biggest fad in the late nineteenth century was a sport called pedestrianism, competitive walking events where men vied for money, belts, and acclaim by walking around a track for days. More puzzling than the walkers, however, were the spectators who paid to watch them walk around and around. By 1902, the sport was waning, but there were still plenty of walking contests to be had. Although, originally, these events pitted one man against another, eventually the sport evolved into teams of two or more who spelled each other on the track. There are remnants of this even today in fund-raising community "walkathons," where donors pledge a certain figure for each mile walked. However, spectators in the stands at these modern-day events are primarily comprised of family, friends, and contestants.[5]

It's hard to imagine that competitive walking would attract the likes of the thrill-seeking Bedford Avenue Gang. Yet, many of the walkers were showmen as well and entertaining to watch, while there were always plenty of vendors who wandered about hawking refreshments. The walk that began on February 9, 1902, in Madison Square Garden, was a six-day "go-as-you-please" event, which meant that contestants were free to walk, run, or jog.[6] The two-man teams could divide up the walking any way they wanted, but no team member could be on the track more than twelve hours of a twenty-four-hour period. The team of Hegleman and Cavanaugh would break the existing record with a total of 770 miles over these six days. Originally, the limit was six days because no walking could be done on Sunday, but, as this race began on a Sunday, that restriction had obviously gone by the board while still keeping the traditional six-day limit.

In pedestrianism's heyday, the big international stars were Edward Payson Weston of Great Britain; Dan O'Leary, an Irishman representing America; and Frank Hart, a black man from Haiti. Walkers attracted sponsors, and there was even a scandal with some athletes being suspected of using what today would be called performance-enhancing drugs, such as coca leaves.[7]

MONDAY, FEBRUARY 10

That day, Florence showed up at Walter's office at 9:30 A.M., the first of four visits that week. Each time, she would ask the office boy, fifteen-year-old Joseph Cribbins, "Where is Walter?" Brooks was usually out. Under oath, Cribbins would say that he never saw any other women in the Brooks and Wells office, but when Florence showed up, he told her that lots of women came to call on Walter Brooks. He could see that it bothered her, which was probably his intent.

Walter was not in at that time, so Florence went away and came back at 2:30, then waited for him until he got back at 4:00. He took her out into the hallway to talk, after which she left.

After work, Walter took Ruth Dunne to dinner at Silsbe's Oyster House and then to the Orpheum Theater.

TUESDAY, FEBRUARY 11

Once again, Flo went to Walter's office. Once again, he was not in and did not come in at all.

Ruth Dunne. Her name was uniformly misspelled as "Dunn." (*New York World*)

That evening, he took Ruth Dunne to a Sagamore Club Dance at the Hotel St. George in Brooklyn.

WEDNESDAY, FEBRUARY 12

As this was Lincoln's Birthday, Walter must have taken the time off. He spent the afternoon ice skating with Ruth Dunne in Brooklyn's Prospect Park.

THURSDAY, FEBRUARY 13

Flo came yet again, this time at 5:00 P.M. She must have been truly at her wits' end to have displayed her desperation so openly. This time, Walter was in his office and took her to dinner. Harry Cohen went back to Madison Square Garden to watch the progress of the walking match.

FRIDAY, FEBRUARY 14

That morning, Walter and his partner, Harry Cohen, took the train to Newark, New Jersey, then went on to Paterson to see a man on business. When that was finished, they had lunch and went to the Delaware, Lackawanna, & Western Railroad depot in Newark, where they saw two young, attractive women, strangers to the men and to each other, and chatted them up. Soon, all four left the depot to rent hotel rooms to have sex. When they were finished and Harry had to get back to the office, Walter took the woman who had been with Harry and went back to the hotel room with her.

While Harry and Walter were dallying with the chippies in the Newark hotel, Florence had written a note to Walter to say she would come by the office at 11:00 to say good-bye, as she was leaving for Detroit. It was a lie, her final ploy to shock him into a commitment rather than lose her. Joseph Cribbins, the office boy, slipped the note under Walter's rolltop desk. At 11:00, Flo showed up at the office to find that, once again, Walter was not there. Cribbins did not know when he would return, so Flo wrote another note and slipped it under his rolltop. Then she left the office and went to lunch at Childs' Restaurant, very close to both Jay Street and the Glen Island Hotel on Cortlandt Street.

Meanwhile, Harry Cohen had caught the 1:30 train to Manhattan and arrived at his office about an hour later. Florence was not there at that time, but when he returned at 3:00 after running an errand, she was there, dressed the same as the day before: she wore a black hat and a black dress with a tight-fitting jacket and carried a muff. Cohen told Flo that Walter would not be in until late and that it was entirely possible he would not be in at all but would just go straight to his home in Brooklyn. Florence left again but came back at 5:00. She told Harry she was going to Detroit the next day and wanted to see Walter once more.

When Walter arrived at his office at 5:30, he said a somewhat perfunctory "hello" to Florence and went right to his desk to go through his mail and papers. They said little to each other. Her morning notes to him would later be found in his wastebasket, where he had thrown them. At 6:30, Harry Cohen was leaving and asked Walter, in shirtsleeves after taking off his suit coat, to walk him out. Cohen begged him not to go with Florence that night and to come out to dinner with him instead. He had a bad feeling about it. But Walter could see the finish line of this relationship and did not want to do anything to ruin it by making Florence angry and, subsequently, prolonging

Harry Cohen, Walter's business partner and friend (*New York World*)

H.L. COHEN

it. She would be going to Detroit, and he intended to "give her a big blowout" that night, then give her sixty dollars for her trip expenses. He would not be staying with her for more than four or five hours, he said. Harry made Walter promise to meet him later that night so he would know his friend was safe.

Because Walter wanted to send Florence on her way with "a big blowout," he had to break his date with Ruth Dunne for that night. He sent her a note saying that he would have to postpone it because of his desire to—finally—be rid of Florence Burns. It would be the last time, he assured her.

That night, when Harry Cohen went to the Ralph Avenue station of the Kings County L line for the prearranged meeting with Walter, Walter was not there. Nor would he be.

Cohen never saw his friend and business partner alive again.

ARREST

A heartbroken Thomas Brooks helped the two policemen carry his son down the stairs to the lobby of the Glen Island Hotel and out to the waiting ambulance, which sped them to the Hudson Street Hospital. The doctors removed the bullet from Walter's head—it was a .32 caliber, the same as Fred Burns's pistol—but "the boy merchant," as he would mostly be referred to thereafter, never regained consciousness. He was pronounced dead at 11:15 A.M.[1]

Harry Cohen was also at the hospital and told the police that they should question Florence Burns about the shooting, as she had threatened Brooks several times. That made two people who had named her, so Det. Sgt. William Colby of the Central Office and Detectives Parker and Schultz of the Church Street station went to the Burns home in Flatbush. They identified themselves to Mrs. Burns and asked to see Florence. Florence seemed neither surprised nor particularly disturbed. Here is the dialogue that transpired at the Burns home:

COLBY TO FLO: Do you know Walter Brooks?
FLO: Yes, I do. I saw him yesterday in his office.
COLBY: Did you have [dinner] with him?
FLO: No, I left him at his office, then came straight home. I got here about 7:00, but my parents were at the theater and my sister had gone to bed, so I went to bed.
COLBY: Did you know Walter Brooks was shot in a hotel?
FLO: No. I wonder who could have done it. Have they found the pistol?
COLBY TO MRS. BURNS: Do you know what time she got home last night?
MRS. BURNS: Please don't ask me any questions. Mr. Burns told me not to answer any questions about this.
FLO: I know I am suspected and I am in a hole.[2]

At this point, Colby felt he had heard enough and decided to take her to the station. However, he was hoping to get more self-incriminating statements from her, so he did not inform her that Walter was dead. Instead, he told her he would be taking her to the Hudson Street Hospital to see him. Although there was a rumor that he also told her Walter had regained consciousness and had named her as the shooter, the police uniformly denied this and there was never any proof of it, nor did Florence ever claim they had said this. Mrs. Burns asked the officers if they would agree to meet her husband at the hospital, then she sent her live-in nephew, Willie Von derBosch, to send a telegram to Fred Burns in Manhattan.[3]

Willie was Mrs. Burns's brother Oscar's son, born in 1878, a construction engineer like his father and grandfather. He must have had a falling-out with his father, however, as he lived with the Burnses for most of his life once he reached his teen years.[4] Willie's presence in the house at this time underscores two things: first, that the Burnses had no telephone, as he had to go out to send a telegram, which we also know from Flo's frantic message to Walter to call her at Speh's Drug Store; second, that someone besides Flo's sister Gladys could have known what time she came in—assuming Willie was there at the time. Yet he was never asked about this.

The lack of a phone is important because the detectives were at the Burns house around 1:30, only two hours after Walter died. So, even if word was leaking out and Fred Burns had happened to hear about it at work, he could not have made a call to his house. It was unlikely that he sent a telegram from Manhattan, as the prosecution's assertion—that the Burnses already knew about the shooting when the detectives arrived at their house—went unchallenged by the family and by Florence's attorney. Therefore, the Burnses must have known before anyone else did, and most likely from Florence herself.

The detectives, who were dressed in plain clothes, which would not have alerted the neighbors, walked Florence the short distance to the Brighton Beach line to take a trolley to the Brooklyn Bridge and into Manhattan. Along the way, Florence told them that she never got excited or anxious about anything and had always been that way. Nothing rattled her. This was probably to explain her noticeable lack of reaction both to Walter's shooting and to her being taken to Manhattan in connection with it, but, in fact, it summed up her demeanor throughout the entire proceedings. When Detective Parker took out his watch to check the time, Florence asked to see it. She examined it, said, "No, that ain't it," and handed it back. It was what was called a "dollar nickel watch," a nickel-plated watch costing a dollar, very similar to Walter's, which had been given to Thomas Brooks at the Glen Island.

On the trolley, Colby noticed a news headline declaring Walter's death, but he did not point it out to Flo. He wanted her to continue to think that he was still alive, although she easily could have seen the headlines for herself.

Once in Manhattan, however, the detectives proceeded directly to the Church Street station and not to the hospital. If Florence questioned it or protested it, there is no record of that. She was taken into Captain Halpin's office and told she was being charged with a felony, but not which one, and murder was not mentioned. She was informed that anything she said could be used against her. It was then about 2:40 P.M.

A detective named Riordan came into the captain's office to question Flo at that point. Because of the hair comb found in the hotel room by Thomas Brooks, Riordan asked her for her combs. She took out the two side combs and gave them to him but said she did not wear a back comb, which was the kind left behind in Room 12 of the Glen Island. These were combs that kept women's hair in place. The back comb had longer teeth than those at the sides and was usually more ornate than those on the sides. Some combs were quite elaborate and could be made of bone (fanciest), metal, or celluloid (cheapest). Flo's were celluloid, as was the one found in the hotel.[5]

While Flo was being questioned, the door opened and George Washington, the bellboy from the Glen Island, poked his head in and said, "That's the lady I saw last night."[6] He had been told to see if he recognized the woman talking to the detective, but, although Washington was adamant about this and would never waver for an instant throughout the entire proceedings, it was a flawed identification because Flo had been the only woman in the Glen Island office. Further, her presence in the office and being questioned could lead to the conclusion that she was suspected of the shooting, thereby causing a witness to assume her guilt as a matter of course. A version of this—what used to be called "the one-man lineup"—is, "This is the person who has been arrested. Is this the one you saw?"

Some of Flo's interrogation that day went like this:[7]

RIORDAN: Why did you want to hurt Walter?

FLO: I didn't hurt him. I loved him more than anyone, even my parents.

RIORDAN: His money is gone. What happened to it? [This was not true and he knew it.]

FLO [*surprised*]: It's gone?

RIORDAN: Yes.

FLO [*taking her right hand, balling it into a fist, and vehemently striking it against her left palm*]: Then that coon took it!

RIORDAN: How much was there?

FLO: $32—a $20 gold bill, two $5 bills, and a $2 bill.

RIORDAN: How do you know that?

FLO: I saw it counted out.

RIORDAN: Walter Brooks was shot.

FLO: Did they find the pistol?

RIORDAN: I won't tell you.

FLO: Was a woman seen leaving the hotel?

RIORDAN: Yes. Did anyone see you leaving the hotel?

FLO: I decline to answer under advice of counsel. I've already said too much.

Advice of counsel? Flo had yet to see her lawyer, although that man—Foster L. Backus of Brooklyn, a former district attorney for Kings County and now a criminal defense lawyer—had been trying to do just that for a couple of hours, as had Fred Burns. They were both being given the runaround because the police wanted to question Florence further before an attorney could stop the flow of information. So the police told Backus he would have to get clearance from the district attorney's office, which, in turn, told him he would have to get it from the chief of police. They batted him back and forth like a shuttlecock until finally Backus threatened a lawsuit and bad publicity if he could not see his client *right now*.

The fact that Backus was on the scene so quickly and that Florence had—albeit, belatedly—decided to follow his advice indicates that he must have been consulted even prior to the arrest. What likely happened is that Fred Burns hired him the first thing Saturday morning, then told his family to say nothing when or if the police came for Florence.

Florence's unfortunate performances with Detective Colby at her home and with Detective Riordan at the station indicate exactly why attorneys tell their clients to say nothing, even though they may be innocent. A defense lawyer could possibly characterize her questions about the pistol and the woman in the hotel as natural curiosity and concern about things pertaining to the shooting of her boyfriend, but what would he do with the money she saw "counted out"? Because that counting out could not have happened anywhere else but the Glen Island Hotel, where Brooks had paid two dollars for the room. If she had seen it before then—for example, in his Jay Street office, where she claimed she had left him—she would have given a higher number, to account for the sixty dollars he intended to give her, the dinner he was supposed to have had with a woman (who she insisted was not her) in a restaurant, as well as the two dollars for the room.

The statement about "the coon" (a pejorative term for African Americans) would have been more damning if she had made it *before* George Washington had stuck his head in to identify her. But the money can't be gotten around. Brooks had told Cohen that he intended to give Florence sixty dollars to help with her fares and expenses, which was the exact amount he put in the hotel safe. If he had said good-bye to her in his office at 6:30 as she claimed, then picked up some other woman to take to dinner and then to the hotel, he should not still have the sixty dollars if he gave it to Florence, as he had intended.

THE BURNS FAMILY CLOSES RANKS

It was clear that Mr. and Mrs. Burns probably had advance knowledge of the shooting of Walter Brooks, and there was only one person who could have given them that knowledge: Florence. From that moment on, no member of this household revealed anything to the press about any possible alibi they could provide for her. Their clever and hardworking attorney, Foster Backus, would soon spirit them out of the state and into New Jersey to stay with family so they would be out of the range of subpoena service by the New York district attorney. What might Florence have told them that would put them so firmly on her side?

Naturally, in a high-profile case such as this one, rumors fly thick and fast. The bulk of these can be discounted completely or scaled back, but there was one—actually started by Florence's one-time boyfriend Harry Gimpel—that might have hit on the truth of what Florence said to her parents: that she and Walter had made a suicide pact, but after Walter shot himself, or after she shot Walter, Flo got frightened and changed her mind.[8] And here's where she might have gotten the script for this concoction: In 1900, an impressionable young woman, Helen Southgate, the adopted daughter of a wealthy, prominent New Yorker, fell under the spell of that man's suicidal, despondent brother-in-law, Henry Barbour. Barbour talked her into committing suicide with him and they checked into a Brooklyn hotel under the name of "G. N. Bartlett and wife,

New York." They lay down on the bed together and Henry leaned over and shot Helen in the side, then stuck the pistol in his mouth and pulled the trigger.

Helen Southgate was injured, but not fatally, and she jumped from the bed to summon a bellboy and tell him what happened. By the time the bellboy arrived, she was afraid to say anything and asked him what time it was instead. She took herself to a hospital for treatment and said she had accidentally shot herself while cleaning a pistol, but the truth soon came out. Because of the social standing of the people involved, this case was a prominent one that Florence would have been familiar with. It is a scenario that could have convinced Florence's parents to protect her.[9]

Florence would have remembered that Helen Southgate had rung for the bellboy, so Florence may have ordered the lemon soda as proof that she had thought about contacting someone about Walter's "suicide" but then changed her mind. The extant rumor about the suicide pact had Walter shooting himself, but his wound was in an extremely awkward location to be self-inflicted. Then, too, it was possibly Flo's pistol, or one belonging to her father, that would have been used, and she was an accomplished markswoman, so it would make more sense that she would shoot him, then shoot herself, rather than each one of them using the pistol separately. Possibly her parents did not wish to examine these facts too closely.

Harry Cohen portrayed his friend as a happy-go-lucky guy who seldom let things get him down or keep him there. Suicide would have been entirely foreign to his temperament: "He was a fellow who was always jolly, no matter what happened to him. When he had a hundred dollars, he spent it, and when he had a quarter of a dollar, he got along on that."[10] While there may have been motive for Florence to kill herself, given the disgrace she was possibly facing, there was no such impetus on Walter's part. He already had a bad reputation for his "love-'em-and-leave-'em" mentality. His behavior in Newark on the morning of what was effectively the last day of his life—having sex with two strange women—does not exactly indicate the kind of depression that is called for in a decision to commit suicide.

FLORENCE AND THE TOMBS ANGEL

From beginning to end, Florence's demeanor provoked a constant commentary in the press. Although there were very occasional instances where a tiny bit of emotion could be discerned, for the most part, her attitude could best be characterized as indifference. Throughout the proceedings, the most frequent report in the many newspapers covering them was that Florence seemed to be the least interested person in the room. Nobody could believe that a nineteen-year-old girl could be this calm, this unflappable, under these circumstances: questioned by police for two hours about the murder of her boyfriend; taken to a cell in the Tombs, New York City's infamous prison; stared at by reporters and spectators; and subjected to a rigorous hearing to determine the likelihood of her guilt.[1]

At the police station, however, there was one thing that rattled her: the press's attempts to take her picture. When she finally spied her father, the only friendly face in the Centre Street Station, she threw herself on him, hysterically screaming, "Oh, Papa! They are trying to take my picture!" It seems an odd choice of complaints as this was the first time she had seen her father since her arrest. It would have been more appropriate for her to proclaim her innocence instead, and the fact that she did not is another indication that they had already discussed the incident at home that morning. When her mother arrived, Florence—fully aware of the reporters surrounding her—cried to her, "Mama, you don't believe that I killed Walter, do you?"[2]

That night, in the Centre Street Station, Florence ate heartily of the meal sent in to her by her father (inmates could have meals purchased for them instead of eating the regular jail fare) and slept soundly on the wooden bench that served as a bed. Even the "serenade" by the only other woman prisoner, who "sang, yelled, hooted, and screeched" all night did not interrupt her sleep.[3]

Although the arresting officer had a warrant based on "information and belief," which was most likely provided by the statements of Harry Cohen and Thomas Brooks pointing the finger at Flo, the police wanted time to get more evidence that would connect her to the murder of Walter Brooks. Her attorney maintained that this was not strong enough to hold her without bail. Moreover, he insisted that this matter be heard in Magistrate's Court so it could be resolved there with the district attorney instead of directly proceeding to the grand jury. Magistrate Cornell, who had known Fred Burns from Cornell's connection with sports at Yale, agreed to what amounted to a preliminary hearing, but he refused to allow bail. Consequently, Florence was sent over the Bridge of Sighs to a section of the Tombs that housed forty women serving sentences for theft and prostitution. Flo was soon seen chatting with her fellow prisoners.[4]

THE TOMBS

New York's City Prison was referred to as "the Tombs" not because it was dark, dank, depressing, and the place where some inmates would meet their deaths—although it was all of these things—but because, in an earlier iteration, it was constructed to look like an Egyptian pharaoh's tomb.[5] In its various sections, it housed those waiting for trial, those serving sentences, those sleeping off the previous night's drinking binge, and—sometimes—those awaiting execution. The Bridge of Sighs connecting the prison to the courts was so called because condemned inmates crossed over it on their way to the gallows.

There was a Women's Prison, a Boys' Prison, and a special section with more spacious and comfortable cells reserved for privileged inmates. The Women's and Boys' Prisons were served by a prison matron, Roman Catholic nuns, and laywomen known as Tombs Angels.

THE TOMBS ANGEL

The original Tombs Angel, the one who defined the role, was Rebecca Salome Foster, the fifty-four-year-old widow of a decorated Civil War general.[6] When he died in the early 1880s, Mrs. Foster began her volunteer service as minister to the inmates of the Tombs, particularly the women and young boys. Over those twenty years, she became connected with some of the most famous prisoners ever to be housed there: Augusta Nack, who, along with her lover Martin Thorn, had killed her current boyfriend Willie Guldensuppe, then cut him up into pieces and threw them into the Hudson River; Mary Alice Fleming, accused of poisoning her mother with clam chowder laced with arsenic; Maria Barberi, on trial for slitting her boyfriend's throat because he would not marry her; George Appo, the boy pickpocket; and now Florence Burns.[7]

The Angel's self-appointed duties were to attend her charges in court and give them moral support, and sometimes physical support, as well, with a ready supply of smelling salts if they were in danger of collapsing. She also took it upon herself to exhort them against continuing a life of crime if they were to be released, to encourage them to turn to God and ask for his forgiveness, and to intervene with the courts if she thought the prisoner had been falsely charged or deserved a more lenient sentence. While at first many judges were dismissive of what they thought of as "sentimentalism" on the part of Mrs. Foster, they soon came to rely on her as a liaison between the court and the prisoner. Indeed, at times this liaison position ran the risk of turning Mrs. Foster into a spy. When she was accused by a reporter of being a "stool pigeon" for the district attorney in the Fleming case when she was able to get confidential information from the defendant, Mrs. Foster vehemently denied this charge.

In fact, Mrs. Foster was responsible for creating, at her own expense, a hidden retreat for battered women and for those women who wanted to escape lives of crime and rehabilitate themselves. She got donations from New York's most famous millionaire families, such as the Rockefellers, Vanderbilts, and Astors. She enlisted society women to come to the Tombs and host special teas for the female prisoners as a way of brightening their lives and demonstrating a lesson in manners.

If a woman prisoner were pregnant, Mrs. Foster intervened with the warden to allow extra time and a special place for the woman's daily exercise. It was rumored that she had done this for Florence Burns, although the warden denied that Miss Burns was getting any privileges that others could not also have—not exactly a ringing denial of a pregnancy.[8]

The Tombs Angel was primarily a source of sympathetic support and companionship for Florence, and she promised her that she would always accompany her to the court hearings. Thanks to Florence's attorney, Foster Backus, these hearings would be held at the Court of Special Sessions before a magistrate and not in a trial before a jury.

FOSTER L. BACKUS

Fifty-three-year-old Foster L. Backus was exactly the kind of lawyer you would want to hire if you found yourself in legal difficulties. A former district attorney, he was aware of all their tricks and knew how to use the system to his client's advantage. Backus had been a star athlete at St. Lawrence University, so this is possibly how he became acquainted with fellow Brooklyn resident and Amateur Athletic Union official Fred Burns, who probably hired him even before Florence was arrested.[9]

Backus was well aware that because of the nature of the grand jury, where no defense attorneys were allowed and great leeway was given to the district attorney, there would be an indictment against Florence. There was just too much evidence against her. He would have known that Florence and Walter had been sexually intimate and, if there was a baby on the way and the Burnses were aware of it, he would have known that too. And he *probably* knew either the suicide pact story or even the real story. All of those things would have been cards he did not want to play unless he had absolutely no other choice. Consequently, Backus's strategy was to lobby for what today would be considered a preliminary hearing, designed to ascertain whether there was probable cause to bind this suspect over for trial. It was up to the district attorney's office to present sufficient evidence to convince the judge that, more likely than not—the standard for a preliminary hearing or an inquest and not that of "beyond a reasonable doubt," which kicks in at trial—this suspect committed this crime. The advantage to the accused was that she did not have to put on any evidence, but she would be able to see what kind of proof the prosecution had in the likely event of a subsequent trial. The prosecution had to walk the fine line between showing enough to convince the judge that there was probable cause without revealing all its cards.

Foster Backus would contest every fact and piece of information (including a refusal to concede that the man in the hotel room was Walter Brooks) yet make the prosecution think that he would be cooperating. In fact, this was one of the constants throughout the hearing: Backus, nearly every day, asserted that he would think about producing the Burnses to testify and "probably" bring them in "next week," but he never did.[10]

For his part, the district attorney William Travers Jerome had his own constant, especially when he realized that the "check" so often promised by Foster Backus would never be "in the mail" or brought to the courtroom. Jerome

William Travers Jerome in 1905
(Library of Congress, 2002711837/)

threatened to withdraw from the hearing and go to the grand jury *right then* for an indictment, but he never did, even though he was well within his rights.[11]

WILLIAM TRAVERS JEROME

Forty-two-year-old William Travers Jerome, newly elected that fall to the position of district attorney for New York County, was something of an anomaly.[12] Although he was born into a family of wealth and privilege (Winston Churchill was his first cousin once removed), he nonetheless did not hesitate to go after criminals of every station, even friends of his own family. As an assistant district attorney and a judge in the Court of Special Sessions before his election to district attorney, Jerome had been one of the "pit-bull reformers" favored by then Commissioner Theodore Roosevelt and Rev. Charles Parkhurst.

Jerome's career as district attorney would be a stellar one, involving many famous New York cases, and we meet him here at the very beginning of it, having just been sworn in a month earlier.

FOSTER L. BACKUS VERSUS WILLIAM TRAVERS JEROME

Foster Backus, for his part, undoubtedly knowing the truth about the shooting and about a possible pregnancy, was trying to protect his client's reputation for as long as he could before he would be forced to admit her condition or claim that she had been "dishonored" by Brooks. Jerome, in turn, was madly searching for the pistol and some ironclad evidence to prove that Florence was the girl in the Glen Island, all the while with the threat of the Unwritten Law hanging over his head. He had no choice but to tread lightly. The two of them would play cat and mouse with each other throughout the proceedings.

In the normal course of events, the district attorney would have gone to the grand jury for an indictment against Florence. He would have gotten it, too, as the evidence that existed at the time was adequate to bind her over for trial. After the indictment was handed down, the next step would be a murder trial.

Foster Backus was a master negotiator here in convincing William Travers Jerome to go along with a special sessions hearing in front of a magistrate instead of the grand jury, just to see if the evidence was sufficient. Backus assured Jerome that at any time, the DA could go to the grand jury, but that the circumstances warranted extra caution: the girl was young; her family was well respected; some of the evidence seemed to have been tainted or unreliable.

District Attorney Jerome knew that his case could be undone by the Unwritten Law[13] and he wanted to make sure that it was solid before he proceeded. His aim was to get as much information from the witnesses as possible and to get Backus to reveal his defense. He had to strike a balance between vigorous prosecution and cooperation with the defense in order to get cooperation in return.

Jerome was hoping to get the Burns family to testify at the hearing, or even just talk to him in his office, without his having to issue subpoenas and come off as heavy-handed against people for whom much of the public had a great deal of sympathy. He made the mistake of trusting Foster Backus's constant assurances that he would produce the Burnses "next week some time" before coming to the realization that he'd been tricked—the Burnses were never going to appear because they had no exculpatory testimony that would help Florence. Anything they had was likely to incriminate her and contradict what she had told the police. When Jerome sent out his officers with subpoenas, he found that Backus had hastened the family out of the state to remove them from New York's jurisdiction.[14]

Florence Burns in court with her lawyer, Foster Backus (*New York World*)

Although Fred Burns continued to work at his brokerage job at the Custom House in Manhattan, somehow he managed to avoid Jerome's process servers, but reporters had no trouble finding him. Burns claimed he had stopped reading the newspapers and had no idea that subpoenas had been issued. He assured reporters that the family would stand by Florence "come what may, though it beggars us," and they would mortgage the house, if necessary. In truth, the Burnses did not own their home but were renting it, so this was just a matter of hyperbole on Fred's part. It was not revealed until months later that the cost of Florence's defense was being borne by her uncle, Oscar Von derBosch. The total would come to $6,000.[15]

Backus continued to insist that they would "present a complete alibi and explain everything on the stand," but he wanted to see what kind of evidence the prosecution had before proceeding. It was puzzling to all as to why—if, indeed, such a "complete alibi" existed that would exonerate Florence—he did not produce it immediately to get his client out of jail and have her declared as no longer a person of interest. It seemed absurd to go through a lengthy hearing if there was proof that Florence was "elsewhere" (which is what the Latin word *alibi* means). In actuality, her defense, if it came to needing one, would rely on something else entirely: the Unwritten Law.

THE UNWRITTEN LAW

On September 4, 1908, a twenty-six-year-old farmer named James Bachus was found dead of a gunshot wound outside his own home in rural Gifford, Idaho, and the house on fire. It did not take long for suspicion to fall on his twenty-two-year-old wife, Nancy, who told several versions of her story, some of which implicated various men who lived in the area. Eventually, she admitted that she had shot her husband. Everyone in Gifford knew—and some testified to it at her trial—that Jim Bachus was a physically and emotionally abusive husband. Nancy's lawyer could not claim self-defense, as Bachus had been shot in the back, so he argued that the police officers had forced a confession from her. Even though Nancy testified on the stand that she had shot her husband, the all-male jury acquitted her after only twenty-six minutes of deliberation.[1]

In 1895, New York City resident and Italian immigrant Maria Barberi found herself pregnant by her live-in boyfriend Domenico Cataldo, who had long promised to marry her but kept putting it off. Now, however, Maria needed him to come through for her and save her reputation. But Cataldo was not in the marrying mood and told her, "Only pigs marry." The day he uttered that nonsensical statement was his last. As he played cards in a nearby bar, Maria slit his throat from behind in front of several witnesses. Her death sentence at her trial set off a nationwide uproar of protests. Her lawyers got her a new trial on the grounds of an insanity defense. On the stand, she claimed, probably untruthfully, that she had been "a good girl" (a virgin) before meeting Domenico Cataldo, and she was acquitted after an hour of deliberation.[2]

In 1909, Verna Ware of Texas was acquitted of killing her druggist boyfriend, and an innocent bystander as collateral damage, while he was on trial for drugging her, raping her, and not marrying her when she subsequently gave birth to their child. In 1915, also in Texas, Winnie Jo Morris was found not guilty for killing the father of her unborn child because he would not marry her.[3]

What was going on here? For about a one-hundred-year span from the mid-nineteenth to the mid-twentieth centuries, there was a construct referred to as the Unwritten Law. Originally arising in the South, it eventually spread to all parts of the country. In its essence, the Unwritten Law applied to men whose wives had been found cheating on them or to husbands/fathers/ brothers who discovered that a man had "dishonored" their wives/daughters/ sisters, which could refer to anything from unwanted advances or harmful gossip to seduction and rape. This violation of a woman's honor called for the man to shoot the offender and not be held responsible for it. Sometimes he was not even arrested for the murder, but if he were, then prosecutors quickly discovered that no jury would convict him in those circumstances. Naturally, the Unwritten Law—being neither written nor a law—could not be used outright as a defense, but everyone understood it to be in operation. The law and the jury were happy if they could use something to legitimize the verdict, such as "temporary insanity," which was often the supposed defense. In fact, the Unwritten Law was often referred to as "dementia Americana."[4]

Eventually, the Unwritten Law came to apply to women who found themselves in circumstances where their own honor was besmirched or who were physically abused by their husbands or boyfriends. As women became more and more independent at the turn of the century, it was no longer assumed that men would come to their aid in matters of honor or abuse. Added to these cases was the very patriarchal attitude of male juries toward womanhood, and so there were probably more egregious cases of ignoring the fact that perhaps the woman had not been ruined after all but was a willing participant in her own downfall.[5]

As late as 1977, the Unwritten Law was applied in the famous "Burning Bed" case, where a woman abused by her husband for thirteen years set fire to his bed and killed him. Self-defense could not be used as the victim was asleep and not an immediate threat to her at that time, so the jury came back with a verdict of "not guilty by reason of temporary insanity."[6]

In fact, although it was often the case that male defendants successfully invoking the Unwritten Law were prosperous members of the upper classes, when it came to women on trial, juries did not always distinguish between rich and poor, as they almost certainly did with men. In 1902, at the same time New Yorkers were eagerly reading the salacious details surrounding the murder of Walter Brooks and the arrest of his girlfriend Florence Burns, a working-class German woman named Lizzie Madaus killed her husband William with a potato knife she was using to prepare their supper.[7]

Lizzie Madaus was pregnant with her sixth child, and her husband was an alcoholic who frequently beat her up. On the day of the murder, Lizzie was peeling potatoes when William came in, drunk, and began punching her in the face. He knocked her down and proceeded to beat her in a fury. The potato knife had fallen to the floor, whereupon Lizzie grabbed it and tried to fend off her husband's blows with it, stabbing him multiple times and killing him. The two oldest children testified on behalf of their mother, and Lizzie herself took the stand and admitted to the killing, although she claimed she had gone into something of a fugue state and didn't remember it all. And that was the hook the jury could hang its hat on. To the absolute outrage of the judge and the prosecutor, Lizzie was quickly acquitted on the grounds of "temporary insanity."

Of course, Lizzie Madaus's acquittal was more in the realm of self-defense, although husbands were allowed to beat their wives and children at that time, so it would not have been seen as justifiable homicide. Nonetheless, the jury saw the justice of protecting this woman and her children from the written law against murder by applying a version of the Unwritten Law, similar to what happened in Nancy Bachus's and Francine Hughes's (Burning Bed defendant) trials.

As for Florence Burns, it was clear that, once it was revealed that Walter Brooks had refused to marry her after having supposedly taken her virginity and possibly getting her pregnant, the Unwritten Law was a subtext in the case. It was there in the rumor that Florence was being allowed extra exercise reserved only for pregnant prisoners.[8] It was there in the question asked of Thomas Brooks as to whether he and his wife allowed Florence to stay in their home for three weeks because she "had a claim on them."[9] It was there in the sermons of ministers that Walter Brooks had deserved what he got, and in the opinions of newspaper editorial pages that Florence was justified in killing him.[10] And it was there in attorney Foster Backus's insistence—more than once—that if the true facts of the situation were known, not a jury in the land would convict Florence Burns.[11] Seldom mentioned by name, the Unwritten Law was understood by everyone to be the solution to the mystery of the murder of Walter Brooks. Why else would her attorney allow her to languish in the Tombs if she had a legitimate defense?

FLORENCE IN JAIL AND A CITY OBSESSED

All things considered, Florence Burns was not having a terrible time in jail, nor was she languishing there. She was the focus of attention throughout the city and reveled in reading the newspaper accounts about herself.[1] She was out of what she thought of as the oppressive atmosphere of her home. She received many visitors, although some of them were using bogus excuses (that they knew her; that they were looking for a missing relative who might have been incarcerated; that they had been in or near the Glen Island on the night of February 14 and could possibly identify the woman they saw) just to get an up-close glimpse of Florence. She was fussed over by the matron and the Tombs Angel. She got a lot of mail, some of it from "cranks" and some of which contained marriage proposals. One letter of encouragement came from Helen Southgate, whose suicide pact probably gave Florence the idea for an excuse.[2] And, with all of it, she enjoyed the "distinction," along with Roland Molineux and Albert Patrick, of being one of the Tombs' most famous current inhabitants.

There was a lighthearted moment despite the seriousness of a smallpox scare in the Tombs when it was determined that all 392 prisoners and 27 attendants were to be vaccinated. Awaiting vaccination with Florence were Molineux and Patrick. Molineux had been convicted of murder in his first trial and was awaiting a retrial for the 1899 poisoning of a woman who swallowed the tampered Bromo Seltzer intended for Molineux's romantic rival. Albert Patrick was an attorney on trial at that time for having forged the will of William Marsh Rice (the patron of Rice University), leaving all the money to himself, then murdering Rice.

In the vaccination room, Patrick waited his turn by reading while Molineux received his shot:

CURRY (the Tombs keeper in charge of the prisoners getting vaccinated): What are you reading, Patrick? The New Testament?

DOCTOR: Maybe it's the Old Testament.

MOLINEUX: Maybe it's someone's Last Will and Testament.[3]

There were articles about the Brooks case, or about the principal players in the case, every day in every paper, even when court was not in session, and it became the primary topic of discussion in the New York area. A young clerk in New Jersey, who should have known better, put a gun to his friend's head to show him how Florence could have shot Walter Brooks. The gun went off, as guns do, and the friend was wounded, although not fatally.[4]

Calls were made claiming to know who really killed Walter Brooks: a sister, a brother, a friend, a stranger overheard confessing, or even the caller himself or herself. These caused the police much wasted time as they were unable to locate the caller or the killer because false names had been given.[5]

A twenty-eight-year-old woman suffered something of a nervous break-down as a result of becoming obsessed with the Brooks-Burns case. In late February, she left her home to ride a couple of streetcars, then got on a ferry and traveled back and forth between Manhattan and Brooklyn for five hours. When she finally "came to" at the foot of Broadway, she claimed she was the one who had shot Walter Brooks.[6]

As for Florence herself, although there was the stigma of incarceration and being the talk of the town, she must have seen this time as something of a respite from the frenetic life she had lived up to the time of the murder. She had been constantly at odds with her parents and with Walter, and she had to move from place to place, all with an anxious uncertainty as to her future. In the Tombs, she had a routine to follow where she was free from having to make decisions. There were times for rising, for meals, for church services, for court attendance, for recreation, and for bedtime. Florence's parents could not visit her because they were avoiding prosecutorial subpoenas, so she was free of their hand-wringing and recriminations. And she was under the loving care of the Tombs Angel, who not only steadied her in court but declared that Florence Burns was innocent of the charge against her.

THE FUNERAL OF WALTER BROOKS

Walter Brooks's funeral was held in the midst of the second-worst blizzard ever to hit the New York City area up to that time. Today, it does not even make the top five. Ten inches of snow and gale-force winds brought the city to a halt.[7] Yet hundreds braved the storm to get to the Brooks home on Decatur Street in Brooklyn. Court was adjourned for that day—February 17—because many of the witnesses were friends of Walter Brooks and would be attending the services.[8]

So many people were packed inside the house and outside it that the choir could not get in. A hysterical Mrs. Brooks was confined to her room and did not attend her son's funeral downstairs, where the open casket revealed Walter's serene and peaceful face.[9]

Officiating at the funeral was the minister who had refused to marry Florence and Walter just weeks before his death: the Reverend Robert Rogers of the Episcopal Church of the Good Shepherd. His sermon that day was a cautionary tale directed primarily at young men, whom he warned to avoid the "thorns" (girls) that would lead them astray, as Walter had been. If they did not keep on the straight path, he told them, the thorns would catch them. Many of the young women at the service took offense at this![10]

One notable absence from the funeral was one of Walter's best friends and the man who had introduced him to Florence Burns: Harry Casey. Determined not to indulge in grief and sadness, the always-upbeat and self-absorbed Casey went to the Orpheum Theater, then to the Argyle Restaurant on Fulton Street, dressed—as always—in sartorial splendor.[11]

At the end of the service, Walter's body was taken to the family plot in the Evergreens Cemetery and buried next to his little sister and his maternal grandmother.

ANOTHER TRAGEDY

Exactly five days after Walter's funeral and the city-crippling blizzard, there was yet another tragedy—this one specifically affecting the court and Florence Burns. Early on the morning of February 22, an ordnance explosion in the basement of the Armory on Park Avenue destroyed that building. Sparks from the fire spread across the street to the Park Avenue Hotel, where many guests blithely watched the Armory fire, unaware of their own peril. Too late, they realized that they were trapped. There were no fire escapes anywhere in the building, a serious safety code violation even for 1902. People suffocated on the stairways and in the halls, while many leapt from the windows to their deaths. The death toll, originally thought to have been fifty, was a surprisingly low twenty-one. One of these was the Tombs Angel, Mrs. Rebecca Foster.[12]

The Park Avenue Hotel before the fire (*New York World*)

The death of Mrs. Foster was a shock to New York City court regulars, as well as to the inhabitants of the Tombs prison whom she had counseled. Florence Burns, who was not told of her death until after the court session that day, was grief-stricken in a way that she never exhibited over Walter Brooks's death or her own legal situation. But, at the same time, her focus in this grief was self-directed because it meant that the Tombs Angel could no longer accompany and support her in court, as the older woman had promised she would.[13]

For the first time in its history, the Court of Special Sessions adjourned for a woman. And, two years later, a marble memorial tablet was placed in the court with a bas-relief bust of Mrs. Foster and that of an angel comforting a woman. The inscription read: "On her lips was the law of kindness. Rebecca Salome Foster. Oct. 24, 1848–Feb. 22, 1902."[14]

THE COURT OF SPECIAL SESSIONS

New York City's Court of Special Sessions, replaced in 1962 by the New York City Criminal Court, was the equivalent of a Municipal Court, the venue for misdemeanor criminal cases and civil cases valued at under a certain dollar amount. Although Florence Burns would be subject to the death penalty if convicted of murder, she had not been formally charged as yet and this was not a trial, even though she was under arrest. A felony trial would be held in the Court of General Sessions, like today's Superior Court, but the hearing to determine whether that trial would take place was held in the inferior court.

Magistrate Cornell had agreed to this hearing, in lieu of one in front of the grand jury, but because he was an acquaintance of Fred Burns, he recused himself from presiding over it. However, he did not let his friendship with Burns prevent him from denying bail for his daughter. Still, this was an enormous concession to a murder suspect.[1]

Florence's future would be determined by the judge who had been recently appointed to take the place of William Travers Jerome on the court after Jerome's recent election as district attorney: thirty-six-year-old Julius Mayer, "a stickler for the dignity of the court," who would be described in his later career as "more a Czar than a Judge." Lawyers who would appear before him over the course of his career would remember one of his most frequent remarks as, "Come to the point and be brief."[2]

During the Burns hearing, Judge Mayer was incensed at the circus-like atmosphere that frequently attended it, with spectators coming and going at will, laughing and talking and eating, and generally acting as if they were at an entertainment—which, of course, they were, as high-profile murder cases were great sources of public enjoyment. This would cause the judge to stop the proceedings and issue an ultimatum: Sit still, be quiet, or leave. At one

Judge Julius Mayer, presiding over the
Burns hearing (*New York World*)

point, frustrated by his inability to effect any change in spectator behavior, he issued an order to his deputies that no one could come in or go out while there was a witness on the stand. This, at least, cut down on the commotion during testimony caused by curiosity-seekers who were constantly entering, looking around for fifteen or twenty minutes, then leaving.[3]

Although William Travers Jerome was in charge of the Burns case, he spent much of his time interviewing witnesses in an attempt to find a "smoking gun" that would link Florence to the Glen Island Hotel at the time Walter Brooks was shot.[4] Consequently, much of the day-to-day testimony was handled by Assistant DA George Schurman. Of the many potential witnesses brought before Jerome, only a small percentage testified under oath at the hearing. This was for several reasons: first of all, Jerome did not want to reveal all his evidence at the hearing; second, some of the witnesses were not credible; and third, some of them seem to have refused to testify under oath, either because they were not telling the truth or because they did not want the notoriety that public testimony would bring. It is interesting to note that of all the witnesses Foster Backus procured on behalf of Florence, not one testified in court. Of course, it was not necessary, as the defense had no obligations at this hearing, but it would seem that if any of them had convincing exculpatory evidence, Backus would have insisted that it be presented.

However, many of the witnesses' names and their testimony, albeit unsworn, leaked out to the press, which dutifully printed it. In fact, the press was so aggressive in pursuing witnesses for statements that when Walter's former fiancée Charlotte Eaton and her sister Edith wanted to leave, a detective had them climb out a window in the courthouse, then onto a roof ledge in ankle-deep snow to inch their way to another window, which would in turn lead them to a back entrance unhampered by the pesky press.[5]

Always aware of the many thousands of people who would not be attending the court proceedings, reporters described everything: the behavior, dress, poses, and physical characteristics of witnesses and spectators alike. If you were a resident of New York City in 1902, you would feel that you had been in the courtroom yourself. For example, you would read that Florence's outfit for court on February 22 consisted of a "black velvet Russian blouse with tiny silver dots, a black skirt, a belt with a gilt buckle, a big black picture hat, white ruching about her neck, black suede gloves, and a red and white enamel winged Mercury's-foot pin in her blouse." When she first arrived in court, she was wearing a veil and a short jacket, both of which she promptly removed.[6]

Florence's various poses were also the subject of attention. She yawned a lot, which gave the impression of complete indifference, even though yawning can also be a sign of nervousness. She put her elbows on the table, rested her chin in her palms, or spread her arms on the chairbacks on either side of her—more the behavior of a restless child than that of a young woman facing the death penalty. She claimed to hate being "stared at by all the fools who crowd into the court-room," she told a *World* reporter, then, pointing out two young policemen who were watching the conversation, said, "There are two fools staring at me now."[7]

The most frequent attendees at murder trials in the Victorian and Gilded Ages were women, and reporters commented on their numbers, their behavior, their looks, and sometimes interjected opinions as to whether they should even be there instead of at home getting their husbands' dinners. A *Brooklyn Eagle* reporter ruminated on the different types of women at the Burns hearing, which devolved over the weeks from a "typewriters' gathering" to an "old maids' convention" to a "soubrettes' show." The latter category featured "peroxided" actresses from the local theaters.[8] The women arrived each morning, long before the doors opened, and offered as much as five dollars for an admission card. The admission card requirement was installed by Judge Mayer to manage the attendance, but these were free, to be issued to anyone with a valid connection to the case. And when they were gone, they were gone.[9]

Harry Casey and his Bedford Gang cohorts "dressed in the very extreme of fashion and appeared to enjoy the situation thoroughly." Casey and "other sartorial wonders" were "all clad in most irreproachable garb." But Casey, described as a "gilded youth," angered observers with his bragging and bravado in court. He gave copies of his picture to the reporters and told everyone that he lived up to his nickname of "Handsome Harry," as his good looks had been the ruin of many a young woman. Some listeners were tempted to beat him up for this, and for the unprintable language used by Casey and the other boys in discussing the women they had seduced.[10]

The Bedford Avenue Gang had a field day, dressed in their standard outfits and preening in court over their importance in the case. Scam artists par excellence, they had gone to a newspaper office and offered to sell them a new photo of Florence Burns for twenty-five dollars, but the sketch artist recognized it as that of a local actress known as "Pink Pajama Girl," whose photo was selling for mere pennies. Undaunted, our lads tried again at another newspaper, this time successfully, as that sketch artist was obviously unfamiliar with "Pink Pajama Girl."[11]

EXPOSING THE BEDFORD AVENUE GANG

The Bedford Avenue Gang got their comeuppance in a series of articles in which Foster Backus's brother Erastus, a detective with the Kings County Court, revealed what he knew about their activities, and an anonymous member of the gang gave out the salacious details of orgies, thievery, and confidence games.[12] (The reporter writing these articles had to clean up the language of both the informant and Det. Erastus Backus, as both were fairly profane.)

This informant claimed that the number of young women who were hanging out with the gang ("and you know what that means," he confided, hinting at sexual activity) was five times the number of young men. They all knew Walter Brooks and Florence Burns and "there wasn't a member of the gang who was not as well acquainted with her as was Brooks." He recounted that a young woman in the grandstand at the Aqueduct Race Track was approached by seven gang members she knew. They took her out to one of the stables and "held a wild and shameful orgie [sic]." It was not clear whether this was voluntary on the young woman's part. Another time, five of the gang members took a girl to a Bedford Avenue pool hall and "indulged in revels which would have put a Nero to blush." Again, there is no indication as to whether this was a gang rape, although the informant commented that "there is an absolute absence of any moral standard among the young women."

After the first article appeared, the Bedford Gang members were worried about this exposure and met in a saloon to discuss what should be done. "Who has been peaching?" they wondered. The decision was made that from then on, they should not admit to knowing Florence Burns at all and that they only knew Walter Brooks by sight. "And the one who opens his head again gets his roof blown off."

Many readers were thankful to the *Eagle* for the exposé, which they hoped would stop the outrageous behavior and be a wake-up call to clueless parents. Backus went even further: He had a list of sixteen boys under the age of seventeen, all with criminal records, and all having respectable parents, many of them wealthy. If there were to be one more robbery or fake purchasing or other gang transgression, he would give his list to the *Eagle* for printing.

THE ISSUES

In order to have Florence Burns bound over for trial, the prosecution would need to prove that she intentionally killed Walter Brooks—not "beyond a reasonable doubt" that she did it, but "more likely than not" that she did so—and that the state had probable cause to proceed with a trial.

Anyone familiar with courtroom dramas on television knows the phrase "means, motive, and opportunity," the establishment of which can result in a verdict of *guilty* for the prosecution. But what do these words mean in legal terms? *Means* is not just access to the murder weapon but the ability to use it. If it is determined that the victim was killed with a heavy sledgehammer, then it is not likely that a frail, arthritic, eighty-year-old woman would have the strength to wield it effectively, despite her having access to it. In Florence's case, the prosecution would have to prove that she had access to the .32-caliber pistol used to kill Walter and that she knew how to use it.

Motive is the one thing that everyone, especially a jury, wants to know: "Why was this victim killed?" Yet, it is not necessary for a criminal case. An 1897 California Supreme Court case still cited today, *The People v. Durrant*, held that the ways of the human heart are boundless and it is not always possible to divine an individual's motive. It would be an undue burden to require that a prosecution do so.[13] Yet, prosecutors ignore motive at their peril. Notwithstanding its being legally unnecessary, motive is critical to proving guilt to a jury, even if it has to be postulated: Why would Florence kill the man she claimed she loved even more than her parents?

Opportunity is the proximity to the scene of the crime at the time of death, or (in the case of a poisoning or a hired hit) the ability to effect the chain of events that results in the victim's death. This is where alibi comes in—to place a suspect too physically far away for travel, or seen to be in a different place, however near, at the time of the murder, or having no access to the poison used. Hence, the importance of placing Flo at or near the Glen Island Hotel between 9:00 and 11:00 P.M. on February 14.

GEORGE WASHINGTON

The most critical witness for the prosecution was the Glen Island bellhop, George Washington, who had seen the woman with Walter Brooks that night. Even though Washington was a young newlywed, he was treated as a child on the stand. For example, on February 22, Backus, in a condescending tone, reminded the witness of the truthfulness of his namesake, whose birthday it was that day, and so he must be sure to tell the truth. While everyone else in the courtroom found this humorous, Washington did not. He was never addressed as Mr. Washington, but as George. He was never referred to without race descriptors: Negro, mulatto, copper-colored, "little and yellow as bright copper"; and never as a man, but as a boy. Yet, Washington was a sharp observer, and although he had a slight stutter, he was an articulate and thoughtful witness on the stand.[14]

Although George Washington fretted about not being able to support his wife because of the court obligations that took him away from his job, he took those obligations very seriously. He made sure that he understood each question and thought about his answer before speaking. If he were asked to identify someone in the courtroom, he stood up and pointed at the individual.[15]

During his testimony, Washington fell prey to a standard (and still used) trial attorney's device of breaking down a witness's estimate of the duration of time. The bellhop had said that, upon arrival in Room 12 and after lighting the gas for "J. Wilson and wife," he conversed with the woman "for two or three minutes" as to any other needs she might have. At this point, she had lifted her veil, so that he got a good look at her face, and this was critical in placing Florence Burns at the scene. Judge Mayer, in what would normally be the defense attorney's role, asked Washington to sit silently until the same amount of time passed as that in the hotel room as he looked at the woman. It turned out to be thirty seconds instead of two or three minutes—still a long time to be looking at something, although it suffers by comparison.[16]

However, Washington had made a critical error, subject to misinterpretation, when he spoke to responding police officers at the Glen Island Hotel on February 15. In his identification of the woman who had accompanied Walter Brooks to Room 12 the night before, he stated that she "was not a clear white woman," which most people—especially Foster Backus—took to mean that she was not white but black. But Washington said he did not mean this, that he was talking about her complexion, not her race. As Florence Burns was very pale, Backus milked this for all it was worth to destroy Washington's identification. The most likely answer is that, in the dim gaslight of the hotel, the woman he saw did indeed appear to have a darker complexion, as well as darker hair, than Washington at first thought. He had not seen her without her wide black picture hat until he went to the police station the following day to identify her.[17]

Washington stood his ground and never wavered from his identification of Florence Burns as the young woman with Walter Brooks. He even described what she was wearing that night, which matched what Harry Cohen said she had worn to the Brooks and Wells office that day. Nevertheless, this identification was undone, not just by the confusing "not a clear white woman" statement but by two separate lineup incidents at the police station that were out of his control. In the first, Washington had been told to poke his head into the room where Florence was being interrogated. His immediate recognition of her was discounted because she was the only woman there. In the second instance, Florence was put with two other women—both older, both shorter, both stouter, neither looking anything like her—and this invalid lineup also negated Washington's picking her out as the woman he had seen.[18]

George Washington's testimony was critical for the prosecution, as it put Florence Burns—or someone who looked very much like her—at the Glen Island with the victim. It is likely that if only one error had been eliminated—the "not a clear white woman" or the invalid lineups—the prosecution would have prevailed. But Judge Mayer thought the combination was enough to negate Washington's identification testimony, and so he refused to consider it.[19]

John Earl, night clerk at the Glen Island Hotel (*New York World*)

JOHN EARL

The other Glen Island employee who might have put Florence at the scene was the night clerk, John Earl. He was the one who had signed in the three couples and was on duty at the time that Brooks's companion would have left the hotel. Newspapers back then pulled no punches in their descriptions of people, so Earl was described as "not as astute as the Negro bell boy" and with a face "that does not display a sharp intellect."[20]

Although Earl was all over the board with the time line, there were three items that locked him in: the victim's 9:00 signing of the register, the 10:30 order of the lemon soda, and another couple's signing in at 10:50. Earl claimed that the woman would have had to pass by his desk in order to leave the hotel and that he did not see her. He could not have identified her in any case, as all three women who came in at 9:00 stayed in a parlor and did not approach the desk while the men signed in.[21]

The woman must have left sometime between 10:35 (assuming five minutes for the lemon soda to be brought to her, the last reliable sighting being by George Washington) and 10:50 (when Earl was at the desk signing in the fourth couple). But she may have had a wider window of opportunity when it is recalled that John Earl, when it came to Glen Island Hotel activities, deliberately overlooked any untoward occurrences. Suppose he *had* seen a woman leave. He would not have known who she was, but in 1902, an unescorted woman leaving a hotel would have been noteworthy, and Earl would have been required to ask if she needed assistance had the Glen Island been other than a "Raines Law" hotel.

Because the Glen Island "asked no questions," however, John Earl would not have done so. Probably there were prostitutes who frequented the hotel as well. After the murder, when he was being questioned about a solitary woman leaving the hotel, he may even have remembered that there was one, but if he admitted it, it would not reflect well on the Glen Island Hotel and could have cost him his job. He did admit that he might have turned his chair around for a better light while he read the newspaper, so that his back was to anyone leaving the hotel at that time. At any rate, Earl stuck to his story that he could not identify the woman with Walter Brooks, and this statement was undoubtedly true.

THE BRIGHTON BEACH "L"

But all was not lost in placing Florence near the Glen Island during the critical time frame. She had an admirer—nineteen-year-old Arthur Cleveland Wible,[22] a conductor on the Brighton Beach division of the Kings County Elevated Railway. Florence Burns was a frequent rider on the Brighton Beach line since his hiring in May 1901, and Arthur and his fellow conductors always noticed her and the other pretty girls who rode with them. "She is the prettiest girl out there," said one of the conductors.[23] For the late-night trains, which ran only every half hour, the railway removed all but two of the cars that were necessary for the workday, so Wible easily noticed Florence on the shortened 11:15 train from the Brooklyn Bridge terminus. She was sitting three or four seats in back of the front door of the rear (second) car. He noticed her before she got on, and he nodded to her when she got off at her usual stop at Beverley Road, just a few minutes' walk from her home. In court, when Wible took the stand, Florence gave a reaction that indicated familiarity with him and looked somewhat disconcerted.[24]

Thomas Smith, proprietor of a newsstand at the Brooklyn Bridge terminus, corroborated the testimony of Arthur Wible. Smith, who knew Florence by sight and by name, was just closing up his stand when she came across

the bridge and got on the 11:15 train. These
sightings contradicted Florence's claim that
she was home by 7:00 that Friday night.[25]

The Glen Island Hotel, today the site of
the World Trade Center Memorial for the
victims of the attack on September 11, 2001,
was approximately half a mile from the
Brooklyn Bridge. Even today, pedestrians can
use the bridge walkway to go from Manhattan to Brooklyn, and back in Florence's day,
it was the only way to go from one side to the
other unless one took a shuttle trolley or had
an automobile. Eventually, the trains went
all the way through, but that was still a few
years away in 1902. How might Florence have
crossed the bridge? The newspapers report
that it would have taken her ten minutes to
walk from the Glen Island to the Manhattan
side of the bridge. From there, she must have
taken a shuttle to the Brooklyn side, which
was a mile away (and would have taken a
brisk walker fifteen to eighteen minutes), as

Arthur C. Wible, the young
street car conductor (*New
York World*)

she got to the 11:15 train a little after 11:00. Flo's parents had been to the theater
in Manhattan that night and in all probability were on the 10:45 train. What
an awkward encounter if they had been on the same train!

Foster Backus, of course, maintained that Florence was not on the train.
He produced Peter Bielman, a clerk in the Brooklyn surrogate's office, who
claimed he had been on that same 11:15 train and sitting in the car where Flo
was supposed to be, and that she was not there. In fact, there was a "spoony"
couple sitting in the exact seat where Wible said Florence was, and their public
displays of affection were embarrassing to the other riders, so this incident
stuck in his mind. These young people got off at Beverley Road. Bielman
even provided Backus with the names of some of the other passengers on
that train. Investigation must have discovered that Bielman was mistaken
as to the day, however, as he did not testify under oath, and neither he nor
those other passengers were heard from after that.[26]

THE TWO COUPLES AT THE GLEN ISLAND

As the hearing proceeded, the police were desperately trying to find two things: the pistol that was used to kill Walter Brooks and the two couples who signed in at the Glen Island Hotel around the same time as Brooks and his companion. Since the other two women spent time in the parlor with "J. Wilson's wife," the prosecution assumed they would have noticed what she was wearing. Apparently, they would rather have heard this from white women than from a black man.

Needless to say, the other two couples had no intention of exposing themselves to notoriety, as it was obvious what they were doing in that hotel, which was considered scandalous back then even if they were not cheating on spouses. They must have told other people, though, because eventually they were discovered. The women were sisters living in New Jersey, one unmarried and the other married with two children. Of the two men, one (unmarried) also lived in New Jersey and was in the brokerage business with the second man, who was married. Although no names were printed in the newspapers, there was probably enough identifying information to get these people in trouble. They were not put on the stand (one of the women said she would rather go to jail than testify, as it would ruin her), but the women were able to describe the third "wife" in the parlor, and the description matched Florence Burns.[27]

The pistol, however, remained elusive, although even the storm drains were being searched for it.[28]

THE MEDICAL TESTIMONY

The three physicians who testified could agree on only one point: Walter Brooks was killed by the bullet in his head. Otherwise, they disagreed as to whether Brooks could have moved after being shot or had been paralyzed by the shot. Dr. Philip Johnson, who assisted at the autopsy, held that the victim had been paralyzed, while Dr. John Sweeney said he was not. Moreover, Sweeney had tickled the bottom of Brooks's foot and claimed that he got a response, which would negate paralysis. There was also some confusion as to whether Brooks had changed his position over the course of the night, which would supposedly have been impossible if he had been paralyzed.[29]

Foster Backus grabbed onto Sweeney's theory and hinted that Brooks had been shot between the doctor's first and second visits—which would mess up the time line for Florence's involvement, even if she had been in the room with him. But as this would posit yet another woman wishing Brooks harm, who managed to sneak into the room after the first hypothetical woman had left, it strained credulity and so was not vigorously pursued.

Dr. John Vincent Sweeney, the on-call physician for the Glen Island Hotel, was born in New York City in 1858, the son of Irish-born immigrants. He graduated from the New York Homeopathic Medical College and his practice consisted primarily of obstetrics. Dr. Sweeney held some crackpot theories, among them a belief that when a community is not engaged in war for an entire generation, warlike tendencies become inert in unborn babies, which will then be awakened when war is actual or threatened . . . if their mothers are patriotic! "Virility begets virility," he wrote. Sweeney himself never married.[30]

On his first day on the stand, Dr. Sweeney presented the time line of his three visits and denied having seen a comb in Room 12. But on the next day, he said that he had seen a comb and some hairpins in the room—just an ordinary comb, five inches long and made of celluloid, but missing some teeth. On cross-examination, he said he did not remember having been asked about it before and that possibly he had not understood the question. He was sure he could recognize the comb if he saw it again. After this, Foster Backus injected some humor into the proceedings by requesting that Assistant DA George Schurman produce the comb and hairpins because "combs and hairpins have been disappearing from my family at a great rate, and perhaps I'll be able to trace them to room 12 in the hotel." Everybody got a kick out of this, even Florence, who was usually stoically impassive in court.[31]

Schurman showed Dr. Sweeney the comb Thomas Brooks found in Room 12, but he did not recognize it. The one he saw in the hotel was lighter in color, had more teeth broken off in the middle, and was more perfect at the ends.[32]

The most puzzling medical testimony was that of the coroner, Albert T. Weston, who had performed the autopsy. The muzzle of the gun had been placed right against the victim's skull at a point two inches behind the top of the right ear. From there, the bullet had progressed to a point that was over the left eye. This, of course, was not disputable. However, Weston was convinced that Walter Brooks had committed suicide! It was not physically impossible, of course, but it was such an awkward position that it's hard to imagine that anyone seriously bent on killing himself would have attempted it.[33]

Furthermore, if Brooks had killed himself, where was the gun? Backus claimed that a hotel employee took it to prevent the other guests from being upset at the commission of a suicide, but the hotel countered with the argument that a suicide would be less upsetting to patrons than a murder. (In fact, there had been several suicides at the Glen Island over the years.)[34] The most puzzling aspect of this is how Dr. Weston could have come to this conclusion. If he had a connection to Foster Backus or the Burns family, it was not revealed.[35]

Besides not having the temperament to commit suicide, Walter Brooks had made plans. He had arranged to meet with Harry Cohen that same night; he had promised Ruth Dunne that once he was free of Florence Burns, he would make another date with her; and not long before his death, he had ordered a new suit to be made for Easter (March 30, 1902) so that he could be in the Easter Parade.[36]

During the autopsy testimony, Florence fanned herself and yawned, giving the impression that she was completely uninterested in it.

MR. AND MRS. THOMAS W. BROOKS

The most dramatic testimony was that of Walter's parents, Thomas and Mary Brooks. That day, many "fashionably dressed women" came to court. In general, over the course of this hearing, women outnumbered men by approximately ten to one, but on this particular day, so many showed up that "there was no room for a man in court." Instead of the young "belles," however, this day's audience was "like an old maids' convention," with row after row of older women garbed in funereal black, much to the disappointment of the young *Brooklyn Eagle* reporter.[37]

Another visitor was the famous artist Charles Dana Gibson, creator of the Gibson Girl, who had come to observe Florence Burns, possibly with an eye to sketching her. If he ever did so, it has not surfaced.[38]

Also attending the hearing was the eccentric, way-ahead-of-her-time Dr. Mary Edwards Walker, sixty-nine, who had been awarded the Medal of Honor (the only woman and one of only a handful of civilians ever to receive it) for her bravery in the Civil War as a doctor and as a prisoner of war. A staunch feminist and suffragist, Dr. Walker usually wore men's clothing because women's clothing was too restrictive and because the long skirts and dresses picked up and spread disease. She was correct on both counts. At the Burns hearing, Dr. Walker had a tendency to voice her approval or disapproval, sometimes even clapping her hands, and was invariably scolded by Judge Mayer, which stifled her not at all.[39]

Mrs. Brooks stops to glare at
Florence Burns on her way to
the witness stand (*New York
World*)

As for Florence, she just kept on fanning, even when Mrs. Brooks stopped
on her way to the stand and stared at her "with hatred and disgust." This
meeting was exactly what the many women in court that day had come to
see, and they were not disappointed. It was a thirty-second stare down and
caused Florence to blush.[40]

Walter's mother's emotional testimony consisted primarily of her many
encounters with Florence during her three-week stay with them when Florence constantly threatened to kill Walter. As Mrs. Brooks recounted it, it
seemed to happen every time they met, every single day.[41]

When Mrs. Brooks had been on the stand for approximately half an hour,
she was shown the watch found in the hotel room and identified it as her
son's. Holding Walter's watch, which she tenderly kissed and held close to
her face, caused such emotion in her that she collapsed from a seizure-like
fit and had to be carried out of the courtroom by four attendants—right past
Florence's end of the defense table. Mrs. Brooks's garments even brushed her
slightly. Yet Flo kept on fanning and gave no reaction whatsoever, not even
looking at the unconscious woman.

Mrs. Brooks was able to continue her testimony forty-five minutes later, when she gave the time line for Florence's involvement with the Brooks family and identified the comb her husband found in the hotel room as one she had seen in Florence's room. On cross-examination, Backus pulled a trick on her and removed the evidence tag from the comb, then asked her to identify it. She said she could not, that it did not resemble the combs she knew that Florence used, and she had never seen this particular comb. This, of course, was like the "one-man lineup," in that the identification tag tipped her off to the comb found in the hotel room where her son had been shot. But she couldn't really identify it.

Mrs. Brooks was also confused by Backus's constant changing of combs, then removing them from her sight and asking her to identify the comb she had just held, without looking at it. At one point, pressed to answer whether she had ever seen a particular comb, she said, "I am getting dazed and tired out." Backus thought she was shamming to avoid answering and asked that the incident be noted in the record.

Backus had a dilemma in cross-examining Mary Brooks. She was a grieving mother who received much sympathy for the loss of her son, so if he came on too strong in his questioning, he would be viewed as a heartless monster and, by extension, Florence would as well. Yet, he had an obligation to defend his client, and he knew there were some holes in this witness's testimony. Although there was no jury to consider at the moment, a potential jury pool was following the hearing every day in the newspapers. So, instead of attacking her, he let her own answers illustrate the essential contradiction in her testimony—that despite the many threats Florence Burns uttered, nobody but Mrs. Brooks ever heard them, and the Brookses allowed her to continue to live in their home for three weeks:

FOSTER BACKUS: Did Florence ever make any threat she would shoot your son before she was sick in your house?

MARY BROOKS: Yes, sir.

FB: When?

MB: About the third time I saw her.

FB: How many times and in how many conversations did Florence Burns tell you she would kill Walter?

MB: The last week she was in my house she told me on Monday, Tuesday, and Thursday.

FB: She told you before that also?

MB: Yes.

FB: Did she tell you every time she saw you?

MB: No, sir.

FB: Did she tell you pretty nearly every time she saw you?

MB: No, not as often as that.

FB: Did she ever tell you that in the presence of anybody else?

MB: No, sir.

FB: She and Walter kept going together after she had told you that, didn't they?

MB: Yes, sir.

Asked if anyone else was present when Florence told her about trying to get her father's pistol, Mary Brooks admitted that there was not:

FB: What did you say to her [about getting her father's revolver]?

MB: I didn't say a word.

FB: Did she stay there and talk to you after that?

MB: Yes.

FB: Now how many times that week did she tell you she'd kill Walter?

MB: Every day that she was in my home that week. She ended every conversation by saying: "I will kill Walter unless he marries me."

Thomas Brooks, who had picked up the comb in the hotel room, had never seen, or at least had not paid attention to, any combs that Florence Burns had worn, nor had he seen any in their home. He thought the comb in the hotel room might have been a clue, so he took it and gave it to a policeman, who later came to the Brooks home. When he described getting to the hotel, where his son lay dying, he broke down briefly before he could continue. While spectators were moved by Mrs. Brooks's emotional collapse, they were far more affected by her husband's sobbing when he recounted the scene.[42]

THE "FAT BABY" FROM BAYONNE

If you were living in the Victorian or Gilded Ages and were unlucky enough to find yourself part of a high-profile murder case, you would hope to be entirely free of any physical flaws or personality quirks because these would be described in the newspapers as part of the entertainment for their readership. This is what happened to nineteen-year-old William Armit Eyre of Bayonne,

New Jersey, "a very fat young man," standing six-feet-two and weighing approximately 250 pounds, which makes him obese according to today's body mass index scale. After testifying, he was known to all as "Fatty" Eyre, and then as "that fat baby" in a scathing summation by Foster Backus.[43]

Eyre claimed that he, Walter Brooks, and Florence Burns had gone to the theater in September 1901. He was already acquainted with Brooks, but it was his first meeting with Florence. In the streetcar on their way to Weber & Fields' Music Hall to see the play *Hodge Podge,* Walter and Flo quarreled constantly. Unwisely, Walter interrupted the quarrel to point out a pretty girl to Eyre: "Billy, she's a beauty!" Eyre replied, "Yes, she's a peach." Florence's response was to look at Brooks angrily, "as if she was going to eat him up right there in the car," and told him, "If you say that again, I'll crack your nut." In the play, an actress told her boyfriend she would kill him if he ever left her, and Florence told Walter she would do the same.

Eyre's connection to Walter Brooks was through the grocery business. "What kind of goods?" Backus asked him. "Everything from sauerkraut up," Eyre told him, an answer that, for some reason, caused much laughter in the audience.[44]

"Fatty" Eyre supposedly told acquaintances over in Bayonne, New Jersey, that he had fabricated the whole story—that he had not been on the streetcar with Walter and Flo. Rather, that it was Walter who told him that Flo had threatened to kill him. When challenged about the discrepancy, Eyre insisted that he had heard her say this herself and that he never told anyone otherwise.[45]

However, there was a better than even chance that he had lied about some or all of this. He also claimed to have gone to Lehigh University and played left guard on their varsity football team in 1899 and 1900. Like Theodore Burris's false claim about having attended Cornell and playing football there, Eyre neither attended Lehigh nor played on its football team.[46]

Eyre had a money stunt that he pulled in bars, whereby he would drink a glass of whiskey, then offer to eat the glass for five dollars. Invariably, someone would take him up on it, whereupon Eyre would break the glass, then chew it up and swallow it. A surgeon who took out Eyre's appendix noticed there were shards of glass in his intestines, along with a quantity of pus. Although Eyre denied that he swallowed glass on purpose ("How I ever swallowed it, I don't know, nor do I have any idea"), his friends verified the whiskey-glass story, and a witness at the operation said that Eyre had notified the surgeon in advance that there would be glass in his intestines.[47]

So, "Fatty" Eyre was quite capable of lying and may have done so in the

Brooks-Burns hearing, possibly—as do so many in high-profile cases—to gain a measure of fame by inserting himself into the story. In his defense, however, his quote of Florence on the streetcar sounds very much like her, so if he was not in her presence, Brooks probably told him this.

THAT COMB AGAIN

Today, with all the advances in forensic DNA technology, we would need only a strand of hair from a comb or a brush used by a victim or a suspect. Unfortunately for the prosecution in the Brooks-Burns case, unless there were some distinguishing characteristics in Florence's combs that could tie her to the one found in Room 12 at the Glen Island, none of the comb testimony was probative. And it was all so tenuous. Thomas Brooks had picked it up from the dresser next to the bed, thereby tainting this evidence, from today's standpoint. It could be argued that he had taken one of Florence's combs left behind at his home and claimed he found it in Room 12, but he was oblivious to what kinds of combs Florence had and saw none when she was living in his home for three weeks. Mary Brooks claimed to have identified the Room 12 comb as one belonging to Florence, but it became very obvious that she wished it to be so rather than knew it to be so. Dr. Sweeney at first said he did not notice any combs in Room 12, then later said he had, but that it didn't look like the one placed in evidence.

In 1902, women's combs were so ubiquitous and common as to be indistinguishable unless they were made of very expensive material or had unusual designs. But the everyday combs worn by most middle-class women were plain celluloid ones, the same material that made up men's detachable collars and cuffs. Unless the Room 12 comb could be definitively tied to Florence, all the testimony in the world about her combs would be useless.

That did not prevent the prosecution from trying yet again, this time with the young chambermaid in Mrs. Hitchcock's boardinghouse, where Florence had lived for a month. Julia McCarthy, always described as "a mulatto" or "a Negress," had found a comb underneath the dresser in the room occupied by Florence Burns. She put it on the dresser, where it stayed for three days, so she got a good look at it during that time, and she also remembered it because it was so dilapidated, "a horrible sort of comb to be in a lady's room." McCarthy was adamant that it was the same comb as the one placed into evidence, and she could not be shaken by Backus's cross-examination, drawing great praise from the *Brooklyn Eagle* reporter for her firm and straightforward testimony. While Julia McCarthy was on the stand, Florence Burns was noticeably nervous and seemed to be embarrassed, turning red and biting her lip.[48]

THE DETECTIVES

The three detectives involved with the arrest and questioning of Florence Burns—Colby, Riordan, and Parker—repeated what she had said to them at her home and at the police station on February 15. Her admissions were damning and amounted to a confession, so Backus fought hard to keep them out. Detective Sergeant Parker, "a fat fellow with a mustache—a typical policeman," got so tangled up in his cross-examination that the audience roared with laughter until Judge Mayer threatened to empty the courtroom.[49]

Backus focused on Parker's refusal to allow Fred Burns to see his daughter and also on whether Florence had been advised of her right to keep silent:

BACKUS: Did you see Mr. Burns . . . [at] the Church street station?

PARKER: Yes, as I was coming out of the captain's room where she was, and I met him at the door. He said he wanted to go in and see his daughter. I told him that it was impossible then and asked him why he wanted to see her. He said he wanted to tell her not to say anything. I told him she had already been told that.

BACKUS: Now, had you heard any one tell her not to say anything?

PARKER: No.

BACKUS: Then why did you tell him that?

PARKER: You misconstrued my words. I said she had been told she was entitled to her rights.

[It was in here that Parker got confused and made "ridiculous statements," not transcribed in the newspapers, to the great amusement of the spectators.]

BACKUS: Why did you tell Mr. Burns he couldn't see his daughter?

PARKER: Why, because she was charged with a felony and no one could see her until she was turned over.

BACKUS: Turned over to whom, for God's sake?

PARKER: I don't know.[50]

After the testimony of the three detectives, Judge Mayer made it clear that he did not trust their evidence and had grave doubts about its admissibility because Florence had not properly been apprised of her rights before she was questioned in her home or at the station. Colby and Parker were in plain clothes and did not inform her that they were detectives. Nor was she told why she was being arrested—just that it was a felony, not that it was a murder. She had not been taken directly to a magistrate before she was questioned. Moreover, he leaned toward Backus's assertion of Florence's having been given the "third degree," although she had not been threatened and had been questioned for, at the most, only two hours, while many of the witnesses were routinely questioned for three. Mayer asked the attorneys to come back the next day prepared to argue these points as he was inclined to throw out Florence's statements. If he were to do so, the prosecution would have virtually nothing that would allow them to go ahead with a trial, although the district attorney would still be free to get there by way of a grand jury indictment, and there was still an inquest hearing in the offing. It must have looked very bleak to Assistant District Attorney Schurman at the end of court that day.[51]

RUTH DUNNE

Like Florence Burns, seventeen-year-old Ruth Maria Dunne was pretty, blonde, and in a constant battle with her parents, Thomas and Bridget, both of whom were born in New York to Irish immigrants. Ruth, born in 1884, was the oldest of four children (a fifth had died before 1900) and three years younger than Walter Brooks.[52] When her parents were not around, she told reporters that she was engaged to Walter, but when they were on the scene, she said she saw him only a couple of times. Her mother was convinced, or claimed she was, that Ruth barely knew him and was definitely not engaged to him. (Did Ruth think her parents did not read the newspapers?)[53]

Ruth probably exaggerated her relationship to Walter as they had been dating for only a month, so were probably not engaged. And Walter, already averse to such a commitment, would not have been likely to take it on when he was still somewhat tied to Florence—especially if there might have been a baby involved. But under oath, Ruth testified to having been with him nearly every day for the week before he died. And he was supposed to meet her the night of February 14 but broke it off so he could give Florence a "blowout" to send her off to Detroit and be rid of her at last. If these somewhat checkable assertions were true, then they were definitely spending a lot of time together.

Ruth preened and chatted with reporters and was dramatically hysterical during some of the testimony to the sarcastic amusement of Florence Burns, who recognized it for what it was. But when Ruth got on the stand, she was so timid and nervous that she could barely be heard in the courtroom.[54]

Ruth's testimony was very precise as to time and place, so it was probably true, but none of it tied Florence Burns to the Glen Island Hotel, although her presence in Walter's life could provide further motive on Florence's part. Ruth had never heard Florence threaten Walter and had only heard of her temper tantrums from Walter himself. It's not even clear that she and Florence were more than marginally acquainted. Still, they practiced the same lifestyle: staying out all night, going to cheap theaters, and hanging out at Coney Island and Bader's with boys of the Bedford Gang.

Although the prosecution claimed that it had much stronger evidence that it did not want to bring out for the defense to see, it had a hollow ring—like that of Foster Backus's mythical alibi claims. And, if Judge Mayer did not allow Florence's admissions into evidence, the district attorney did not have much of a case at all.

THE VERDICT AND AN INTERMISSION

When Judge Mayer sparred with Assistant DA George Schurman on the third degree, on Florence's rights under the Sixth Amendment, and on the general unfairness of the police officers in dealing with her on February 15, the press noted that Foster Backus might just as well have stayed home that day. That's how defense-oriented Mayer's approach was. So, by the time the judge's decision was to be announced, everyone was about 99 percent sure that Florence Burns would not be held to answer for the murder of Walter Brooks.[1]

It took Mayer an hour and a half to get to the conclusion that everyone already knew he had made. During this time, with the entire courtroom on pins and needles, waiting to explode, Florence sat calmly fanning herself and yawning. Here were the salient points made by the judge:[2]

1. Walter Brooks was murdered. He did not commit suicide.
2. Florence Burns's verbal threats against Walter Brooks, testified to by William Eyre and Mrs. Brooks, were worthless because they took place months before the murder and did not place her at the Glen Island. Moreover, Florence continued to live with the Brookses even after these threats, which were not heard by anyone other than the victim's mother. (In a classic understatement, Judge Mayer commented, "It is enough to say that the situation in that house is a peculiar and doubtful one.")
3. The identification of the comb was worthless as none of the witnesses was able to connect it sufficiently to any comb used by Florence.
4. As for the statements made by Florence at her home and in the police station, these were all thrown out. It was not clear when or if she was told she did not have to say anything; the plainclothes detectives did not identify themselves to her at her home; she was not told she was under arrest for

murder, but for a felony; and they should have brought her immediately to a magistrate. Consequently, they should not have questioned her at all.
5. George Washington's identification of Florence was worthless because of his statements about her skin color and because of the defective lineups.

Judge Mayer seemed to accept Arthur Wible's testimony as to Florence's presence on his streetcar at 11:15 (but did not connect it to her lie about having arrived home at 7:00) and admitted that her question about the pistol was something of a confession. Still, he announced that he was discharging her because nothing successfully put her at the Glen Island Hotel with Walter Brooks—even though the hotel was within walking distance of the streetcar and within the time frame of when the woman who killed Walter would have been there.

It was an outrageous conclusion with regard to Florence's statements, which clearly implicated her and indicated that she knew exactly what the detectives were doing in her house. They might not have been in uniform, but they had informed Mrs. Burns immediately who they were before asking to speak to Florence. Despite the detectives' "felony" gaffe (possibly done on purpose), Florence stated that she had not shot Walter and wailed, "I don't know why I should be suspected" after George Washington identified her in the captain's office. The detectives were scolded for not telling Florence that Walter had died, but she could have seen the headlines in the newspapers in the streetcar. Today, it is perfectly legal for law enforcement to lie to witnesses and suspects in order to get information from them.

Mayer's decision to throw out Florence's incriminating statements was not supported by any of the existing case law presented by Assistant District Attorney Schurman, but, of course, it *was* supported by another kind: the Unwritten Law. The judge needed something he could "hang his hat on" from a legal standpoint in order to apply the Unwritten Law, and he chose to interpret the written law in a way that had not been done before. It was a classic situation for the Unwritten Law, although the facts of the Burns case did not comport completely with the traditional narrative of a young, naive, good (i.e., virginal) girl seduced by a scheming man who led a risky lifestyle and then refused to protect her honor by marrying her.

Everyone knew what had gone on here. William Travers Jerome knew it too. He ruminated about needing stronger evidence to place Florence at the Glen Island, but the failure to convince Judge Mayer probably meant it would be difficult to convince twelve men, so it might be useless to try her. Then, too, Jerome admitted, the "influence of the negative value of the unwritten law upon a jury was well illustrated in the Marie Barberi case." He knew what he would be up against if he rearrested her.[3]

CHAOS IN THE COURTROOM

As soon as the judge announced Florence Burns's discharge, the courtroom erupted "with a wild shriek" and pandemonium ensued. Spectators jumped over chairs to get to Florence to congratulate her. A woman fainted and others had their clothing torn. Mayer's gavel was completely ineffective and the police had to form a cordon around Florence so she could be safely removed from the room. What were her first words? "O, how hungry I am!"

In the back of the room, Walter Brooks's father, described as a "little, pale-faced man," was visibly upset as he ran down the stairs and into the street.[4]

FOSTER BACKUS FOILS THE CROWD

For the first time since her arrest, Florence Burns made a statement to the newspaper reporters who thronged around her, carefully protected by Foster Backus: "Of course, I am very happy at the result of the hearing. But it was just as I expected. I was innocent and I knew that Justice Mayer realized it. I cannot say now what I will do. I expect to go with some friends and rest up, as the experience I have passed through has been a dreadful one."

Backus took over at that point and told the press that Florence would be going away "to the country" to rest and would later "join her family," which evidently she would not be doing right away.[5]

Meanwhile, the crowd was milling around outside, hoping to get a glimpse of Florence Burns as she got into the waiting hack (a horse-drawn taxi). A detective came out and told the hack driver that Backus and Miss Burns would be coming out soon but that he should try to avoid the following crowd by driving the horse as fast as it would go.

Soon, out came Backus with his arm around his charge, who was wearing a picture hat and a black feather boa, and hustled her into the hack. Immediately, the cry went up: "It's Florence Burns! It's Florence Burns!" And hundreds of people ran, bicycled, or drove after the carriage. One desperate man grabbed onto the rear axle and hung on as it zigzagged a crazy route, then eventually ended up at the Hotel St. Denis. There, the pair got out and Backus addressed the crowd: "Gentlemen, allow me to present Mrs. Backus. We thought we would dine here this evening."[6]

While Backus was playing his bait-and-switch trick on the crowd, Florence and her uncle, Oscar Von derBosch, quietly escaped out another door and walked a few blocks to get a streetcar. Although Backus did not divulge where Florence would be staying until the danger was over for her (the inquest was still to be held), it is most likely that she went to Von derBosch's summer home in Cortlandt, New York, near Peekskill, or maybe to relatives' homes in New Jersey. Later, she would complain of having been hidden away in houses of relatives "in dreary little country villages," which really rankled the big-city girl.[7]

When Florence was asked if she would be going on the stage—it seems to be something that had to be on the resumé of every notorious defendant in the Victorian and Gilded Ages—she said she doubted it. And Foster Backus was even more vehement—this would be a bad move for her. She should be keeping a low profile and not exposing herself.[8]

THE RESPONSE

Newspaper editorial responses to the discharge of Florence Burns were mostly sympathetic to her and approving of the decision. Some viewed the Brooks-Burns saga as a cautionary tale for young people and their parents to ignore at their peril. And there was more than one nod to the Unwritten Law.

The Watertown, New York, *Daily Times* compared Walter Brooks and young men of his ilk to insects that needed killing. So, even if Florence had done it, "it served him right" to be removed from society "by one of the many victims of his vanity and lust." The editorial smugly asserted that this sort of behavior was unique to large cities "where dual lives and deception are so easy."[9]

The New York *World* praised Judge Mayer for standing up for Florence, who had been "subjected to a frightful ordeal by the police and the District Attorney" when she was "questioned, threatened, browbeaten" by them in their imposition of the "Third Degree." This, of course, was a gross exaggeration, as most of the incriminating evidence from her own lips came while she was still at home.[10]

The *Brooklyn Daily Eagle* acknowledged that many people believed that Florence had shot Walter out of a motive that should exonerate her:

Indeed, this feeling is so general that if on her trial, Florence Burns, instead of keeping silence, avowed the motive and avowed the shooting her chance of conviction by any jury would still be remote. . . . But with all the uncertainty of procedure and with the rooted objection of juries to convicting women of murder *when they act from the motive which must have been the ruling one in this case,* if any murder was committed, it is not risking much to guess that Florence Burns will never be convicted and probably will never be tried.[11]

The Troy, New York, *Press* urged young people and their parents to take a warning from this case: parents ought to know what their children are doing, but many are ignorant of the fact that their boys and girls "are in the initiatory stages of the careers of Walter Brooks and Florence Burns."[12]

The *Evening Post* of Charleston, South Carolina, printed an editorial from the Richmond, Virginia, *News* criticizing the double standard applied in the Brooks-Burns case and in that of the trial of Jim Wilcox for the murder of his girlfriend Nell Cropsey in North Carolina. Wilcox was convicted on the same day that Florence was discharged. "The evidence against Florence Burns . . . was in every way stronger than that against Wilcox. . . . The woman goes free while the rope is put around the man's neck." If women want equal rights, the editorial concluded, it should include the right to be hanged.[13]

There now remained the coroner's inquest, whose evidence would be heard by a jury, after which it would issue a verdict of how the victim came to his death and, if murder, by whose hand.

THE INQUEST

Another unusual aspect of the Brooks-Burns case was the delay in holding the inquest until after the special hearing. The normal procedure at that time was for the coroner to summon a jury immediately, often from the crowd of onlookers at the crime scene, with the examination of witnesses and evidence to take place on the premises, even in the victim's own house.

The function of the inquest was to determine the *legal* cause (referred to as "manner") of death, whether by accident, homicide, suicide, or the delightfully quaint "misadventure" (i.e., through the victim's own carelessness, often by doing something he or she should not). In the case of a verdict of homicide, the jury was to recommend either the name of the most likely suspect or conclude that it had been committed by "a person or persons unknown." The standard, as at the preliminary hearing to determine probable cause, was the same as for civil cases: "more likely than not" or at least a 51 percent probability that the suspect named was guilty. The suspect was then bound over for trial, where the standard of proof would then rise to "beyond a reasonable doubt."

The inquest jury, unlike that at a trial, was allowed to ask questions of the witnesses brought forth by the prosecution. There was no presentation by the defense, but Foster Backus asked for and received permission from the coroner to cross-examine the prosecution's witnesses, which he did with a vigor that frequently had to be tamped down by the coroner.

New York City's coroner in 1902 was Nicholas T. Brown, a fifty-two-year-old former alderman who, in campaigning for election as coroner, got himself arrested for being drunk and disorderly. As alderman, he had been accused of corruption as the henchman of the notoriously corrupt police justice Patrick Divver in Tammany Hall and, as a result, some important groups did not endorse him for coroner. Nonetheless, he was elected, and with quite a large margin. In 1918, New York City would change over from the system of coroner to that of chief medical examiner.[1]

The district attorney's office was anxious to get Florence Burns back under its jurisdiction by serving a subpoena on her to appear as a witness so that the jurors could observe her demeanor for themselves. But that subpoena could not be served outside the state of New York, and, in any case, she could not be forced to testify against herself. Backus would not reveal where she was or even which state she was in, but he promised to produce her if a valid arrest warrant were to result from the inquest.[2]

There was a supposed sighting of Florence at the River Styx resort area of Lake Hopatcong in New Jersey, and shadows of a woman were seen through the curtains on the top floor of Oscar Von derBosch's summer home in Cortlandt, New York, which was occupied by the family of Von derBosch's sister during the other seasons. But nobody knew for sure where Florence was.[3]

Notwithstanding the absence of the "main attraction" from the coroner's inquest, the courtroom was crowded with spectators throughout the eight days it lasted. Many of the witnesses who had testified at Judge Mayer's hearing came to repeat their testimony, or a current version of it, except for William "Fatty" Eyre and Julia McCarthy. Eyre refused to submit himself to ridicule again, and McCarthy could not be located, having moved out of state for another job. Their testimony was read into the record.[4]

Ruth Dunne was there, as were Walter Brooks's parents, the bellboy George Washington ("Yes, I could identify her among a hundred women"),[5] the physicians (Dr. Weston, Dr. Johnson, and Dr. Sweeney), the streetcar conductor Arthur Wible, and Walter's business partner Harry Cohen. Some new witnesses added spice to the proceedings, the most notable of whom were members of the Bedford Avenue Gang.

BAD BOYS

William Maxwell "Max" Finck, twenty-four, and Joseph Wilson, twenty-three, were currently serving forgery sentences in the Elmira Reformatory, now the Elmira Correctional Facility, in upstate New York. A fellow forger, George F. Jackson, was not brought down for the inquest as he had no probative testimony to offer. Max Finck belonged to a socially prominent family, but, like Theodore Burris and Harry Casey, he could not stay out of trouble. When he was seventeen, he felt he was not making enough money working as a typist for his uncle, so he ran away to become a traveling salesman. (Given his later history, he most likely stole the items he was selling.) Two weeks into his new life, Max tried to jump a freight train carrying coal near Ansonia, Pennsylvania, and missed. The train ran over his right leg and severed it above the knee. From then on, he had a wooden leg.[6]

In 1901, Finck and Jackson had made up fake advertising contracts, passed them off on Finck's employer, then went to Richmond, Virginia, with the money they got for those. In Richmond, the boys presented a bad check for five dollars, and moved on to Washington, DC, where they presented another one for fifty dollars. In Brooklyn and Manhattan, they solicited ads for nonexistent college football and track programs.[7]

In September 1901, Max Finck and George Jackson picked up a couple of girls at the popular Brooklyn resort, Bergen Beach, and took them to a nearby dance at the Prospect Park Hotel. The four of them were drinking quite a bit and, as Jackson said later, were "ossified" to the point of not knowing, or claiming not to know, what was going on. They roused a minister from his bed and got him to marry George and one of the girls, Dolly Nicholson. Then the boys disappeared.

The next day, Dolly declared she had been married, but she had been so drunk she was confused as to which one was her husband. She thought it was the one with the wooden leg (Finck), but it turned out to be Jackson, who had given the name of a relative in Pennsylvania instead of his own. When reporters tracked down the families, Max's mother was furious—her son was not married to Dolly Nicholson, despite what the girl said, and possibly some other young man was using Max's name. When George Jackson got back to town, he claimed to know nothing of his having been married. Yet, certificate No. 5919 shows that he was![8]

When Finck and Wilson were arrested, Finck agreed to turn state's evidence against several members of the forgery ring in exchange for a suspended sentence. But the judge, who had discovered some of Max's other antics, refused to uphold the district attorney's deal and sent him to Elmira.[9]

The reason Max Finck had been brought to the inquest was to testify to an incident from February 1901 at the Palace Hotel in New York. This was before Florence had met Walter Brooks and, at the time, was dating "Handsome Ed" Watson. Florence was wearing a muff, from which she had taken a .32-caliber pistol and threatened to shoot Watson. Max Finck managed to disarm her, with difficulty, removed the bullets, and threw them away. He did not remember what the pistol looked like, only that it had a light-colored handle. Florence

Florence Burns with muff; friends testified that she carried a pistol in it (*New York World*)

told him the pistol used to belong to her father. He never heard her threaten Walter Brooks.[10]

Joe Wilson was also there to testify to Florence's possession of a pistol. Wilson had dated her after Ed Watson, and he knew she kept it in her muff because he had seen it. He asked her why she carried a pistol and she told him that she lived in a "lonely part of Flatbush and might need it for self-protection." Like Finck, Wilson could not describe it, other than that it had a light-colored handle. He knew that Florence and her mother were both very skilled with firearms and had won prizes at shooting contests, which was corroborated by Harry Cohen.

Wilson was a good friend of Walter Brooks and had known the family for about six years. When Wilson was on trial for forgery, he was defended by Mr. Brooks's lawyer, and when Wilson and Finck were in the Tombs, Walter visited them there. Joe had met Florence at the Haymarket Dance Hall in Manhattan and told an inquiring juror that, yes, this was before he had been introduced to her: two major faux pas for that era.[11]

The Haymarket Dance Hall, at Sixth Avenue and West 30th Street, and located in the Tenderloin district, known as "Satan's Circus," was notorious for its bawdiness, despite its respectable outward appearance and its restriction against too-close dancing. Prostitutes frequented the Haymarket, as did shopgirls and those of the higher classes who were "slumming," like Florence and her cohorts. Authors Greg Young and Tom Meyers call it "a veritable shopping mall for sin" with "curtained-off rooms in the balcony and upper floors." The colorful eroticism of the Haymarket is depicted in a famous painting by John Sloan.[12]

As for Wilson not having been introduced to Florence before speaking to her, that was a tradition that—thanks to informal places like Coney Island—was fading out with the younger generation. For older folks like the juror who asked about it and the parents of these young people, it was proof that a girl was "fast" and had compromised her virtue by allowing a young man to speak to her without a proper introduction by a mutual acquaintance—and at the Haymarket, no less.

Another bonus for the inquest attendees was the presence of Edward Cole Watson, who had not been at the Mayer hearing. "Handsome Ed" corroborated Max Finck's account of the Palace Hotel incident where Florence threatened him with a pistol. Neither of these boys gave the exact day in February for this, but February 15, 1901—exactly one year before the death of Walter Brooks—was the date Florence gave to Mrs. Birdsall as to when she "went wrong" with Ed Watson.[13]

MRS. BROOKS CHANGES HER STORY

Undoubtedly realizing that her possibly exaggerated story of Florence's constant threats against her son was not rational in light of the Brookses' three-week tolerance of her presence in their home, even after these threats, Mrs. Brooks now testified that they had thrown Flo out of their house after the first threat. Asked about the discrepancy with her previous testimony in front of Judge Mayer, she said she could not remember that. Since Judge Mayer based part of his decision to dismiss the case against Florence Burns on this testimony, it was obvious that Mrs. Brooks was hoping to avoid another dismissal.

However, she did reveal something interesting that had not come up before, which was the supposed statement made by a physician called in to attend to Florence when she was sick: that the young woman was faking illness and should be sent away from their home immediately. Given that Mrs. Brooks had already been caught in a lie, had never brought this up before, and a doctor had already diagnosed Flo's illness as real, this was highly suspect. It was also hearsay, which would not have been allowed in a trial. If it were true, why didn't the Brookses get a written statement from the doctor who said this, or even bring him to the inquest hearing?[14]

When Thomas Brooks was on the stand, a juror asked him about the Brookses' invitation to Florence to stay in their home, their tending to her illness, and their allowing her to stay for three weeks. In a subtle allusion to the application of the Unwritten Law, the juror wanted to know if it was because they felt that Florence "had a moral claim on them." Mr. Brooks denied any such claim. But the fact that he was questioned so closely in both hearings regarding the nature of Flo's illness indicates that there was always that suspicion of a pregnancy, which would have been a very large moral claim indeed.[15]

As she sat in the courtroom with her husband day after day, Mrs. Brooks frequently burst out crying or shouted disapproval. One time, she stood up and insisted that Walter had been drugged with chloral when he was drinking with friends at Bader's and that they never found him until the next morning. There is no doubt that Mrs. Brooks believed (or chose to believe) this outrageous story, but what was really odd is that Walter's second partner—Thomas C. "T. C." Wells—proclaimed from his courtroom seat that he remembered that very time as well.[16] It's not likely that Brooks was drugged because what would have been the point, other than maybe as a bad practical joke? Was he left all night at Bader's? Maybe T. C. Wells did not want this distraught mother to doubt the goodness of her son, who had stayed overnight at the roadhouse and needed an excuse for not going home.

THE TIMING EXPERIMENT

The detectives from the various police stations repeated their observations and Florence's incriminating statements, hoping that this time these statements would be allowed into evidence. There was a new aspect in the testimony of a detective who had done timing experiments to test Flo's claims. It took him nineteen minutes to get from the Glen Island Hotel to the Brooklyn Bridge at a "leisurely pace." "Leisurely," indeed: it was only half a mile, and Florence's pace would have been brisk to distance herself from the hotel and get to the streetcar on time. His next experiment was more to the point: it took him forty-one minutes to get from the Brooks and Wells office at 17 Jay Street in Manhattan to the Beverley streetcar station in Brooklyn (about a two-minute walk from her home). Florence claimed she had left the office at 6:30, although others said it was more like 6:45 when she left with Walter. With either time, however, she would not have made it to her home by 7:00, which is the time she said she arrived there.[17]

THE REST

Except for the addition of a young man who claimed he had seen Florence's combs in his mother's boardinghouse (but could not conclusively connect them with the one found in the hotel),[18] the other witnesses were all carried over from the preliminary hearing.

The "fair and pretty" Ruth Dunne recounted her last days with Walter Brooks and mightily disappointed the spectators by not being allowed to read the letters she identified as having been exchanged between them. Ruth was there every day, having been hired by one of the "yellow" papers, probably the *World* or the *Herald,* to report on the inquest. Walter's partner Harry Cohen said that Florence had a muff with her when she visited their office on February 14, important testimony after what Max Finck and Joe Wilson said about Florence keeping a pistol there.[19]

THE VERDICT

In his charge to the jury, which was heavily prosecution-oriented, Coroner Brown emphasized the testimony of conductor Arthur Wible and the detectives' report of Mrs. Burns that indicated she and her husband already knew about the shooting. Throughout this charge, the jury acted bored and inattentive. The reason for this, as a juror later gleefully confided to a reporter, was that they had already made up their minds.[20]

The verdict of "murder by a person or persons unknown" took exactly fifty minutes and "no single juror had favored a verdict placing the responsibility of Brooks' death on Miss Burns."[21] With such unanimity, it is not hard to imagine the jurors all taking out cigars or pipes or cigarettes to enjoy a smoke and give the illusion of an actual deliberation. The fifty minutes occurred over a lunch hour, so maybe they also had something to eat.

It's not hard to read beneath the reasoning (not wanting to put the responsibility for Walter's death onto Florence) and see the workings of the Unwritten Law—not that she didn't do it, but that they did not want to hold her responsible.

Mrs. Brooks had stayed home for the verdict they must have known was coming. Her husband was quite upset about it: "This verdict is, indeed, a blow to me." At the opposite side of the spectrum was Florence's attorney, Foster Backus, who had surely earned every penny of the $6,000 her uncle paid him. With obvious relief that the three-month ordeal was over, he was "completely overcome and sobbing like a child."[22]

Now having failed twice in his attempt to try Florence Burns for the murder of Walter Brooks, District Attorney Jerome decided to hold off on going to the grand jury. But he and everyone else knew that the Brooks-Burns case was over. The Burnses could now return to their home, free of subpoena servers. And Florence could attempt to get back her life and her reputation.

HERE'S WHAT MIGHT HAVE HAPPENED

Florence Burns was desperate. Somehow, she needed to convince Walter Brooks to marry her so she could redeem herself in the eyes of her parents. She had always had sexual power over him, and she was banking on that if she could only get him to see her. She made up a story about moving to Detroit the next day and waited for him to show up at his office. With the Detroit story, however, Walter—rather than fearful of losing her—could see light at the end of the tunnel of their relationship and agreed to go out with her "one more time." He even generously offered to give her $60 for her trip. It is remotely possible that Florence presented the Detroit trip as a trip to an abortionist, as she did not seem to have any connections in that city. This would also explain the money Walter gave her "for expenses."

They left the office around 6:45 or 7:00 and went to dinner, probably at Walter's favorite place, the Cosmopolitan on Chambers Street. Florence suggested that they find a Raines Law hotel where they would not be questioned about luggage and have one final "fling." Walter was feeling expansive because, after that, he would be free.

Florence must have thought that sex could persuade Walter to change his mind and agree to marry her. When she could not get him to budge, she might have been so filled with rage that she decided she would get even by shooting him. She waited until he was asleep (or maybe chloral was used, as Dr. Sweeney said he had smelled it), put the pistol right up against his head to minimize the sound and to make sure of a direct hit, and pulled the trigger. When she called for the lemon soda, she had no doubt already shot him and probably assumed he was dead. Then she got into her clothes, blew out the gaslight on the radiator without turning off the gas, and left.

The mystery here is why, if Florence were angry at Walter for not changing his mind, she did not confront him with the pistol so she could get some satisfaction by letting him know why he was going to die. Instead, she opted for drugging him and shooting him as he lay unconscious. Perhaps part of the answer lies in the cases of Nancy Bachus and Francine Hughes, who were a good deal smaller and weaker than their husbands. Walter was over six feet tall with an athletic build and would have put up noisy resistance, and Florence would have had to stifle the sound of the pistol to prevent attracting attention so she could slip out quietly.

Was John Earl at his desk when Florence walked by? If so, was he busy checking in the couple at 10:50 and unable to pay attention? Or was his back turned to her so he had better light for reading his newspaper? Or did he notice her and say nothing because of the Glen Island Hotel's policy of employees keeping their mouths shut?

Florence would have wanted to dispose of the pistol as soon as possible in case the shooting was discovered and someone came running after her. We know she didn't keep it because her first question was whether they had found it. Throwing it into the East River would have been her best option, and maybe she could have accomplished this before getting on the trolley that took her to the Brooklyn side of the bridge.

When Florence got home, her parents were already there, having arrived about a half hour earlier from their theater date in Manhattan. It was at this point that she told them whatever story she had concocted, probably the murder-suicide one. Fred ran out, either then or early the next morning, to enlist his friend Foster Backus, who agreed to take on the case if Florence were arrested. Before leaving for his office the next morning, Fred Burns enjoined his family to say nothing to anyone who might ask about the shooting of Walter Brooks.

The most damaging evidence against Florence Burns was that she had been with Walter Brooks earlier that night; she knew exactly how much money he had *after* he paid for dinner and the two-dollar hotel room; she had obviously told her parents he had been shot; and despite a three-month high-profile case covered by every newspaper in the country, not one person came forward to give her a solid alibi. Not even her own family could do so.

WAS THERE A BABY?

Nothing that is known of this case goes toward proving that Florence Burns was not pregnant when she killed Walter Brooks, and there is much to indicate that she was. However, without an actual baby or a statement from her or someone with access to the truth, it cannot be definitively proved. Here are seven indicators that make it more likely than not that she was:

1. *Florence was sexually active:* We know this not only from the extant rumors about all the Bedford Gang boys, not just Walter Brooks, being intimate with her but from her own statement to Mrs. Birdsall that she "went wrong" with Ed Watson in 1901.
2. *Flo's parents:* The Burnses' extreme reaction to their daughter's relations with Walter Brooks—to the point of throwing her out of the house and refusing

readmittance unless she married Walter—indicates there was a pregnancy. Fred Burns said that Mr. Brooks was a "criminal" and should be in jail for objecting to the marriage. He told Walter that if he did not marry Florence, he (Fred) would go to hell. Since the Burnses did not exhibit this same reaction to Florence's relationship with Ed Watson, even though they also kicked her out of the house for that, there must have been more at stake.

3. *Flo's admissions to Mabel Cooper:* In September 1901, Florence confided to her friend Mabel Cooper, as well as Mabel's mother, that she was "in serious trouble" and that Walter Brooks was to blame. If she could not "regain her health," she told them, she would take her revenge on Brooks. (Readers of a certain age will be familiar with the term *in trouble* with regard to an unwed young woman.)

4. *Walter's parents:* The Brookses clearly did not like Florence Burns, and they particularly objected to their son marrying her. Yet, they consented to her extended stay in their home during her illness, whatever the cause, paid for a physician to attend her, and allowed this to go on for three weeks, despite Florence's threats against their son. This seems unreasonable indeed unless they felt she had a "moral claim" on them because of a pregnancy for which their son was responsible.

5. *The timing of Florence's desperation:* Florence seems to have stepped up her demands that Walter marry her. When he asked her where and how they would live, as he had no money, her response was, "But we must get married." (Again, readers will recognize "they had to get married" as a code phrase used in past eras when there was a pregnancy involved.) And when did Florence's desperation intensify? Right around the time when a pregnancy would be noticeable, in the fourth or fifth month.

6. *Florence's special treatment in the Tombs:* Pregnant prisoners were given special exercise privileges, and these were extended to Florence. Unfortunately, by the time this became known, the Tombs Angel—who would have asked for it on Flo's behalf—had died in the Park Avenue Hotel fire and could not be asked about it. The Tombs administration did not deny it, only stated that Florence was not given any privileges not extended to others. The rumors persisted in the press. "She is about to become a mother"[23] was about the most straightforward assertion, but there were strong hints throughout. (It should be noted here that the word *pregnant* was rarely used in print at that time, even into the midcentury.) Foster Backus denied this and said that he was willing to leave Florence in jail for any length of time so they could

see there was no baby,[24] but it was an empty promise, and he made sure to remove her from sight as soon as the Mayer hearing was completed.

7. *Florence's extended absence:* If there were a baby on the way—and we use Florence's statement to Mabel Cooper in September as a benchmark—it would have been born in May or June 1902. Florence won her discharge on March 22 and the inquest hearing—with District Attorney Jerome's decision not to proceed further—ended on May 19. Soon after that, Mr. and Mrs. Burns and their daughter Gladys moved back to their home. But Florence was not with them. Nor did she rejoin them until mid-July. This time span would allow for the birth of a baby in June and Florence's recovery from that. Although today's new mothers are up almost immediately after giving birth, this is a recent phenomenon. Up until the late twentieth century, mothers and their newborns stayed in the hospital for a week after the birth, followed by the mother's bedrest at home for another week. In the middle of April, there was a brief comment by Foster Backus that, despite the rumors from an unknown source, Florence was not seriously ill.[25] This was an odd report and the subject of her ostensible illness was never referred to again. Alone of all newspapers, the Columbia, South Carolina, *State* proclaimed that Florence had gone to Charleston to "make her future home."[26] There are several pronounced references to the physical intimacy between Florence and Walter, possibly insinuating that Florence was leaving to have a baby there. However, in her own article written for the *Herald* in November, she mentioned only the small towns of New York and New Jersey. But it gives her an excuse to have delayed her return to Brooklyn, so she may have made up the story about moving to Charleston.

So, there are many hints that Florence was indeed pregnant, and if she was, it makes a lot of her behavior, as well as that of Walter and the two sets of parents, more understandable. But what might have happened to the baby? It definitely did not go back home with Florence, so someone must have taken it. The most logical adoptive family would have been one related to Florence to avoid the possibility of the baby's existence leaking out to the public. Yet, a search in the 1910 census of the known Burns/Von derBosch relatives did not reveal the presence of a child of the right age: seven or eight years old.

Florence Burns never addressed this issue, at least in a way that was made public. In the 1910 census, there is a question for married and widowed women to indicate how many children they have borne, and how many of those are still alive. At that time, Florence was married, so she would have been asked this question, but in the circumstances she found herself at the time, she was probably avoiding the census taker. Those circumstances will be the subject of the next chapters.

FLORENCE'S NEW LIFE

When Florence Burns finally rejoined her family at their home in July or August 1902, the reunion was unlikely to have been a joyful one. Her parents, particularly her mother, were mortified beyond belief by the court hearing and the attendant publicity. (Mrs. Burns constantly referred to the entire incident as "our trouble.")[1] Now that they had their daughter back, they had no intention of allowing her to parade herself before the neighbors or take up her former life with the Bedford Avenue Gang and her other friends.

Florence then sulked her way through the rest of the summer and the fall, constantly resentful of being a prisoner in her own home. She refused to do any housework, but this was nothing new: she had never done any, so Gladys pitched in instead. Oh, there were the (very) occasional visits to Bergen Beach on hot days, but she was always accompanied by an adult relative. She was not allowed to venture out of the house by herself. And she described her situation, past and present, in melodramatic terms: "During the past year, I have suffered as no other woman of my age has been called upon to suffer in the memory of this generation."[2]

Who was to blame for Florence's situation? In Florence's thinking, it was anyone but herself! She blamed her overly strict parents, who never understood her. She blamed her teachers, who hated her for doing whatever she liked because she "chafed at the imprisonment of school." She blamed the "scoundrels" of the Bedford Avenue Gang, "a crowd of worthless young wretches, who took advantage of my innocence and ignorance with a skill that was simply devilish." She blamed Harry Casey, who "ought to be—well, there is nothing bad enough for him on earth." She blamed Ed Watson, who "caused all her trouble." She blamed Walter Brooks's friends, who interfered with their relationship when they loved each other so much.[3]

Despite the Burnses' attempt—or maybe because of it—to keep Florence out of sight, and hopefully out of mind, of neighbors and the press, the rumors swarmed like blowflies to a corpse. Her lawyer, Foster Backus, had to defend her constantly: No, Florence was not engaged to a Southern boy with a big red car. No, she was not being taken riding in elegant automobiles by other young men. No, she was not cavorting with friends at Manhattan Beach. No, she was not buying expensive designer fashions. No, she was not contemplating going on the stage. Her primary focus was to put the Brooks case behind her and try to reestablish her good reputation. She would lead a quiet life from then on.[4]

This plan worked until Foster Backus and his wife went on a vacation to Europe. With her primary monitor in absentia, Florence took matters into her own hands and effected her escape to freedom: She eloped with a young man ten years her senior whose past was very much like those Bedford Gang "scoundrels." His name was Charles White Wildrick.

CHARLES WHITE WILDRICK

Charles White Wildrick was born in 1872, the eldest of four sons of a Civil War hero, Brevet Brig. Gen. Abram Calvin Wildrick, and his wife, Marion White Wildrick, both from prominent and accomplished families. Brevet Brigadier (really Colonel) Wildrick, a West Point graduate, had fought valiantly at the Battle of Petersburg. Even as a very young child, Charles had a tendency to be "wild and venturesome," according to his mother.[5]

Two of Charley's brothers followed their father's footsteps to West Point and served in the army with distinction for over thirty years, as did his third brother after graduating from Princeton (eye problems kept him from West Point). All three boys attained the rank of colonel.[6] Not so Charley, however, who dabbled in military service as some kind of "cadet and embryo officer" (but not at West Point), then abandoned that in 1888 at the age of sixteen to work for the New York Central Railroad as an auditor. From then on, according to his own account (and unable to be completely verified), he lived the life of a dime novel hero, a boy's idea of a man: a swashbuckling, dueling, lady-killing, modern-day D'Artagnan, drifting from place to place, searching for adventure, seducing women, and spending as much as $100,000 (almost $3 million today) in the process. His relatives believed that he had stolen the family jewelry.[7]

Somewhere in his youth, Charley was given the nickname of "Tad" and from then on, that is what he was known by.[8] The origin of it is a mystery

Charles White "Tad" Wildrick.
Ned and George are Tad's
brothers. (Courtesy of the
Wildrick family)

to his family even today, although there is a feeling that it might have been
after Abraham Lincoln's son, who the president thought was like a tadpole
because he squirmed and also because of his large head. Tad Lincoln was also
a "wild and venturesome" child. Another guess is that it stands for "The Art-
ful Dodger," which accurately sums up Charley's nature and his ability to talk
himself out of the trouble he got into. For example, when he was twenty, Tad
and two friends were in Salt Lake City and found themselves short of cash.
They began begging money from passersby, after which they purchased beer.
Three policemen saw the transaction and arrested them for vagrancy. Tad's
two friends were given the choice of being jailed or getting out of town, while
he himself declared that he was simply borrowing the money that he got from
the "donor," not panhandling, and that two prominent doctors in town could
vouch for him. The judge decided that he was "a gentleman in hard luck" who
had "fallen among bad associates," so nothing came of the charges.[9]

After his time with the New York Central, Tad went to work for the Southern
Pacific Railroad in the West. He claimed he had saved Collis P. Huntington,

one of the Big Four of Western railroading, from a serious fall, after which Huntington got him the position of assistant customs house agent. In Tulare, California (sometimes he said it happened in New Mexico and at other times in the country of Mexico), he shot two Mexicans to prevent them from holding up his train.[10]

When General Wildrick died in 1894, just after he retired from his thirty-seven-year career with the army, Tad inherited quite a bit of money (possibly the $100,000 he bragged of having gone through in a six-year period), after which he went to Bard's Ranch on Bear River in Wyoming to work as a cowboy. This does not seem to have kept his attention for long because he soon ended up managing a hotel owned by a woman in Laramie. When the woman's brother got wind of an affair between Tad and his sister, he challenged him to a duel. They were both such poor shots, however, that neither got hurt. On his way to Laramie, he had stopped off at the Republican Convention in Cheyenne and fought an eighteen-round boxing match with another cowboy.[11]

In 1896, now twenty-four, Tad went to Chicago, where he was hired as a buyer for Montgomery Ward. His manager there considered him a very smooth talker and a stylish dresser, but a young man who felt he was too good to have to do any work. Tad was about to be fired after eight months on the job, but he quit first. In 1898, still in Chicago, he signed onto a volunteer regiment preparing to fight in the Spanish-American War, but the regiment was never activated, so he went back to New York.[12]

That same year, 1898, Tad met the rich, beautiful, and cultured Jennie Armstrong of Louisville, Kentucky, who was visiting in Detroit, where she was also planning to buy some racehorses. When Jennie went away with him, her parents were furious and cut her off, but she and Tad eventually quarreled, and they parted on bad terms. (In 1900, desperate for money, Tad asked a friend to cash a sixty-five-dollar check for him, signed by J. F. Armstrong, his former girlfriend. The signature was forged and the check bounced, so Tad's friend had to cover those funds with the bank.)[13]

Then Wildrick went to Marion, Ohio, where he connected with the young social set and was all the rage with the girls—much to the dismay of the boys. Tad Wildrick was the stereotype of the tall, dark, broad-shouldered, handsome man, who also had the power of seductive charm, which he used to his advantage, making every woman feel as if she were the most important one in the world.[14]

Soon after his sojourn in Marion, Tad met a married woman named Mary Cockley in Philadelphia. In June, she left her husband of five years and ran away to New York City to live at the Winthrop Hotel with Tad. Cockley followed them there, but Mary refused to go with him, so he filed for divorce and named Tad as a co-respondent. Soon after that, Tad "threw her over," according to Cockley.[15]

Late in 1900, Tad Wildrick met twenty-seven-year-old Mabel Strong, the daughter of a wealthy man in Cleveland. Mabel's mother had died in 1883, and her father remarried. There may have been some tension between Mabel and her sister on the one hand, and their father and his new wife on the other, as the girls lived with their paternal grandmother for several years. They also had inherited money from their grandfather, with Mabel's share variously reported as $10,000, $13,000, $15,000, $40,000, and $80,000.[16]

Mabel was infatuated with Tad Wildrick to the point of folly. In January or February 1901, she "eloped" with him to New York City, where he convinced her that they had an oral contract of marriage because they recited vows in front of witnesses, although there was no clergyman or other official. They got a thirty-dollar-a-day suite of rooms at the Hotel Girard, registered as Mr. and Mrs. Gordon Sterling, and, by all accounts, proceeded to see how much money they could go through in the course of a day. Soon any money they had between them was gone. While they were assiduous about paying for the suite in the early days of their stay there, that eventually stopped, probably in March.

Either before they left for New York, or soon after they got there, Mabel contracted consumption (tuberculosis), but she was under the impression that it was in one lung only and curable. However, it became evident that she was getting worse and needed medicine, so their money was now diverted to paying for that. When Mabel began to realize that she might very well die, she went to a lawyer to have him draw up papers transferring all her assets to Tad and giving him power of attorney, but the lawyer—possibly suspecting some undue influence on Tad's part—refused to do it. Earlier, Tad had bragged to friends that Mabel had given him $8,000 of her money, but she later said she had not. At the time she recanted, however, she was trying to save him from prison, so he was more likely telling the truth here.

In April, the Girard's manager was getting impatient with not getting paid for the expensive suite. Tad did what he normally did in such situations: he gave him a phony check signed by a fictitious person, supposedly his brother, for $375. Then, without checking out, and also leaving some of their clothing behind, Tad and Mabel relocated to the Hotel Normandie, where she had stayed many times over the years and was well known. It was there that Tad was arrested on April 25, after his check to the Girard was discovered to be bogus. A guest at the Normandie, who knew Mabel's father, told the hotel to give the young woman whatever care she needed and to put it on his bill.

When it was clear that Mabel was getting worse and would not survive for long, the Normandie contacted Clayton Strong in Cleveland to tell him his daughter was ill with consumption. He scoffed at this and said she was faking it, as she was "very resourceful" and only pretending to be sick in order to cover for Wildrick and get him out of trouble with her playacting. No, the Normandie personnel insisted, she really is dying of consumption and hasn't long to live. Alarmed, Strong left for New York.

As weak and emaciated as she was, Mabel Strong got into a carriage with a nurse and went to the courthouse to see Tad: "I am Mrs. Wildrick. I want to see my husband before I die. Let me go to him, I implore you." The magistrate agreed to let her go up to the second tier of cells, where Tad was being kept, but she had such difficulty navigating the stairs that she fainted on the way. Tad was brought down to her instead and allowed to hold her. The scene, as reported, was a melodramatic one, with Tad's the only dry eyes in the house. Even the magistrate was touched. Mabel sobbed, "I know I am dying, Tad, but I could not die without seeing you again. I am come to tell you goodby, darling Tad." Then she addressed the magistrate: "Have mercy, judge, on my husband. If my life is spared for another day, I will see, I swear to you, that every cent of this money will be paid." She promised to bring the money on Monday, April 29, hoping to get it from her father. She was unaware that out of their affection for their friend at Fort Wadsworth, the late Col. Abram Wildrick, several army officers had paid off the debts left by his son.

Mabel fainted one more time and Tad was allowed to carry her to the waiting cab before returning to his cell. Tad was reportedly unmoved by this scene and insisted that she had no claim on him, that they were not married as she had said they were. "She was awfully stuck on me, poor girl," was his comment, accompanied by a smirk. Needless to say, he did not come off well in the eyes of the press and the public for this callous attitude toward a girl who had given him everything, even getting out of her sickbed to plead his case.

In Tad's slight defense for such callousness, there might be a somewhat benign interpretation of his lack of concern for Mabel's condition. It may have been, on her part, a performance designed to elicit the very response that it got from the magistrate. There is no doubt that the girl was ill, but she and Tad may not have realized it was as bad as it soon became, despite her claims of being on the brink of death. She herself thought she only had consumption in one lung and believed it was curable. Some of the drama may have been the result of exaggeration, such as the two fainting spells, which was a quite common response of women in that time period to extreme emotional duress—like that of Mrs. Brooks on the witness stand. Mabel's own father believed her capable of pretending to be ill, and Tad might have assumed she was putting on a show to help him out.

There was a great deal of sympathy for Mabel Strong, and both the magistrate and the trial judge were inclined to be lenient with Tad because of that and also because of his father's reputation. But three communications doomed that inclination: a letter from a US Army colonel, who denounced Tad as a scoundrel; a letter from Tad's former friend telling about the sixty-five-dollar forged check from 1900; and a telegram from the cuckolded Willard A. Cockley, who urged full prosecution of this "rascally hotel beat." This, then, was obviously not Tad's first brush with the law, the unfortunate result of an honest but misguided effort to procure medicine for his dying fiancée; rather, it was part of a pattern of behavior. On May 4, he received a six-month sentence to the penitentiary at Blackwell's Island. He would never see Mabel Strong again.

When Clayton Strong arrived in New York to get his daughter, he was overcome with remorse for having disbelieved her illness. His statement to the press hints at past difficulties: "Whatever follies my daughter has done in the past, whatever sins she has committed, I have fully forgiven her. I only remember that she is my little girl, that she is in great trouble, that she is dying. I have not a single word of reproach for her, only a great yearning. But I would gladly kill the man. A more despicable wretch never drew breath. He is absolutely without a shred of honor. . . . He is in for the penitentiary, but I wish he was to sit in the electrical chair." Strong hoped to take his daughter home to Cleveland, "where she was so happy as a girl." But she grew weaker and was taken from the Hotel Normandie to St. Luke's Hospital, too ill to be moved to Cleveland.

Mabel Strong proved to be strong indeed. While her doctors were predicting that she had but a few days to live back in late April, she lasted until July 14, 1901, dying on her sister's birthday. "Tell Tad I loved him," she commissioned her father, who was at her deathbed. These were her last words. When newspapers recounted the story and praised her loyalty, they also showered Tad with such epithets as "worthless," "scapegrace," and "hotel beat." Clayton Strong took his daughter's body back to Ohio, where she was buried in a family plot in Fredericktown, next to her mother.

Is it any wonder, then, that the press was deliriously joyful at the news of a marriage—an elopement, no less—between Charles White Wildrick and Florence Burns? Two sensational histories in one package!

THE COURTSHIP OF FLORENCE BURNS

Tad Wildrick would have finished up his six-month sentence around November 4, 1901. Supposedly, he soon made the acquaintance of Florence Burns and asked her to marry him, but at that time, she was heavily involved with Walter Brooks and had no eyes for anyone else. In another month, the relationship would deteriorate, but in November, she probably believed she would marry Walter. Although the newspapers claimed that Tad was a member of the Bedford Avenue Gang, this is unlikely. For one thing, he was about ten years older than most of the members of that group, and, for another, he was not one to join such an organization and submit to a leader and a set of rules. Tad Wildrick followed nobody's directives but his own. In all the publicity given to this gang during the Brooks-Burns case, not once was Tad Wildrick's name ever mentioned, despite the constant references to other members.

It's obvious that the paths of Tad and Flo crossed at some point, but it is unclear whether it was before or after the Brooks murder. They both stuck by the probably fictional story that they had been friends for a long time and that he had loved her for many years, but when would he have had the time between his multi-state adventures and his prison sentence? Florence claimed that during her "imprisonment" in her Brooklyn home, she sought his advice as to how to gain her freedom, that maybe he could find her a job that would get her out of the house.[17] However, she had exploded in anger at Walter for this same suggestion, declaring that she would never "ruin herself by working," so there most likely was no discussion of job-seeking at their meetings. At that time, Wildrick may have been living in Brooklyn and, once Foster Backus left for Europe, Florence was probably taking advantage of his absence by either boldly leaving her home or sneaking out of it to meet Tad.

At some point, the idea of marriage came up, and there is no doubt that Florence would have grabbed at any chance to get out from under her parents' stifling repression. She depicted herself and Tad as two lost souls in that they were scorned and misunderstood by the world—"the playthings of fate," she called them. Tad professed to take on the cause of proving her innocent of the murder of Walter Brooks. He would be her knight in shining armor. "I will devote my whole life to clearing this sweet girl's life of the cloud of this infamous accusation," he declared.[18]

The marriage was supposedly a sudden "Why don't we get married?" impulse, but it was probably planned in advance. In fact, Florence had quarreled with her parents shortly before that—maybe deliberately—and stormed out of the house, never to return. A week later, reporters sought the Burnses' reaction to the marriage, but they knew nothing about it. Fred Burns was shocked to hear it and refused to comment: "I have nothing to say. I will stick to my policy of saying nothing, the same policy I have always maintained concerning my daughter."[19]

Shortly before 9:30 P.M. on Wednesday, November 26, 1902—the day before Thanksgiving—Tad and Flo showed up at the Thirty-Fourth Street Reformed Church in Manhattan, where the regular weekly meeting was just breaking up. They told the minister, Rev. John H. Elliott, that they wished to be married. Elliott thought it odd as the hour was late and they had brought no witnesses, but the prospective groom answered his questions "in a straightforward, manly way," so he summoned two parishioners to serve as witnesses. The couple signed their names as Charles White Wildrick and Florence Wallace Burns. Elliott did not recognize either name, but one of the witnesses, twenty-three-year-old Edythe Mariani, thought she did: "Wouldn't it be funny if the bride was the Florence Burns of the Brooks case?"[20]

When Mariani and the other witness, James Cromie, discovered the truth a day or so later, they were angered and upset at having unwittingly played a role in the marriage. Mrs. Mariani was outraged: "My daughter is horrified at this publicity. She does not know Florence Burns, and was a witness to the marriage lately at the request of Dr. Elliott." It was the first of many indications that, although Florence was dismissed as a murder suspect by a judge and the coroner, and to thunderous approval in the two courtrooms, most people believed she had killed Walter Brooks.

Reverend Elliott said that he never connected the bride with the woman accused of murder, and he supposed his fellow ministers would criticize him for it. But, he argued, if he had not married them, someone else would have. Nonetheless, he capitalized on his brief fame by giving an address at a conference on supporting a bill to punish adultery. He was known as the minister "who recently married Florence Burns to Charles W. Wildrick."[21]

Editorials around the country weighed in on the probable success of the Burns-Wildrick marriage. Typical of these was one from Montana: "Will they live 'happily ever after'? They may. But it's a 50 to 1 shot that they don't."[22]

FLO'S FOLLIES

Before he left for Europe, Foster Backus addressed the issue that most intrigued the public: What will Florence Burns do now? Would she go on the stage? Backus had assured everyone that pursuant to a family consultation (likely without input from Florence herself), it had been decided that Florence would not go on the stage but instead live a more subdued life. She should not attempt to "coin her notoriety into money." "As to Florence's future, she has now seen the error of her ways, and is a changed girl. She never was a really bad girl, but she liked gay life. It appealed to her. She is dignified and reserved. The examinations in this case have enlightened her as to the kind of men she has been going with. They have revealed to her what she would have become if she had continued to live the way she had been living."[23]

Quite possibly, Backus's speech was intended to send a message to his client, who did not seem to be so inclined to "live a more subdued life." But the *Brooklyn Daily Eagle* urged Backus to press home this point to Florence—that although most people in the community were on her side during her hearings, its "moral sense . . . will rise in protest against any attempt to make capital for her out of the tragic publication of her shame. This is a time for plain talk."[24] In other words, we may have been on her side because of the circumstances (the Unwritten Law), but that doesn't mean we will support her flaunting herself on the stage through notoriety acquired by the death of that young man.

Foster Backus and the community at large reckoned without the independent and headstrong nature of Florence's character. No sooner was Backus off to Europe than she arranged her liberation by eloping with Tad Wildrick and, two weeks later, signing a vaudeville contract with Irving Pinover, a dramatic actor and former reporter with William Randolph Hearst's "yellow" newspaper, the *New York Journal*. A skilled agent, Pinover had successfully managed the comedy team of Weber and Fields, famous for its slapstick and satire, which included a sketch done in the German dialect.[25]

The plan was for Florence to begin her vaudeville career with a tour of twenty weeks, to begin in New Jersey or New York, then to the Midwest cities, but instead it was decided that she should start in her hometown of Brooklyn. Her performance was to stay completely away from the Brooks case and would consist of songs, little sketches, and maybe some solo dancing. It was an interesting omission in that theatergoers would expect someone involved in a high-profile murder case to sate their curiosity by discussing it. Someone smarter than Florence—Tad? Her agent?—must have reminded her that there was no statute of limitations on murder and, guilty or innocent, she could say something onstage that would trigger an arrest. Since there had been no trial, double jeopardy did not apply.

Florence was to get $1,500 even though nobody knew if she could act or sing. How did the community react to this news? On the joke page for Friday, December 12, 1902, the *Eagle* included a jibe at Florence in the guise of a conversation between two women:

> No. 1: So, Florence Burns is going on the stage again, eh?
>
> No. 2: Again? Has she ever been on the stage before?
>
> No. 1: Well, she played an important part in a considerable farce a few months ago, I believe.[26]

Most people believed she had killed Walter Brooks, and most did not mind that she got away with it—probably a majority even believed he deserved it—but making money off it, whether she was going to talk about it or not, was crossing a line. However, for her agent and for the proprietors of the houses she was booked in, the only success was not in the quality of her performance but in how many paying customers would line up to see her. When Florence and her new husband showed up to watch a play at a local theater, the audience was much more interested in them than they were in what was happening on the stage. Now, added to the titillation of a sensational murder case was the romantic derring-do history of Tad Wildrick. This fascination would carry over to Florence's own stage appearances.[27]

It's a good thing it did, too, as her debut at the very popular Hyde & Behman's theater was a disaster. The managers had no idea what she was going to do or whether she could sing or recite a monologue. She had not rehearsed at all either. Hyde & Behman's, however, was not in the least concerned about this because they knew she would be a big draw. In fact, even though it was universally discussed and decided that this vaudeville career was a bad move on Florence's part, most of those who criticized her still showed up to see her.[28]

By this time, with the vaudeville contract on top of Flo's elopement with a man who had only the year before been released from prison, in addition to her autobiographical article written for Hearst's *Journal* criticizing her parents, the Burnses had washed their hands of her and cut her off from the family.

On the day of Florence's inauspicious debut, Foster Backus was on his way home from Europe, ignorant as to how far his former client had regressed

The vaudeville ad promoting Florence Burns's Brooklyn appearances (*Brooklyn Daily Eagle,* reprinted in www.newspapers.com and used with permission from www.Ancestry.com)

since he last saw her, and there was much speculation as to how he would react to it.[29] History, however, is blessedly silent as to this.

The debut consisted of two performances, one in the afternoon and one in the evening. Tad hung about in the wings to give her encouragement. The crowd, consisting mostly of women, applauded madly before Florence had even opened her mouth. For the afternoon session, she began with an imitation of that kangaroo walk that was the current craze and then was to sing a current popular song called "Gracie Brown (A Sly Naughty Girl)" by Maurice Jacobs (lyrics) and Harry Robinson (music). It was a somewhat suggestive song insinuating that Gracie was a flirt who took money from the boys, then left town:

1st verse:
Gracie Brown was a maid with a sly naughty wink
was Gracie Brown.
She wore a straw hat and a dress that was pink
did Gracie Brown.
She lived in a village where boys there were few
But the boys that were there had hearts that were true
And now they all sigh with a tear in their eye
for Gracie Brown
Chorus:
Gracie Brown, she is out of town

She's the kind of girl that is hard to find
is Gracie Brown.
We're all blue and we sigh for you.
If you change your name we will know you the same
as Gracie Brown
2nd verse:
Reuben Glue came to town and his whiskers were pink,
met Gracie Brown.
She's a nice little girlie I think
is Gracie Brown
He is waiting for Gracie, she said she'd be back
'Cause Gracie was honest, he gave her his cash
But he'll see her no more, Gracie's gone to the shore,
Sweet Gracie Brown.
(Repeat chorus)[30]

Florence's performance was "a dismal and pitiable failure." Her voice was
so weak that she could not be heard at all, not even in the first row. She tried
three times to get this song right, but she kept forgetting the words. She had
not practiced and didn't even have a copy with her on the stage, and then she
had to start over. Finally, the band leader handed her a copy, but she wadded
it up without looking at it and left the stage. The stage manager mercifully
brought the curtain down and not even the audience's raucous calls for Florence to come back and finish could change her mind.[31]

Although newspaper reports said she was not nervous, only unprepared, it
was obvious that Florence was a victim of stage fright. Anyone who has ever
dreaded speaking in public has known that breathless feeling where the lungs
don't seem to fill up completely and that powerlessness to project the voice.
A few times, when Florence forgot the words to the song, she looked at Tad
in the wings and laughed—again, a sign of self-conscious nervousness and
not, as many felt, her failure to take the performance seriously.[32]

For the evening show, Behman did not want to risk a repeat of the afternoon
debacle and arranged for a group of nine female singers—Turner's Rialto Belles,
fresh from a tour in Pennsylvania—to come onstage with Florence and be sort
of a warm-up/backup act. The ensemble was billed as "Turner's Rialto Belles
and Florence Burns," although, strictly speaking, Florence did not belong to
this group. The Belles, managed by Frank Turner, had a singing and dancing
routine consisting of three presentations, after which Florence was to join them

"Gracie Brown" music sheet sung by Florence Burns (Author's collection)

on the stage. But Behman sent her out after the second act, which threw the Belles off, as they had not been prepared for this interruption.[33]

For this performance, Florence was decked out in a "very becoming dove-colored gown, trimmed with immense turquoise bead flowers, mingled with silver flowers. The gown was cut very low and at the shoulders were trimmings of black chiffon." She accessorized her outfit with black gloves and a black hat.[34]

Florence came out, "swinging her arms and moving her body like a village belle trying to be real graceful," but something about this entrance—was it viewed as arrogant? seductive?—was completely off-putting for the audience. They gave her the silent treatment: no clapping, no shouting, no sound at all. She started "Gracie Brown" but still did not know the words, or else they were frightened right out of her head. As she stopped and started several times with the same four words, the orchestra frantically tried to keep up. By this time, the audience took pity on her and there was a smattering of applause to encourage her to get through it, but she could not. Nor could she be heard any more than at the afternoon performance, with her thin, reedy voice. The reviews were merciless: "It was like some five-year-old child giving an exhibition of its prodigious skill." "The only thing she had going for her was beauty." "Very ungraceful in her movements."[35]

Florence left the stage before the song was finished, singing as she left and with the same sauntering gait she had used for her entrance. There was very little applause, which lasted for mere seconds. The stage manager tried to coax her back onto the stage to finish up, but she would only go back for a curtain call.[36]

After a second disastrous performance, Behman decided there might not be any more singing if it did not improve, but only sketches and maybe some dancing. Reporters were astonished to hear that the theater would continue her contract for the week, but the manager was more practical: The theater was turning hundreds of customers away because everyone wanted to get a look at the infamous Florence Burns.[37] Nobody was interested in the other performers—the full house was for Florence alone, as if she were a freak in a circus sideshow. Why would it matter that her performances were flops? Even a lukewarm Keith-Albee Manager's Review of Flo's debut would not have discouraged anyone from attending:

> Turner's Rialto Belles and Florence Burns: The Rialto belles consist of eight women and a leader who render three songs with figure dancing and light effects. The act was a good deal of a disappointment and failed to carry. The introduction of Miss Burns at the close of their set proved to be an unprecedented drawing card, filling the house at each performance with the high class audiences, who watched and listened to her short act with engrossed attention. Miss Burn's [sic] appearance was remarkably prepossessing. Used full stage; time 17 minutes.[38]

Hyde & Behman now had a potential lawsuit on its hands from the Turner's Rialto Belles, who had their sets interrupted without warning. Their manager claimed a breach of contract for that and for what he saw as Florence's "stealing their applause" in coming onto the stage between their second and third acts. ("Stifling their applause" would be more accurate, as the audience had shown its disapproval of her flaunting entrance with a crushing silence.) Frank Turner threatened to quit if changes were not made, but they were not. Behman's reaction to Turner's threat was to get the Newsboy Quintet for Flo and tell Turner he could take his Belles elsewhere. The Newsboy Quintet was an enormously successful act created for Hyde & Behman's in 1896, consisting of five teenage boys dressed as "newsies" in torn, ragged clothes who sold newspapers and sang popular songs. As boys grew too old for the part, they were replaced by others, much like Menudo, a similar band of the 1970s and 1980s.[39]

Frank Turner had one more card to play: he consulted the notorious law firm of Howe & Hummel, the most colorful, creative, and corrupt lawyers in New York City—and the most successful. From 1869 to 1907 (when Hummel was convicted of suborning perjury and sentenced to a year in prison; Howe had died in 1902), they represented gangsters, madams, murderers, thieves, and the vaudeville/theater community. The very tall, very corpulent William Howe generally handled the criminal aspect, while the short, small, dapper Abe Hummel was a master at taking care of theatrical cases. Howe had represented, among many other famous defendants, Martin Thorn for the murder and dismemberment of Willie Guldensuppe, Carlyle Harris for the poisoning of his wife, and George Appo, the boy pickpocket. Abe Hummel's most notable client was probably Evelyn Nesbit, the "Gibson Girl," after her husband, Harry Thaw, killed the architect Stanford White in an "Unwritten Law" case that was prosecuted by William Travers Jerome.[40]

Although Howe & Hummel were not above lying and cheating to win their cases, Abe Hummel did have some sound advice for Frank Turner: he was to have his girls ready, willing, and able to perform every night of their obligation so that Behman could not claim they had breached their contract by not appearing. Hummel suggested that Turner might also have a suit because of the damage to his professional reputation. Behman's response was to laugh at this and put a false spin on it. The Belles weren't really all that good, he claimed, so he had Florence go out on the stage to help them out![41]

Somebody with tongue planted firmly in cheek wrote a letter to the editor with a suggestion of a very melodramatic sketch for Florence and her husband to perform, with several fat women planted in the audience to sob on occasion. Fat women are best, the author wrote, because their voices are "more strident" than those of thin women, and thin people, in general, are less sympathetic than fat ones.[42]

At Newburgh, New York, just fifty miles up the Hudson River from New York City, Florence was billed as "the most persecuted and most beautiful young woman in America." But approximately five hundred people waited outside her hotel and jeered her when she came out to get a cab to the theater.[43]

Florence's eventual debut in Manhattan, after appearances throughout New York State and New England, was in February 1903, at Proctor's Twenty-Third Street Theater, one of several Proctor's theaters in New York City and Newark, New Jersey. There, she was "The Persecuted American Girl" and still singing "Gracie Brown," presumably with some improvement. Among the acts appearing at Proctor's with her was a standard sampling of vaudeville acts of the time: a Japanese troupe of magicians and illusionists; trick bicycle riders; a blackface monologue, probably by a white man, but then also a "colored singing comedian." Including Florence's, there were to be a total of nearly thirty acts—a lot of entertainment for a Gilded Age audience![44]

Vaudeville at the turn of the twentieth century was enjoying a surge in popularity, although it had been around since after the Civil War. But with an increase in both public and private transportation options available, as well as the establishment of the amusement parks at Coney Island and elsewhere, Gilded Age audiences were enamored of variety shows. There were also the dime museums (cheap variety shows for the working class, a level below vaudeville) and the circus with its sideshows.[45]

The staples of vaudeville and other variety acts were the minstrel shows with white men in blackface, magic tricks and optical illusions, short skits, dancing and singing, and—always—actors and actresses with strong ethnic accents, which audiences found hilarious because of the influx of immigrants into the cities. It was an occasion for nonethnic viewers to laugh at the foibles of the newcomers, with the most common accents being Irish, German, Italian, and Yiddish.[46]

Yet another factor driving the proliferation of variety shows was the increase of factories and shops in the cities, which had the effect of luring young men and women from the farms. In their leisure hours, they went in search of entertainment not available in rural areas. In an ironic coincidence, one of these young women who exchanged farm life for the factory was named Grace (but not Gracie) Brown. Her murder in 1906 by a boyfriend who refused to marry her when she got pregnant would form the basis of Theodore Dreiser's *An*

American Tragedy. And, in a further irony, if Grace had killed Chester for not salvaging her honor with marriage, she would have been acquitted under the Unwritten Law. Chester, having no such defense, was executed in 1908.[47]

By the summer of 1903, Florence was appearing at beach venues: Rob's Casino Theater at North Beach in Brooklyn and Morrison's Casino at Rockaway Beach on Long Island. She had never joined the Actors' National Protective Union, which caused a problem for her at Rob's Casino when the other actors, actresses, and musicians refused to work with her. Consequently, she was dismissed.[48]

However, at Morrison's at Rockaway Beach, Florence was the star attraction—so much so that a nearby rival theater was losing business, until the proprietor had a brainstorm. He had a large poster printed up saying, "FLORENCE BURNS" and, on top of that, in very tiny letters, "Pauline Brown will give an imitation of." Florence, accompanied by Tad, went to the local police court to get a restraining order against the rival establishment, but the magistrate informed her that it was a civil matter, not criminal, and she would need to get an injunction against the proprietor, as well as Pauline Brown, from the proper court.[49]

In the fall, the proprietor of Morrison's got the bright idea of featuring Florence with the temperance scold, the hatchet-wielding Carrie Nation, famous for attacking saloons with her weapon. The juxtaposition of the fifty-seven-year-old morally upright matron and the twenty-one-year-old morally challenged Florence Burns Wildrick was too tempting for him to resist. The wonder is that Mrs. Nation actually agreed to it! She saw it as an opportunity to lecture against alcohol and tobacco, but she was unprepared for the two-pronged shock that was in store for her.[50]

In the "green room" while she was waiting to go onstage, Mrs. Nation encountered another performer, the perennially popular vaudeville singer/actress Lottie Gilson, on the downside of her career at the age of forty-one. Nation, never passing up an opportunity to preach, told Gilson that she should never marry a man who smoked cigarettes (no mention was made of pipes or cigars, so possibly they were not on the Carrie Nation Hit List of Forbidden Indulgences). "If I do," the younger woman responded, "he will buy his own. He won't get any of mine." Nation was so shocked that Lottie Gilson was a smoker—and admitted to it without shame—that she shrieked, "Let me out of here!" and remained outside on the theater grounds until the time of her appearance with Florence.

When Carrie Nation saw Florence's low-cut dress, she experienced another shock and refused to go on with her dressed like that until someone put a shawl on Florence to cover up the offending area. "You're a faker," Florence said. "Maybe I am," Nation responded, "but I'm no woman to appear with such a woman with no more clothes on than one of the park statues." She took out her Bible and waved it at Florence as if warding off evil, gave her scheduled lecture, and collected fifty dollars for it. In the end, like Florence Burns and Lottie Gilson, Carrie Nation was herself an entertainer.

Carrie Nation had to know who Florence Burns was and probably had some inkling as to her vaudeville act. Quite possibly, she realized that appearing on the same stage with her would provoke the very kind of confrontation that resulted, and she would have yet another opportunity for a "teachable moment" that would find its way into the press. Otherwise, it would have been more in keeping with Nation's straitlaced persona to have given lectures, not on vaudeville, which was solely for somewhat low-brow entertainment, but in more high-brow venues such as formal lecture halls or Chautauquas.

So it went, until December 1906, when the conflict between the desires of Flo and Tad came to a head.

THE BREAKUP

At the beginning of January 1907, Florence left Tad Wildrick and moved back in with her forgiving parents, now living on Putnam Avenue in Brooklyn. He was back to his old habits of sleeping with other women, in particular one whom Flo seriously thought of suing for alienation of affections. Tad begged her to divorce him, which his adultery gave her the right to do under the divorce laws. But he could not file on his own because he had no statutory grounds, which at that time in New York State were adultery, cruel and inhumane treatment, imprisonment for three or more years after the marriage, and continuous abandonment for one or more years. Flo had committed none of these offenses—not yet, anyway.[51]

If Tad Wildrick really had someone he wanted to marry at that time, he would have done well to force Florence's hand by not giving her any money. Instead, he chose to send her a payment each week with no legal obligation to do so. When he stopped the payments a year and a half later, Flo suddenly had the motivation to file for divorce, which she did in April 1908, on the grounds of infidelity (although she did not name anyone as co-respondent). She asked for twenty-five dollars a week for alimony and $200 for attorney's fees.[52]

WHAT SHE SAID

In her filing papers, Florence claimed that, apart from Tad's adultery with many women, he hit her, neglected her, and spent large amounts of money on these other women, while she suffered from a lack of funds. She claimed she was a "physical wreck" and needed medical attention because of having to deal with Tad's "immoral behavior," which she had finally had enough of. She had no money for whatever medicine she needed, although Tad could easily support her, as he was living "very comfortably and luxuriously."[53] Here, she seems to hint at having contracted a venereal disease.

WHAT HE SAID

Tad actually had a bigger list of complaints against Flo than she had against him. While some of them may have been exaggerated or created out of whole cloth, the very tenor of the first one set out in his countersuit smacks of Flo's vindictive nature. Tad worked for an advertising company, where Flo frequently sent postcards accusing him of things such as being a "morphine fiend" and other "scurrilous statements" that the company's clerks and Tad's employers could read, since the postcards were put in a common area. Contrary to Flo's assertion of his living richly, Tad insisted that he earned only fourteen dollars a week. He had tried his best with her and even sent her to Liberty, a resort town in the Catskills, for four weeks in 1907.[54]

Tad accused Flo of frequently being with "disreputable company," although he did not give any specific examples of this, and of being addicted to gambling and staying at gambling resorts. Flo was earning good money on her own, he asserted, even more than his own fourteen dollars a week, with her "fancy exhibitions of roller skating" at a Manhattan rink.

Tad claimed to have taken good care of Flo. We know that he accompanied her to her vaudeville appearances and was generally a support system for her there. But, he asserted, her harassment of him at his office was causing him "mental anguish." He denied ever having used morphine in his life.

Florence's monetary demands were scaled down quite a bit by the judge: from twenty-five dollars to five dollars per week for alimony pending the divorce trial and from two hundred dollars to fifty dollars for attorney's fees.[55]

Florence must have been chafing at having to live with her parents and was looking forward to having some funds to find her own room somewhere. At some point in 1909, she moved out of her parents' Brooklyn home and began a succession of Manhattan habitations. Unmoored from any settling influence—her parents or her husband or her vaudeville career, now mostly defunct as the novelty of Florence Burns had by then worn off—Florence was adrift and on her own. She began a downward slide that primarily consisted of heavy drinking, then petty scams to support her habit, then soliciting money from men, which led to exchanging sex for money and drinks: prostitution in spirit if not in a more formal arrangement.[56]

Gladys Burns, who had also been living at home at age twenty-four, suddenly eloped to New Jersey to marry twenty-four-year-old Harry West Mettais in Hoboken on November 9, 1909. Once again, the Burns parents were caught off guard at the marriage of a daughter.[57]

Mrs. Burns, despite all the heartache caused by her older daughter, was sending Florence weekly money by registered mail, usually three or four dollars, but sometimes more if she had it. Florence discovered, to her dismay, that the Unwritten Law did not help her so much outside of court. When some of her landladies saw the return address on Flo's mother's envelopes as "Burns" and addressed to Florence Wildrick, they put two and two together and realized she was "that" Florence Burns. Consequently, she was evicted from a couple of boardinghouses, and from then on, her mother had to put her maiden name (Von derBosch) in the return address.[58]

Florence's life spiraled further downhill. She became adept at getting men to buy her drinks, supplies, or just give her money, blaming the troubles in her past for her current situation. Nothing that happened to her was ever her fault, and she seemed to be immune to any self-examination as to why her life was out of control.

Then Florence met two men who would change the arc of her life in a significant way: Charles W. Hurlbut and Edward H. Brooks.

THE BADGER GAME

By the fall of 1909, Florence was living at a boardinghouse at 39 Seventh Avenue in Manhattan. From 1909 to 1910, she seems to have moved every two or three weeks, either for nonpayment of rent or because the proprietor discovered her true identity. Her room and her personal appearance reflected her fall from respectability. No longer a beauty, no longer "the Belle of Bedford Avenue," Florence took on a slatternly, unhealthy appearance. Her hair was rarely combed and her clothes were rumpled and dirty. Whatever room she rented—never an apartment or a flat, but just a room—was littered with empty liquor bottles and cigarette butts.[1]

In November 1909, Florence fell while drunk and broke her arm. On the evening of December 9, she encountered a fellow lodger in the street in front of the boardinghouse and asked him if he would buy her a drink. He could tell she had already been drinking, but he took pity on her because of her broken arm and shabby dress. Whether Florence had targeted this young man or stumbled upon him accidentally, she hit upon the perfect mark: an abstainer of alcohol, a mender of broken wings, a knight in shining armor, a man of character, a perfect patsy.

CHARLES WAYLAND HURLBURT

Charles W. Hurlburt was born in 1879 in Palmyra, a small town near Rochester in western New York, to a prominent but litigiously inclined Wayne County family. In 1884, when Charles was five, his thirty-seven-year-old mother died and his father, Lyman, eventually remarried. Lyman Hurlburt, his brother John, and their deceased brother Theron's widow were involved in a rancorous, contentious legal battle that began in 1884 and did not end until 1895. It was a feud that, in its intensity and its duration, had a profound effect on young Charles, who was a sensitive and gentle soul. Added to that were the other court battles fought by Lyman Hurlburt over properties he had amassed, until, as his brother-in-law put it, "the family was at loggerheads with most of its neighbors." The effect on young Charles was to turn a "bright and cheerful boy" into a "silent and morose" man.[2]

The father of Lyman, John, and Theron Hurlburt put $12,000 in a Rochester bank in Theron's name so that Theron could access it for him, as the father lived in a small town with no bank and had no way to get to Rochester. Theron, however, died unexpectedly in September 1883, when he was just thirty-seven, and the father died four months later. Ella, Theron's widow, claimed that the money in the bank account belonged to her late husband as an outright gift from his father and refused to give any of it back, whereas Lyman, as his father's executor, claimed it belonged to that estate. The case came to a trial three years later and a jury found for Ella, probably because there was no writing to back up the alleged agreement.

Lyman filed his own lawsuit against Ella Hurlburt and got $3,000 from that. When he died in 1893, he left some of his property to the surviving brother, John, who then died a couple of years later, leaving his entire estate to . . . Theron's widow and daughter! John must have had some feelings of guilt for the extended feud, most of which seems to have been perpetuated by Lyman.

Lyman Hurlburt's will left his widow, Anna, a life estate as long as she did not remarry and also stipulated that she take care of his son Charles, then fourteen, and make sure he was educated. Her obligation to house him and take care of him ended at his majority, age twenty-one, unless he wanted to stay in the family home longer, and then she had to continue to provide for him. If she remarried or died, Lyman's entire estate went to Charles. There was also a "secret trust" set up by Lyman for his son when Charles reached the age of thirty-five, as the father felt that nobody under that age was disciplined enough to handle inherited money prudently.[3]

Charles, however, had other plans than to live off his stepmother. He went to law school in Rochester, took the bar exam, and was admitted to the New York State Bar in May 1900. Perhaps his career choice was influenced by his family's perpetual legal difficulties. In December 1900, he applied for the manager's position, or any other available, with the Little Rock, Arkansas, Travelers baseball team, which was to be included in the newly formed

Southern League. In his application, he said he had experience with state league baseball and was hoping to get involved with something at a higher level, like the Southern League, which would comprise several states.[4]

However, Charles probably did not help his chances when he stated that because of his poor health from an unstated cause, his doctors had advised him to be out in the fresh air, and this is why he wanted to manage a baseball team! "One word in regard to the salary," he wrote. "Of course, I can make a dozen times over practicing law what I could running a team, but it is, as I said before, my health that compels me to resort to baseball, together with my love for the game. There would be no trouble about the salary." The Little Rock Travelers eventually became the Arkansas Travelers, one of the most successful and renowned minor league franchises in history. Today, they are the Double-A team of the Seattle Mariners.

Charles Hurlburt, spurned by the Travs and with no choice left but to practice law indoors, opened an office in the Rochester-Palmyra area until 1904, when he decided to try his chances in New York City. There, he was in practice with a lawyer named Madison Haden Haythe until Haythe died suddenly in 1905 at age forty. Eventually, Charles got a position with the Lawyers Title Insurance & Trust Company on Broadway. A Wayne County judge called him "one of the brightest young men [of] the local bar," but his position with Lawyers Title was not so much adversarial as it was research-oriented. This is where he was working when he met Florence in December 1909.[5]

THE FLEECING OF CHARLES HURLBURT, PART I

Although Hurlburt was three years older than Flo, she was way ahead of him in life experience and sophistication. He was a naive country boy from a small upstate town, while she had been surviving on the streets of Manhattan for a year or more. So, when Flo asked him to buy her a drink that evening as he was coming back from his supper, he relented, even though he told her he was "not a drinking man." He took her to a café across the street from their boardinghouse. In spite of her appearance, Flo must have retained something of her former charm and seductive appeal—at least, enough of it for someone like Charles Hurlburt—because when she later invited him to her room, he went.

There, she told him she was about to be evicted for nonpayment of rent and asked him for a couple of dollars to prevent that. Flo played on his sympathy by telling him that her broken arm prevented her from getting a job as a stenographer or a telephone girl but that she would work if only she could. This, of course, was a lie, as she had never sought legitimate work in her life. Charles gave her two dollars and left. If he thought this would be the end of it, he was sadly mistaken.

A few days later, Charles encountered Florence again. She told him she had fallen on the ice and refractured her arm, and indeed he could see that the bone was sticking out in an alarming fashion. He took her to a Dr. McIntyre, who had set her arm previously, and paid the bill for this.

Flo stayed at their boardinghouse at 39 Seventh Avenue for a few more days after this, then moved to nearby 43 Seventh Avenue, where the two of them began a sexual relationship if they had not already done so. Charles gave her money to buy clothes and other necessities. After three or four weeks at the new address, Flo moved again, this time to 247 West 22nd Street in January 1910, then shortly after that to 217 West 22nd Street. Somewhere in here, she got the bright idea to start her own boardinghouse as a source of income. And where would she get the money for this? From Charles Hurlburt, of course! But by now, Charles was getting wary of her—he might be naive, but he wasn't stupid—and began visiting her less and less. He did, however, agree to give her the money for the first furniture payment in the boardinghouse venture: $150 for the residence at 607 West 136th Street.

It is not to be supposed that Florence was interested in Charles Hurlburt for romantic reasons. He was not at all her type, which ran to "bad boys" and those with far more personal magnetism than Charles possessed. She thought of him as "sort of an old fossil who always had a lot of things to tell me." He didn't drink, he didn't know how to play cards, and he was very fastidious and straitlaced. Still, at some level she must have appreciated his genuine kindness, generosity, and sympathy, even as she angled ways to part him from his money.

Now a new player enters our drama, which will become very dark indeed: Edward H. Brooks.

ELDRIDGE HILDRETH BROOKS

Although twenty-seven-year-old Eddie Brooks passed himself off as Edward H. Brooks, his real name was Eldridge Hildreth Brooks III. In an ironic twist of fate, he bore the same surname as the young man Florence was accused of shooting in 1902, but he was not related to him. In 1910, Eddie Brooks stood just under six feet and weighed 150 pounds. He had a dark complexion, dark hair, and dark eyes.[6]

The first Eldridge Hildreth Brooks, Eddie's great-grandfather, was a hero in the Mexican-American War, enlisting in the 1st Dragoon Regiment in 1844 at the age of twenty-nine. He was killed three years later, shot through the head in the New Mexico campaign at Pueblo de Taos, New Mexico, and is buried in the military cemetery there. The name skipped a generation, then was given to Eddie's father, who went by "Ed."[7]

Eddie had a long way to go to live up to the accomplishments of his father, but although he inherited his ambition, he did not inherit his work ethic or his moral compass. Ed Brooks, originally from New Jersey, moved to New York City and married Grace Atkins in Brooklyn in 1881. Their two children, Eddie and Miriam, were born in 1883 and 1889, respectively—he in Jersey City, New Jersey, and she in Lebanon, Pennsylvania.[8]

Ed Brooks had lots of irons in the fire and was always looking for the next entrepreneurial opportunity. In 1885 or 1886, he moved his wife and their toddler son to Lebanon, Pennsylvania, to become the superintendent of the Edison Electric Light Company and began installing arc lights around the city. As an adult, young Eddie would remember Lebanon as the place that where he spent most of his childhood—from age two to age ten, the longest time he had ever lived anywhere when he was growing up. In January 1886, a near-tragic incident occurred when the coal stove in the house the Brooks family had just moved into emitted serious sulfur fumes. They managed to escape just in time.[9]

In 1890, Ed filed a patent for a handle to be attached to axes and hammers to prevent the head from flying off, and his Keystone Handle Company did a brisk trade in the product. In 1891, he was instrumental in establishing the Lebanon & Annville Street Railway. For the groundbreaking ceremony, instead of the usual ceremonial token turnover of a spade in the dirt, Ed, dressed for labor, "stepped forward, spat on his hands, and seizing a pick, for about ten minutes struck lustily into the earth, loosening several cart loads of earth in this short time, while the perspiration rolled down over his forehead." The contractor joked that if Brooks didn't stop, the men he had hired would be out of a job and the railroad would be completed in a day. More than anything else, this vignette sums up the essence of Ed Brooks. When something needed to be done, he did it without hesitation. No matter how lofty his title, he never backed down from manual labor. He was not afraid of hard work.

Ed Brooks once hired an African American as a wiper at the electric company, but this did not sit well with the two engineers on duty, who refused to work "under the direction of a colored man." Brooks and an assistant had to cover their twelve-hour shift, from 7:00 P.M. to 7:00 A.M., which he did without hesitation. Many another superintendent might have delegated this to an underling.

Other enterprises Ed undertook were partial interests in a startup market company, an inn, and an insulated wire company. Brooks himself tested the insulated wire by burying it in the ground for six months to see if it was still good when it was removed. It was.

In 1893, having exhausted his opportunities in Lebanon, Pennsylvania, Ed moved his family to Everett, Washington, to run a vessel—possibly a ferry—on Puget Sound. His friends back in Lebanon were not surprised to hear that his business was doing well, as "Ed has the grit in him to succeed at almost anything."

By 1895, the Brookses were in Red Bank, New Jersey, where they had moved from Asbury Park, New Jersey, then on to New York City shortly after that, where Ed was superintendent of a match company. In April 1898, he went back to Lebanon on a business trip to investigate some financial investment opportunities there. At the Lebanon Iron Company one afternoon, his overcoat slipped off his shoulders and, as he bent to retrieve it, he suffered a massive stroke on his left side. He was taken to his hotel room and a doctor was summoned, but the doctor realized that his unconscious patient was dying. He sent for an ambulance and for Ed's family. Grace and her two children, Eddie and Miriam, arrived the day before he died. Ed Brooks, mourned as "an able and energetic business man, of a genial disposition and honest purpose," was forty-nine years old.

The upheaval of his youth, coupled with the early death of his father, had a profound effect on young Eddie. Despite the many ventures of Ed senior, he must not have left much money for his widow. In the early years of the new century, she would have to go to work, which she did as a clerk in a publishing house. Eddie turned fifteen the year his father died and would also have to help support the family. At seventeen, he was working as a drugstore clerk. In 1902, the family lived in Brooklyn, and from then on, they seemed to alternate between there and Manhattan.

Although Eddie would venture out on his own, he used his mother's residence—wherever that happened to be—as his home base, often giving that as his home address, and just as often going back to live there. His actual residence changed so often (he admitted to twenty different addresses in 1910 alone) that he needed a fixed abode, especially for job hunting. Unlike Florence, Eddie did

Eldridge Hildreth "Eddie" Brooks in his late thirties (Used with permission from www.familysearch.org and the National Archives and Records Administration)

look for work, but he lacked his father's self-discipline and work ethic, never putting himself wholeheartedly into any task and either getting fired soon after starting or finding a reason why he could not continue.

Eddie developed a drinking problem—another thing he had in common with Florence—and was arrested for public intoxication a few times in Manhattan. He was fired from at least one job for drinking.

In December 1909, Eddie went to work for the Erie Railroad as a freight brakeman, which required running on top of the boxcars. This did not suit him, so he quit that aspect of it because of his health, unspecified, and transferred to the passenger service area. But this did not suit him, either, so he quit or was fired around Christmas of that year. He did not work in January or most of February 1910, but at the end of February he was hired by the Union Switch & Signal Company, makers of railroad signals, a job he held for only two or three weeks before he claimed the gas in the tunnels from the steam locomotives was affecting his health and that he had been "knocked out" two or three times.

An ad in the *New York Herald* led Eddie to the Holmes Electric Protective Company, makers of burglar alarms and bank safes. It is remotely possible that he was related to the founders, as his great-grandmother, wife of the war hero, was a Holmes. He started working there in March or April as assistant night manager, but by April 19, he had been fired for drunkenness and for missing two shifts.

From there, Eddie got a commission job (not a salaried one) in June or July with Monarch Realty Company, and from then on he passed himself off as a real estate salesman, although he did very little work and, by September 1910, had earned the paltry sum of $46.50 in commissions.

Then on December 15, 1909, a Mrs. Baker, the wife of someone he had worked with on the railroad, introduced him to Florence Brooks. They all had drinks and he escorted her home. Two weeks later he saw her again, this time in the company of Charles Hurlburt.

THE FLEECING OF CHARLES HURLBURT, PART II

Around the beginning of January 1910, Flo and Charles were coming back from a movie when Flo was hailed by someone across the street: "Why, hello, Flo!"—not "Good afternoon, Mrs. Wildrick," spoken from a closer distance, as would have been the polite standard at that time. It was Eddie Brooks. Flo introduced him to Charles as an "old friend," although it was supposedly only the second time she had met him. Eddie insisted on the three of them going into a nearby café, and when Charles told him he did not drink and saw no need to have one, Brooks overrode him: "We have to have a drink right away!" And the nondrinking person, the only one of the three with a steady job, paid for the drinks: eighteen or twenty rounds, he estimated. (Flo later said he was trying to show up Eddie, who was poor.) If Flo and Eddie had really not met up again since their first meeting on December 15, surely they must have given each other glances throughout this very odd evening that signaled, "Is this a born sucker, or what?" At the end of this drinking session, Brooks escorted Florence home, even though Charles had been her date, where they had sex for the first time—unless it had already happened earlier, which neither cared to admit.

They decided they would need to test Charles Hurlburt further before going ahead with a major plan to get money from him. Charles had always been generous with Florence. He estimated that over the course of their relationship, he had spent $500–$800 in money given directly to her or paid out on her behalf. However, at times, he could be stubborn in not wanting to part with his money. They would need a scheme that would give him plenty of motivation to do so.

Eddie moved into Flo's room on 22nd Street on January 15, 1910, exactly one month after they met. It is doubtful that Charles was aware of this until the night of "the test," which was in late January or early February. Flo invited Charles to visit her in her room, during which they had sex. While they were still in bed, Eddie opened the door and stormed in, roaring, "What are you doing here, you goddamned son of a bitch?" Charles, shocked that Brooks had been so bold as to open a lady's door without knocking, leaped out of the bed and said he had been invited there "by the young lady," then hurried to put his clothes on. Eddie beat him up and Charles put up no resistance. They made such a row that the landlady came in and scolded them all for "causing a rumpus." Charles finished dressing and left.

Now the scheming pair knew another important thing besides his having money: Charles would not fight back if physically attacked.

Two weeks after this episode, Eddie showed up at Charles's office at the Lawyers Title Company and demanded money for Flo's boardinghouse venture. Charles had given her $150 for the first payment on the furniture, but now there was another one due and Eddie wanted it. Charles refused. He had agreed to only that one payment, nothing more. Eddie threatened to tell Tad Wildrick that he had found Charles in Flo's room, which would give Tad the grounds he needed for divorce. He would name Charles as a co-respondent and this would cause him shame and notoriety, especially with his employers. Charles responded that Florence had told him that she and Tad were already divorced, which Eddie informed him was not true. Nonetheless, Charles stood his ground and insisted he would not contribute any more money for the boardinghouse plan. He reminded Eddie that he, Eddie, would be the co-respondent in Tad's divorce, as he was the one who was living with Flo.

The new boardinghouse does seem to have been at least begun, as Charles saw her there once or twice in February or March and then again in April. Flo threatened him to make her payments on the boardinghouse or she would get Brooks to tell Tad. However, Charles would not budge on his stance and Flo had to give up the boardinghouse in February for a lack of funds to pay the bills. He had called their bluff and won. He did not see Flo at all in May or June.

Life with Eddie, in the meantime, was one of squalor, despair, and torment for Florence. He frequently beat her, by his own admission. He had knocked some of her teeth out, dislocated a rib, and given her black eyes.

He pawned two of her rings, along with a watch of his own. There were gin, whiskey, and beer bottles everywhere in the small room, as well as cigarette butts, ashes, and other trash. Flo would stand looking out her ground-floor window and make suggestive remarks to men passing by, which sent Eddie into a rage and caused another beating.

In August, Charles met up with Flo several times at their usual place on the corner of 5th Avenue and 14th Street. She looked awful and confessed that she was not doing well. He often gave her meal money, as she didn't look as if she was eating regularly. She told him she had a new room at 224 West 25th Street and invited him to come and talk, nothing more, but Charles was not risking another beating by Eddie, so he refused each time. Flo would call him at his office, thanking him for his past kindness to her and asking if he would send more money. Her practice, when drunk and alone, was to write a letter to Charles, so he ended up with a lot of letters—letters of thanks, of complaint about her plight, and of supplication.

Charles saw Flo a few more times in September. On the 16th, he took her to a Dr. Dennis O'Leary to be tested for venereal disease, as he had heard somewhere that Eddie had one. Charles had himself checked out on the 15th and he was negative, but when Dr. O'Leary tested Florence, he found that she did indeed have a venereal disease. He advised Charles not to have intercourse with her. Although Flo denied she had been told this and said that what she really had was common to all women—a discharge called leukorrhea, also known as "whites"[10]—she was taking bichloride tablets, an over-the-counter remedy for syphilis. And among the causes of leukorrhea is a sexually transmitted disease.

On Sunday, September 18, Flo met with Charles at 5th Avenue once again, which they had agreed to on the 16th, and begged him to come to her room "to talk" because she was feeling low. Her parents had "turned her down" (presumably for requests of money), her sister and brother-in-law wanted nothing to do with her, and she sometimes felt like committing suicide. Charles had always been kind to her, she said, whereas Eddie—whom she wanted nothing more to do with—often beat her.

Alarmed, Charles advised her not to think about killing herself but to go to her family in Brooklyn, as New York City was not the right place for her in her weakened and desolate condition. He agreed to walk her home but not to go inside. Along the way, she asked him to buy her something to eat, which he did, and then got him to pay for a drugstore purchase: twenty-five cents for a bottle of bichloride tablets.

"Please come in," she pleaded when they arrived at 224 West 25th Street. "Eddie has gone to Boston for the day and won't be back." Charles was still hesitant, reluctant to believe her claim that Eddie was in Boston, but he was concerned about her mental state. Was she really suicidal? He kept asking her, "Are you sure? Could he come back early?" Despite her assurances, however, Eddie Brooks was not in Boston. He was right across the street.

THE BADGER GAME AS GRAND GUIGNOL

Although the Badger Game may have changed its name over the years, it has never gone out of vogue. It was probably practiced by the ancient Egyptians because it is—even today—a more effective extortion tool than threatening someone with groundless or unprovable accusations. With the Badger Game, the victim participates in his own downfall, which is backed up by witnesses or photographs or, in the modern version, a damning video from a hidden camera. In its pre-technology form, the essence of the Badger Game was for a woman to lure the mark (always male, always wealthy) to a compromising location, such as her apartment or a hotel room, where they would have sex. Suddenly, a man—or two men—would burst through the door, claiming to be the woman's husband/father/brother and threatening the mark with death or dishonor . . . unless money were paid to keep it quiet. If the man held a particularly high-profile position in politics or society, it would do no good for him merely to deny it, especially in light of the photo or the testimony of the witness(es). The damage would be done with exposure and would likely cost him his job and his family.[11]

However, Charles Hurlburt had already indicated that he would not cave under a threat of being a co-respondent in Tad Wildrick's divorce suit, since Eddie Brooks was a more likely candidate for that position. Flo and Eddie would have to come up with something much more convincing. What they decided on was sodomy.

In the New York of 1910, and possibly in many other states, sodomy was a felony that included all forms of oral and anal sex no matter who the participants were: a man and a woman, two men, or two women. Although Flo would claim that Charles Hurlburt did not really like sexual intercourse, but preferred oral or anal sex instead, it is doubtful that this was true of this very conventional, very fastidious young man.

The day before the plan was to be put in operation, Eddie had gone to the landlady, Celestine Grygiel, and borrowed a screwdriver from her, then loosened the bolt on the door to their room in order to make it easier for him to break down the door in a "rage." (Mrs. Grygiel assumed that Eddie was Flo's husband because Flo had told her this.) Then he arranged with a friend, Martin Held from Monarch Realty, to play the part of the unassailable witness and also to help with getting Charles's "cooperation," if needed. Martin Held, which was probably not his real name, was thirty-five to forty years old, five-feet-eight, heavyset, with broad shoulders and a dark complexion—an intimidating presence, which was undoubtedly the intent in selecting him.

On that Sunday, Flo got ready for her part in the venture by drinking two half-pints of gin before going to meet Charles Hurlburt—not the wisest of choices for keeping sharp in the midst of what was likely to be a scene of unpredictable confusion. The old military maxim that no battle plan, no matter how perfect—and theirs was not—survives first contact with the enemy was not heeded by these two, who seem to have assumed that all would go swimmingly once Charles was confronted with his options.

In fact, in approaching the house, Charles almost spoiled the whole game by spying two men sitting on a porch across the street. It was dusk and he couldn't see clearly, but he thought he recognized Eddie Brooks and, like a skittish horse, backed off. Florence had quite a job on her hands of assuring him that was *not* Brooks and that he was in Boston. Despite his reluctance, Charles entered the house.

Florence's room in the Grygiel boardinghouse consisted of a bed, a bureau, a rocking chair, a sitting chair, and a stand. For the mostly transient community that populated the boardinghouses of that era, almost all such rooms were furnished by the landlady or landlord. As soon as they entered, Florence made a show of bolting the door without, however, sliding it into the latch, then grabbed Charles and threw him down on the bed, kissing him and begging him to help her "get back on her feet again." He had not removed any clothing. She had said she only wanted to talk, and this was a bit much for him. He stood up and declared he would be going.

Exactly three minutes after Flo and Charles had entered the room, the door burst open with a bang, followed by Eddie and Martin Held rushing in. "You goddamned cuntlapper," Eddie screamed, then slammed Charles against the wall. He told Held he was going to "have the son of a bitch arrested." Flo was gleeful that the plan was working so well. "You goddamned son of a bitch," she crowed triumphantly at Charles, "I have got you now where I have been trying to get you a long time and you have to come through with the goods." Eddie hit Charles again, then Held hit him too.

Charles, as was his wont, did not fight back physically but insisted on his innocence—"I have done nothing wrong"—and asked to be taken to a police magistrate immediately if they really thought he had committed a crime. It is the first indication that the accusation of sodomy in this and past instances (they would say they found him on his knees with his head in her vagina when they entered the room) was not true. A guilty man, especially one as passive and guileless as Charles Hurlburt, would not insist on being taken to a court to prove his innocence. And it should have been a warning signal to Flo and Eddie because this was not at all the response they had counted on.

Yet Eddie blustered on, reminding Charles of his important and responsible job, which would be in jeopardy if his employers found out about this. "These charges of unnatural sexual connections will injure you mentally and morally and physically and financially" if he did not come up with the money.

Brooks and Held searched Charles's pockets, coming up with fifty-seven dollars in cash—quite a large sum of money to be carrying—and a blank form from Lawyers Title Company. Florence told them that Charles was worth about $15,000, which would mean $5,000 for each of them, but Charles protested that he was not worth anywhere near that. They immediately scaled down their demands to $500 apiece.

Eddie took a piece of paper and wrote out the promissory note language, which he then had Charles copy on the Lawyers Title form: $500 payable to Edward Brooks. Then he had Charles write out a second note made out to Florence for a withdrawal from his bank savings account in the amount of $500. At this point, they had run out of paper (poor planning!) and they still had the confession, the third promissory note, and two further orders to be written down. Eddie went out to look for paper and, with only one man guarding him, Charles had a burst of courage and tried to make a break for it. However, he was overpowered by Held, who hit him over the head with a beer bottle. Thereafter, every time Charles stood up over the course of his long ordeal, Eddie and Held would beat him.

Eddie came back with butcher's paper, the only kind he could find. They cut it into pages and had Charles sign them before anything was written on them. They told him one was a confession to the crime of sodomy, one was to access Charles's boardinghouse room, and another was for the title company to access his keys and his bank book. Eddie filled in the sodomy confession over Charles's signature and Florence added her own witness testimony, which was probably composed by Eddie: "He cleaned my clitoris and sucked me until I was faint. He has been in the habit of doing so for several months, namely from December 10, 1909, until the present date." Then Eddie "notarized" the confession paper.

By this time, Charles Hurlburt was a physical and emotional wreck. They intended to keep him prisoner until the bank opened the next day, Monday, at 10:00 to make sure they got their money, so they proceeded to settle in and enjoy themselves with an all-night drinking and card-playing party. The three kidnappers drank quite a bit and played casino. They tried to get Charles to play as well, but he did not know how, so they issued him a hand, which he held, and Flo played that one as well as her own. Throughout the night, they kept reminding Charles of what they would do to him if he went to the police: kill him (possibly defensible under the Unwritten Law) or expose him. Eddie had his confession in his pocket, a confession he asserted would land Charles in Sing Sing Prison. Martin Held bragged about being a "famous lawyer detective" and that Charles could never successfully hide from him. He would pursue him relentlessly.

By 5:30 A.M., the gang was drunk, restless, and bored. There were still four and a half hours left before they could get their money, and they decided to spend it in saloon-hopping. Eddie ordered a taxi in the name of Wildrick, and when cabbie Paul Adamson pulled up to the house, he was astonished to see a woman come out, accompanied by three men in a football "flying wedge" formation: two men with their arms hooked through the arms of the middle man, who was being rushed into the cab.

They first directed Adamson to go uptown and stop at 59th Street and 7th Avenue, where they piled out to go to a saloon. By this time, Charles was evaluating his chances at getting free or getting help and had decided that the cabbie was in on the scheme. (He was not.) When they got to the saloon, there was nobody in it but the bartender, so Charles thought he would wait for more people to show up. However, they left after having only one drink. Next, they went to Highbridge in Yonkers to another saloon. Now it was 7:00—still three hours from the banks' opening. Once again, there was only the bartender in the Highbridge saloon.

At this point, a fight broke out between Eddie and Flo as to what to do next. Eddie thought they should go to breakfast, then get the money, while Flo adamantly insisted on getting the money first. Flo said the scheme was all her idea and that she was in charge of it, at which Eddie hit her in the mouth and stated that *he* was the boss. Flo was unfazed by this as she was used to Eddie's tantrums. Instead, she deferred to Martin Held and asked him to decide. In a surprising move, as he was Eddie's friend, he sided with Flo: money first, then breakfast.

They made one or two meandering stops after this, causing Paul Adamson to grow impatient and demand to know just where they were ultimately headed. They directed him to Hurlburt's boardinghouse at 39 Seventh Avenue, where they intended to collect anything of value from his room. But now it was 8:00 and there were people on the street. Charles did not want his captors to get into the boardinghouse, so when he exited the cab, he made a break for it and ran up the street. Brooks and Held caught up to him, knocked him down, and pummeled him. He got away again and ran into the Surprise Department Store, asking for help from the clerk, a young man named Frank Fanelli.

Brooks, Held, and Flo rushed in after him, with Brooks yelling, "What are you doing here, entertaining the party? You degenerate piece of humanity. I have the evidence right in my pocket to send you to prison, you cuntlapping son of a bitch!" Martin Held claimed to be a doctor from St. Vincent's Hospital whose mental patient (Charles) had escaped and needed to be taken back. Flo sat down and put her head in her hands, moaning, "I was never in such a predicament in my life. You will see all this on the front page of the *Journal* in the morning."

With this ruckus, the store manager came out of his office and threw them all out for foul language, then sent Fanelli to find a policeman.

Fanelli did not come back with a policeman, but he later admitted, "I did not look very hard. I wanted to see the fun. I thought there would be a little excitement." He thought the whole lot of them, except for Hurlburt, were "pretty well soused."

The manager showed Charles a side door he could exit to avoid running into the other three. Hurlburt immediately sought out the beat cop near his boardinghouse, patrolman John Hewitt, and told him what had happened to him. He was afraid they would go to his room and get his things. Hewitt told him to call the landlady and tell her not to let them into his room or give them any of his property, then go to the police station to file a complaint. Charles first went to a nearby Turkish bathhouse to clean himself up, then purchased a gun, then went to his office.

In the meantime, having lost their victim, Florence, Eddie, and Held went down to Hurlburt's office at 160 Broadway and tried to cash the signed note to Florence there. They were told that a company official would have to take care of that and nobody was due in until 10:00—an hour from then. They demanded to see Charles Hurlburt, who would confirm the validity of the promissory note, but he was not in. Flo threw a fit and accused the clerk of giving them the runaround, insisting that Hurlburt was there. She got nowhere with this because he really *was* not there. After the abortive attempt at getting the money at Hurlburt's office, Martin Held took off and was never seen or heard from again.

Flo and Eddie got back into Adamson's taxi and had him take them to the train terminal, where they went in but did not come out. After a while, the cabbie went in and looked for them, but they were nowhere to be found. They had taken a train to New Jersey for Eddie to collect a total of nine dollars from three men. Flo sat in a café there and drank for the rest of the day while Eddie attempted to collect this money.

Adamson was now fuming because he was owed fourteen dollars for chauffeuring these four people all around the city for an entire morning and had not been paid. He did not intend to let it slide. He knew where they lived.

ARREST, TRIAL, AND THE LAW OF UNINTENDED CONSEQUENCES

The next morning, Tuesday, September 20, Paul Adamson went to a police station and filed a complaint for nonpayment of services against the people who had ordered his taxi in the name of Wildrick at 224 West 25th Street. A policeman was detailed to go to that address and place the occupants under arrest. When Florence and Eddie were brought into the station house, they agreed to pay their one-third share of the cab fare, which included Charles but not the now vanished Martin Held, and were then released.[1]

At around the same time, Charles Hurlburt had gone to a police station and filed a complaint for kidnapping and extortion against Flo, Eddie, and Held. As he neared his boardinghouse, he noticed Eddie following him at a discreet distance, so he immediately approached Patrolman Hewitt, handed over the revolver he had purchased the day before for protection, and indicated Brooks—still following—as the kidnapper he had previously told him about.

Hewitt placed Eddie under arrest and searched him. In his pockets, he found the signed confession, the promissory note for $500, and the directives for acquiring Charles's keys and bank books, as well as for gaining admission to his boardinghouse room. On the way to the station house, Eddie warned Charles that he had better not pursue this matter, but Charles told him he would see it through to the end. Given the previous passivity of Charles Hurlburt, and the nature of Badger Game victims in general, this must have been the last thing that Eddie and Flo expected from him. It is another indication that the accusations of his preference for "unnatural" sex were likely fabricated, as he would be reluctant to have this come out in a public forum if it were true.

Eddie was put in the Tombs pending a grand jury hearing and, later that day, an officer was sent out to arrest Florence, who claimed to be "very much surprised" by her arrest. She wanted to do "two or three little things" before going with the policeman, such as finish drinking her gin ("I always drank when I got excited") and fix her belt, but he told her to hurry up or he would call for the wagon by putting his head out the window to tell the neighborhood that she was under arrest for blackmail and extortion. She demanded to see a warrant and was told he did not need one. "I think you do not have a warrant," she responded, then relented. "I have been up against trouble before with the police and I will go with you." Before they left, the landlady, Mrs. Grygiel, came in and took back her key to the room.

On her way to the police court, Florence tried to put a brave face on it. She had been through the "third degree" before, she told them, and nothing they did to her would "jar" her. She had no idea what Eddie Brooks had done to Charles Hurlburt, but he was probably just trying to scare him away, as Brooks was very much in love with her and jealous of any attentions that other men paid to her. He would not have gone through with any threats, she insisted. They were engaged to be married as soon as her divorce from Tad Wildrick was finalized at a hearing to be held later in the month of September.

After hearing Hurlburt's testimony at the police court, Magistrate Steinert called the saga "one of the boldest badger games ever attempted in this city." Once again, Florence found herself in the Tombs, New York City's jail. That evening, Fred Burns showed up at the police station asking to see his daughter but was told he could not. Visibly distraught and with tears in his eyes, Fred begged the lieutenant to keep the name of "Burns" off the police record and use Florence's married name of Wildrick instead. "Enough notoriety has been brought to my name," he wept, "and I should like to be spared this additional humiliation."[2]

Keeping the Burns name out of the newspapers was only a pipe dream on Fred's part, just as Florence had feared it would be as soon as the kidnapping/extortion scheme began to fall apart the moment Charles Hurlburt escaped into the Surprise Department Store. She knew that the Brooks murder case of 1902 would cause this new charge against her to be published everywhere. And so it was, the very next day: "Florence Burns in Bold 'Badger' Game"; "Florence Burns Again in Hands of Police"; "Florence Burns in 'Badger' Plot, Lawyer Charges"; "Girl Once Tried for Murder Held in Badger Case."

Almost immediately after the articles appeared, Charles Hurlburt was fired from his job at Lawyers Title Insurance & Trust Company because of the notoriety it brought to the business and to its employee.

Although they were being held in separate sections of the Tombs and had no contact, it's clear that before they were arrested, Flo and Eddie had gotten together and cobbled together something of a common story to counter the one that Charles would tell. The missing Martin Held would be tagged as the idea man behind the scheme, the one responsible for getting them involved. The police had supposedly searched for Held, but they probably did not do so very assiduously, as they had two perfectly good suspects in custody and it was likely that "Martin Held" was not the third suspect's real name anyway. As a result, the plan to blame Held was not going to work.

TRIAL

Predictably, the grand jury returned an indictment against Florence Burns Wildrick and Edward H. Brooks on September 30, 1910, but the trial would not begin for another twenty-four days while both sides prepared. Because of the potential conflict of interest, Flo and Eddie each had an attorney—not, as might be expected, public defender types, but two very experienced and esteemed practitioners. Either these lawyers—Robert H. Roy for Florence and Clark L. Jordan for Eddie—were working pro bono or the defendants' families had hired them. Charles Hurlburt would be represented by Assistant DA Charles C. Nott, prosecuting on behalf of the people, and Hon. Thomas C. Crain presided in the Court of General Sessions.

Notably absent during the proceedings, which would last five days, was any kind of report of the testimony by any newspaper. They published the arrests and they published the verdicts, but not a word in between. There is very little hint that this was anything other than a standard Badger Game, except for a few vague references to Florence and the victim's previous acquaintance. The reason, of course, is because of the salacious content of the testimony, which even by today's standards would be considered unsuitable for verbatim quoting in a newspaper. One newspaper did explain that the trial was full of "filthy" testimony that it refused to print. Even the "yellow" papers would not dare to cross that line.[3]

Assistant District Attorney Nott, in his opening statement, began by apologizing to the jury for the "rather unpleasant features" they would be subjected to. After giving a detailed summary of the facts of the case, Nott admitted that the victim, Hurlburt, had had "immoral relations" (sex outside of marriage) with Florence, but that he had been led into it and that "if every young man in this city who has improper sexual relations with a woman were to suffer for it as much as this man has suffered, there would be much greater deterrence for such things than there is now."

The elements of the crime of extortion do not take into account whether the threatened accusations against the victim are factually true. Even if they are, the accusers can still be convicted of extortion. However, it would be natural for jurors to feel that if the accusations were true, the victim more or less got what he deserved through his own immoral actions, so Nott strongly hinted that Charles Hurlburt was not guilty of acts of sodomy: "It is for you to say after hearing his testimony whether there is an atom of truth in the filthy allegations they make against him, or is it not just the weapon these people used to deter people from prosecuting them by knowing that if they are prosecuted the complainant will be subjected to this unpleasant notoriety and these sort of charges."

Jurors would also have to decide for themselves whether Charles Hurlburt signed the blank confession paper and the bank drafts voluntarily or because his life was threatened. If he did it voluntarily and under no threat at all, then the defendants were not guilty. If, however, he gave up these papers involuntarily because of the threats to his life and his reputation, then they should find the defendants guilty.

As the complainant, Charles Hurlburt was the main prosecution witness. It had taken much courage for him to proceed with prosecuting Florence and Eddie, a kind of moral courage that they did not think he would be able to muster. He gave his testimony in a straightforward way, without histrionics or outrage or indignation, and came across as extremely believable. Under cross-examination, Charles did not contradict anything he had said on direct and firmly denied ever having engaged in oral or anal sex.

THE TESTIMONY OF EDDIE BROOKS

Eddie Brooks, however, was by turns sullen, sarcastic, smarmy, and defiant on the stand. The judge had to tell him to sit up in his chair and his lawyer told him to speak up. On direct examination, he was boldly lewd in eagerly describing what he and others supposedly said, with a lurid scenario for the confrontation between Charles Hurlburt and the two intruders, Eddie and Martin Held. He estimated that it was no more than three minutes from the time Florence closed the door to the two men bursting in and, in that length of time, Charles was down on his knees with his face "in her private parts." They would have gotten right down to it as soon as that door was closed, by this account. He claimed to be so outraged that after he threw Hurlburt against the wall, he lashed out at Flo, who was trying to calm him down—"Get away, you dirty filthy trollop!"—after which he hit her and knocked her down. However, as Charles did not testify that Eddie had hit Flo except over the argument in the taxi as to who was in charge of the scheme, this probably did not happen. It was all a piece of theater for the jury.

Brooks seemed to delight in his physical abuse of Flo and also of Charles, possibly thinking that it would paint him as a legitimately incensed "fiancé" who could not restrain himself in the presence of such outrageously immoral deeds. The first time he hit Charles was when he caught him in bed with Flo on 22nd Street, he said. Charles supposedly cried and begged Eddie not to hit him. Brooks confided to the jury, man-to-man: "To be candid with you, gentlemen, I felt like a big coward for hitting him because I expected him to fight back. It was the first time I had ever struck the man and I felt a little bit cowardly for doing it, because he did not hit me back."

Eddie's entire narrative portrayed himself as the manly protector of decency and Charles as the weak, womanish hanger-on, forever following Flo around: "If I did not see that man when I was out with Mrs. Wildrick, or spot him on some corner, I thought I was with the wrong woman." As for imprisoning Charles, well, that was just nonsense. Charles was mortally embarrassed by having been caught in an act of sodomy and offered, on his own, to sign a confession to be used against him if it ever happened again. Eddie would always have leverage against him, so he would not need to tell the police about this particular instance. As Charles was too shaken to write coherently, he dictated his confession for Florence to write down. Then Florence added her own confession so that Eddie could have them both arrested if they transgressed in the future.

A few minutes after this, Eddie claimed, Charles offered to give him $1,000 for the return of the very document he had just voluntarily dictated and signed! Moreover, Charles chose to stay in the room with them all night long while they played cards and drank, when he easily could have left at any time. As for why Eddie chased him all around New York on Monday and followed him on the street on Tuesday, that was all about getting Charles's share of the cab fare, nothing more. And that was also why he, Flo, and Held went to Charles's office.

It was an unbelievable performance that soon unraveled under the withering cross-examination of Nott, whose every question demonstrated a profound contempt for and disbelief of this man and his testimony. Brooks found himself in the awkward position of having to explain his previous lies by making up other lies to account for them, which resulted in preposterous statements. For example, he had previously testified that he had once taken Flo to his mother's house to stay for a short while and had told his mother the truth about her (which he had not done): that Flo was still married, not divorced, and that Eddie was living with her as if they were married. When Nott got him to admit that he had sex with Flo on only the second time they had met, the assistant district attorney immediately went to the "I tell my mother everything" lie:

NOTT: Did you tell your mother that?

BROOKS: No, sir.

NOTT: Do you tell your mother every time you have connections with a woman?

BROOKS: Do you think I do?

NOTT: You told me you tell her everything and had no secrets from her, do you or don't you?

BROOKS: I do tell her everything of any consequence.

In reality, Flo had sex with many men, both before and while she was with Eddie, some of which he had encouraged, telling her that if their money situation did not improve, she would have to "go out on the street." So he was little better than a pimp, an image he tried to dispel by claiming, to the point of absurdity, to know nothing of her previous sexual connections with other men: "The subject is very distasteful to me. She does not dare to tell me about people she had met prior to meeting me." So how did he know there had been others? "Don't you think that any ordinary man could read between the lines of that [1902] case which she was mixed up in? . . . I judged from what I have heard. We have heard a whole lot about Florence Burns, you know."

Eddie claimed Flo had not had sex with anyone while she was with him, but then what about Charles Hurlburt? Well, she never told him she was having sex with Hurlburt. It was obvious he knew, though, and of course they had discussed it because it was the basis for setting the Badger Game trap.

There were many instances where Eddie was slippery and sly, not answering a question directly unless pinned down. Had he paid Flo's rent? First he said yes, then said he did when he could, then asked what month Nott referred to, then admitted he didn't always pay her rent but gave her money when he could.

NOTT: Did you tell her that you were not going to support her and she would have to go out on the street and do some work?
BROOKS: Do I look like that kind of a man?
NOTT: If you ask my opinion, I will give it to you. I ask you the question.
BROOKS: No, sir, I never did.

Eddie admitted he beat Flo often, mostly because she talked to men on the street, although he could have been drunk for some of these beatings. He also beat her because she drank.

NOTT: Nobody beat you when you got drunk, you only beat her when she got drunk, is that it?
BROOKS: Yes, that is it.

Eddie was cross-examined at length about his spotty employment history. He denied he had been fired from the Holmes Company for intoxication but claimed he resigned instead because the local agency had no power to fire anyone. Asked why he left the Erie Railroad, he began yet another convoluted answer:

BROOKS: I left the Erie after a bad cold—
NOTT: I don't care a rap about your cold—when did you leave the Erie?

Whenever he truly got stuck, Eddie would give his own version of "I don't recall" with "I won't confine myself to any date/amount." After Nott read Florence's addendum to Charles's "confession," Eddie claimed not to know what the word *clitoris* meant. Told it meant *vagina*, he responded that Charles, who supposedly had dictated it, was the college graduate and would know those technical words.

Nott's cross-examination of Eddie sarcastically referred to Florence as his "intended wife" or his "fiancée" to underline the contrast between how a real gentleman would behave regarding his future wife and how Eddie behaved. In this exchange, Eddie went around and around, exasperating the already-impatient prosecutor:

NOTT: Will you tell the jury why on earth you had him in your rooms all night, that was your home?
BROOKS: Why he was there?

NOTT: That was your home?

BROOKS: Yes.

NOTT: You and the woman you were going to marry?

BROOKS: Yes.

NOTT: Why did you keep him there all night?

BROOKS: We were all drinking, as the complainant says.

NOTT: You went out and got the liquor?

BROOKS: Yes.

NOTT: Were you drunk before you went out and got the liquor?

BROOKS: No.

NOTT: Why did you go out and get liquor to bring in and sit around and drink with that man in the room who had done that to your intended wife?

BROOKS: He did not have anything to drink.

NOTT: Why did you go out and get liquor to bring back to your room and sit around with a man who had done that to your intended wife?

BROOKS: I went out to get it for Held, and Mrs. Wildrick had some and I had some.

. . . .

NOTT: Why did you leave him there when you went out to get liquor, why didn't you kick him out?

BROOKS: Because he stayed there.

. . . .

NOTT: I ask you why did you let him stay there?

BROOKS: I had been drinking.

NOTT: You just said a minute ago you had not been drinking until you went out to get the liquor.

From there, Brooks equivocated about the difference between "drinking" and "being intoxicated," although he had clearly responded "no" to whether he had been "drunk" in the prosecutor's earlier question. In order to account for that discrepancy, he said he had been drinking—just one or two whiskeys—with Martin Held before they entered the room, but those two drinks caused him to be "slightly under the influence of liquor."

Eddie Brooks's testimony was a maddening, confusing jumble of denial and contradiction. Since there was no press coverage of the trial, we can't know whether his mother was there, but she probably was. It must have pained her to see her son, who once had a bright future, sink so low as to even be accused of such a sordid crime, let alone be guilty of it.

THE TESTIMONY OF FLORENCE BURNS WILDRICK

It is an axiom among defense lawyers never to put defendants on the stand unless there is a compelling reason to do so, especially if those defendants would not come off well or would be prone to falling into prosecutorial traps. Of course, if a defendant insists, it is his or her right to testify, even against a defense attorney's strong objection. In this trial, neither defendant was particularly sympathetic to a jury, but the defense really had no other choice. There was no exculpatory evidence and what testimony existed (patrolman John Hewitt, Fanelli the store clerk, Paul Adamson the taxi driver, and Mrs. Grygiel the landlady) backed up Charles Hurlburt's account. They would have to hope that they could spin the facts to at least a reasonable doubt, so that it became a matter of "he said/they said" and that maybe at least one juror might hold out for the "they" side.

If Eddie Brooks's testimony was a mass of wily attempts at dodging the truth and accounting for discrepancies, Florence's was a self-pitying mess of primarily alcohol-induced forgetfulness. Whenever she wanted to avoid answering a question, she pleaded intoxication to the point of not remembering. When it suited her purpose, she had pinpoint accuracy of past events. And, throughout it all, she blamed her current predicament, as well as her alcoholism, on her troubles since 1902. It was not a pretty performance. Her most outrageous statement was that within three minutes (between the time she shut the door to her room and the two men burst in), she was totally unconscious as to what was going on—the result of the two half-pints of gin she had drunk before meeting Hurlburt and the stultifying effects of the heat in the room. Therefore, she had no knowledge of any acts of sodomy and certainly no willing participation in them. When she woke up because of the loud arguing among the three men, she realized something was amiss, but she was at a loss to discern what it was.

Another thing that was not likely to endear her to the jury was her failure to remember the exact year when Walter Brooks had died. She said it was 1901, the same year she mistakenly thought she had married Tad Wildrick. She had no reason to lie about this, so she obviously had misremembered the year, a year that should have sealed itself into her subconscious. That she did not recall when her boyfriend, whom she had been nearly put on trial for killing, had been murdered must have sent a signal to the jury as to her cold carelessness: It was not important enough for her to remember. She had probably gotten away with what most people felt was a deliberate murder, and possibly for justifiable reasons, but then to forget the date? Inexcusable!

There were some questions she simply refused to answer based on a New York statute that allowed refusal if it would "tend to incriminate or degrade her," something of an expansion of the Fifth Amendment of the Constitution. Those answers would probably be in the affirmative, such as whether she had sex with anyone in the year and a half after she left Tad Wildrick; or whether she had sex that December or January (so after she had met Eddie) with a man named Jack Carey; or what she meant by having sex, but not intercourse, with Hurlburt. In one instance, she claimed to have done "something against nature," but then said she had been too drunk to remember. "I had been drinking considerable on account of some of the troubles since I left my husband, and I could not even swear positively at certain times what I had done."

The trial was not without unintended humor. Flo was trying to set up a pattern of "unnatural" sex acts on Hurlburt's part and recounted their walk from the meeting place to her room on September 18. She wanted to stop at a drugstore for a bottle of bichloride tablets and he had given her a quarter for this, along with a request for her to get a laxative as well. She pretended not to know what it was for, but then claimed that he told her, and it was for "a filthy reason," which obviously referred to anal sex. She was just about to give the reason (being directed by her attorney to do so) when Nott objected. Judge Crain, instead of ruling on the objection, quickly said, "Strike out the reason"—even though she had not said what the reason was! Nobody wanted that visual.

Florence admitted to having sex with Eddie the second time she met him but blamed it on Charles for buying them both so many drinks. "At this time, I was under the influence of liquor most of the time through my troubles, and I cannot really tell you exactly" was her response as to how long after meeting Charles Hurlburt she had first met Eddie Brooks. "I had been drinking a great deal in the past year," she went on. "I have had so very many troubles that I have formed the habit of it more or less."

Florence had decided that portraying herself as an alcoholic, promiscuous woman was better than the alternative of telling the truth as to what had really gone on in this very cruel, sordid tale. It did not require her to think or attempt to explain or try to outmaneuver the prosecutor. And maybe she could get at least one juror to feel sorry for her. Her testimony, especially on cross-examination, is peppered with comments like these: "I have a nervous condition." "I am getting tired and I cannot think. What did you ask me?" "This is an awful ordeal for me—I have been through thirteen hours of the third degree in my life [actually, only two hours] and my nerves are not very good." "I don't remember saying anything like that to him." "They usually put everything I do on the front page [of the *Journal*]." "Wait just a minute until I quiet down, and then I will answer you." "My liberty depends upon this—I wish you would give me a minute's rest until I think a little."

Poor Flo! She was not smart enough to think fast. The judge had to keep reminding her not to tell a story but to listen to the question that was being asked and to answer only that question. Some of the exchanges were mind-numbingly confusing, like a rendition of "Who's on First?" She bragged about all the money she had made on the stage, so much money that it left her unimpressed with and unconcerned about the $500 promissory note from Hurlburt. In fact, she averred, she had received several offers to go back on the stage just that year. But, asked to name one of these offers, she could not. And, given the sad state of her appearance at that time, it was unlikely that anyone would seek out the (no longer) "beautiful Florence Burns, the Belle of Bedford Avenue." One can only imagine the despair of her own attorney witnessing this performance.

THE VERDICT

In his summation, Assistant District Attorney Nott emphasized the absurdity of the defendants' claim that an attorney for the Lawyers Title Insurance & Trust Company had voluntarily dictated and signed a confession to the crime of sodomy, then minutes later offered to buy it back for $1,000. Added to that improbability was his voluntarily remaining with these defendants all night long while they drank and played cards, when he himself did neither. Clearly, he was held prisoner and not free to leave without threat of bodily injury, which was backed up by the statements of Paul Adamson, the cab driver, and patrolman John Hewitt, as well as Fanelli, the clerk at the Surprise Department Store.

The jurors had not been fooled at all. It took them only twenty minutes—the approximate time it took to smoke a cigar—to come back with the verdict of guilty for both Flo and Eddie. On November 1, 1910, Judge Crain sentenced Eddie to "not less than seven years and five months nor more than fourteen years and ten months" in Sing Sing Prison in Ossining, New York (the very place Eddie had threatened to send Charles to with his sodomy accusation), and Florence to the same length of time in the Auburn Prison for Women. Because it was their first felony offense, the judge could not impose the maximum of twenty-five years, but he told them he would have done that, given the cruel circumstances surrounding the crime. Newspapers reported that Florence held her head high and smiled, as if she cared not a fig for it, while Eddie turned pale and put his head down, as if in shame. Because there was no newspaper coverage of the trial, the two reactions reported here might lead to a conclusion that Flo was the brains behind this scheme and Eddie her possibly reluctant devoted follower. Nothing could have been further from the truth.

UNINTENDED CONSEQUENCES

If you were living in a boardinghouse in 1910, there was a good chance that you would not actually be getting your "board," but only a room if the owner did not care to provide meals (typically only dinner and maybe breakfast). In that case, you would contract with another nearby boardinghouse for your meals, paying weekly, as you did for your room. This is what Charles Hurlburt had done for the entire time he was in New York City, since 1904. He had a room at 39 Seventh Avenue, where he had met Florence; and he took his dinner meals at Mrs. Mary Kavanaugh's boardinghouse at 140 West Thirteenth Street, just around the corner.[4]

Having dinner nearly every night with the same people meant that they got to know each other fairly well. Mrs. Kavanaugh and her boarders could tell that Charles, who was normally a serious man anyway, had been depressed since the Badger Game incident. What an ordeal that must have been for him! First of all, the crushing betrayal by Florence, whom he had taken care of and loved and spent money on; then the shocking false accusations by her and Brooks, accompanied by physical attacks and threats; their imprisonment of him and the whole harrowing sequence of events the next day; losing his job because of this; and then the trial with its degrading testimony, which was so disgusting that no newspaper would print it. We don't know if people attended it, as they did every other sensational trial, but we must assume they did to see the fall of Florence Burns if for nothing else. On top of that, Charles might have felt some guilt at having caused Flo and Eddie to be sent to prison, even though they were the sole architects of their own fate.

Charles was not in any financial straits because of losing his job with Lawyers Title. His maternal uncle, F. Wayland Foster, said he had accounts in six or seven New York City banks and that Charles never seemed to have less than $100 in his pocket at any time. He may have been looking to start up a business on his own, possibly a law practice once more. Foster wanted them to go into business together, buying out an already-going concern in a western part of

New York State that was a combination of law and real estate sales, but Charles was not keen on this. However, Foster claimed, his nephew had recently come to realize that it would be easier than starting from scratch.[5]

In July 1911, an odd phenomenon occurred, given Charles's fastidious and very tidy habits. He began bringing a companion with him to dinner at Mrs. Kavanaugh's, a man whose appearance and clothing were more than a little off-putting to the other boarders. The norm for dining was a white shirt and an appropriate tie, but this man wore a black shirt with a red tie, as well as a handkerchief around his neck in place of a collar. Charles does not seem to have introduced him by name, instead informing the others that the man was "an old friend fallen on hard times." This mysterious stranger was described as large, heavyset, and with a dark complexion, almost foreign looking. In fact, the description fits that of the elusive Martin Held! However, it is unlikely to have been Held and hard to imagine under what circumstances he could have come back, with his cohorts in prison, himself vulnerable to arrest, and his hold over Hurlburt eradicated. This man came to dinner on July 10, 11, 15 and August 12 and 16.[6]

On August 12, the guest's appearance had improved a bit, and on the 16th, he even had worn a white shirt and a collar and looked "almost resplendent." It was one of the two instances that caused Mrs. Kavanaugh and her boarders to take note of the date. The other instance was Charles Hurlburt's almost euphoric state, the best mood they had ever seen him in. It was the last time they would see either Hurlburt or his mysterious friend, although Charles had paid for his meals up through August 20.[7]

On Saturday, August 19, the dark stranger showed up at Hurlburt's boardinghouse on Seventh Avenue. He asked the landlord, Mr. Fernandez, if he could go to Hurlburt's room. "He's not in," Fernandez told him. "I know," the stranger replied, "but I want to go there, anyway." Fernandez showed him the way, then came back a little while later to look in. He saw the man sprawled out on Charles's bed, sound asleep, and the floor littered with papers and other objects, as if the visitor had rummaged through them to find something. Fernandez declared that nothing was missing, although it's hard to know how he could have determined that.[8]

On Sunday, August 20, a body washed up on the shore at Jones Point in Rockaway County, opposite Iona Island, about fifty miles from New York City. The body was wearing trousers, but no coat, hat, or other clothing. One of the pockets contained a West Shore Railroad schedule with the name Charles W. Hurlburt on it, a couple of coins, and a gold ring engraved "Alva to Lyman." Alva was Charles's mother's nickname, short for Alvesta.[9]

Because of the name on the timetable, the coroner's office thought the body might be that of Hurlburt. Eventually, Charles's uncle Wayland Foster was contacted, and on September 1, he confirmed the identification as that of his nephew, about two weeks later than the probable date of death of August 17 or 18.

In a family of people who tended to conspiracy theories, it is not surprising that Wayland Foster's first reaction was that Charles had been murdered by friends of Florence and Eddie. But what friends? Neither had much in the way of friends other than drinking companions and occasional sexual partners. And to what end? Flo and Eddie were not going to be let out of prison early. Foster alleged that Charles had told him he had received threatening letters from both of them, vowing revenge, like a couple of Mafia capos dealing death from their cells.[10] How would they have orchestrated this from two separate prisons that were 236 miles apart?

Prior to about 1970, with the case of *Palmagiano v. Travisono* in the US District Court for the District of Rhode Island, courts did not interfere with penal institutions' censorship of inmates' incoming and outgoing mail as this was deemed to be part of the necessary maintenance of prison security. In the *Palmagiano* case, a class-action lawsuit by inmates challenging censorship of their mail as unconstitutional, the assistant director stated that he "felt he had a statutory duty to censor outgoing mail in order to 'protect the outside community from insulting, obscene, or threatening letters.'"[11] In 1911, then, it was probably standard penal practice that any mail written by inmates was read prior to being sent, and any correspondence containing threats to outsiders would not have been allowed to go through. Nobody but Wayland Foster mentioned these so-called threats, which means that he either made them up to encourage an investigation into the death of his nephew, or Charles made them up so his family would not believe he had committed suicide, or Charles was growing paranoid as a result of increasing mental illness.

In the meantime, two lawyers who were employed at the Lawyers Title Insurance & Trust Company when Charles was there filed a will for probate that had been drawn up by Charles on January 21, 1910. It left his entire estate to these men, Henry W. Aube and William Murray. Immediately, Wayland Foster telegrammed his brother-in-law's widow (Charles's stepmother) in Palmyra: "Probate Charley's will in Wayne county immediately. Two men here say they have another will making them his sole heirs. None of us ever heard of them here." Anna Hurlburt was the sole legatee of a will that Charles had drawn up in 1901. As a more recent will had already been filed in New York City, she ultimately had to file a contest of it there, which she did in November, alleging that at the time of making out the 1910 will, her stepson was "incompetent . . . and was subjected to imposition and fraud." It was estimated that Charles's estate, before the release of the "secret trust" funds, was $30,000. In an eerie coincidence, at the same time Mrs. Hurlburt filed her contest of her stepson's will in Manhattan, Fred Burns got a writ of habeas corpus in Brooklyn based on his contention that Florence's sentence should have been for a misdemeanor and not a felony. He would lose this appeal in 1912.[12]

It is interesting to note that January 21, 1910, the date on which Charles made this new will, was after he had gotten involved with Florence. Yet nothing was left to her even though he had already spent quite a bit of money on her.

On September 20, some visitors to Iona Island—now part of Bear Mountain State Park—found Charles Hurlburt's hat, coat, and vest under a plank.[13] This indicates that he placed them there, then, wearing only his trousers, entered the water and drowned. Was it a swimming accident? He would most likely have brought more appropriate swimwear if he had intended to swim. Although we know very little about this very serious young man, physical exercise does not seem to have been part of his life and, if it had been, there were many closer places around Manhattan or Brooklyn where he could have gone swimming.

The coroner, A. W. Dutcher, declared that the cause of Charles's death was drowning and that he had not been murdered.[14] There were no physical marks of violence on him, which indicated that he had committed suicide or had died by misadventure. Those who believed in the "threats from prison" rumor thought he might have killed himself through fear of reprisals.

There is another indication that Charles Hurlburt committed suicide, and that is his extremely good mood on August 16, the last time he dined at Mrs. Kavanaugh's. Today, we know that often someone who has entertained the idea of suicide and finally makes up his mind to go through with it is so incredibly relieved that he exhibits a happy sense of peace. Those around him mistake this for real happiness and an indication that their loved one has put his troubles behind him and is looking forward to moving on in life. It is then a shock to hear that he has killed himself because "he seemed so happy."[15]

Wayland Foster thought that another proof of murder was that Charles's usual $100 was not found with him, nor was the gold watch his father gave him. But these items were not found with his folded clothing on Iona Island, either, and it does not seem that anyone had discovered that clothing prior to September 20. Charles had probably given these items away, maybe even to the mysterious stranger—yet another sign of a decision to commit suicide.[16]

What of the foreign-looking stranger? Was he really a former acquaintance? This man never came forward when Charles's body was discovered, which is suspicious and leads to the conclusion that possibly he knew about the suicide. What was he looking for in Charles's room? Obviously, the stranger's newfound sartorial splendor was due to Charles, either through a purchase or a donation of clothing. Since the improvement in his dress occurred on August 12 and 16, and not before, these must have been items given to him by Charles, who would not be needing them anymore.

Why did Charles have the railroad timetable with him? Homer Gardiner, a man living near Jones Point, said that a few days before the body was found, Charles had stopped him to ask directions to the nearest railroad station. This may be how he got to Iona Island. He put his name on the timetable by way of identification. It is, all in all, a very strange story that leaves too many questions.

In December 1911, Mrs. Anna Hurlburt withdrew her contest to Charles's 1910 will and Charles's two lawyer friends—Aube and Murray—received it all.[17]

Charles Hurlburt, age thirty-two, is buried in Palmyra Cemetery with his family.[18]

15

LESSONS NOT LEARNED

With Florence in prison and, in her trial testimony, having admitted to adultery, Tad Wildrick was able to get a divorce decree in his own right and have her right to alimony revoked. In October 1912, he married Caryl Bensel, a marriage that lasted over fifty years.[1]

Despite their deep humiliation over Florence's latest run-in with the law, her parents stuck by her. In December 1915, when she had been in Auburn for five years, her mother applied to New York's Gov. Charles S. Whitman for a Christmastime pardon for Florence, but Whitman declined to act, calling the case "not worthy."[2]

In August 1918, after seven years and ten months in prison, both Florence and Eddie were paroled from their respective institutions. That same year, using the surname Wallace (her middle name), Florence was arrested for a serious but unnamed charge that was probably solicitation. In the spring of 1919, she married a man named Finlay, a man who—like Eddie Brooks—beat her.[3]

Florence continued her downward spiral with alcohol and an abusive marriage. At 2:00 A.M. on July 9, 1919, she was arrested for being drunk and disorderly with an African American musician named William Washington. Florence was extremely intoxicated at the time, and the musician was trying to drag her into a hallway. She was bleeding from a gash in her arm and had two black eyes and a cut lip. She said her husband had beaten her and she was on her way to a drugstore to get something for her wounds. Florence denied being very drunk but claimed she was weak from loss of blood.[4]

Washington said he had been on his way home from performing at a nearby music venue when the woman had approached him and asked him to take her to a drugstore, which he commenced to do. Another man came by and told him the drugstore they were headed for—on Fulton Street—was closed and directed them to a twenty-four-hour place on Atlantic Avenue. The scene sounded contrived and the magistrate did not believe it. He fined Washington ten dollars, which the musician paid. As for Florence, who admitted to having been arrested "several times," the magistrate intended to check with the probation office to see if she had been a good citizen since leaving Auburn Prison.

The fingerprint expert who was processing Florence's booking was a man named Gerard Horn, who had been in elementary school with her, but her appearance had changed so much from the "pretty rosy-cheeked girl" he had played with in the schoolyard that he did not recognize her at first. He was shocked when he saw that her fingerprints matched those of Florence Burns.[5]

This entire event is very strange indeed. Why was Florence "dressed stylishly in a modish gown of blue voile" at 2:00 A.M.? If she was headed to the drugstore on her own, why did she need to accost the musician to help her get there? If he was helping her get to a drugstore, like a Good Samaritan, why was he dragging her into a hallway? It sounds very much as if Florence was soliciting the musician for some quick money in exchange for sex, which was going to transpire in the hallway. Like Eddie Brooks, her husband might have forced her to "go out on the street" and beat her up because she objected to it. Or it could have been that the musician saw her as so intoxicated and unable to help herself that he decided to take advantage of her and beat her up in the process. But as she did not accuse him of this (and, as a white woman accusing a black man of assault, she would have been believed), that is probably not what happened.

Florence was put in a cell until her hearing on July 12. That day, she, along with her husband, her parents, and her parole officer, appeared before the magistrate, where the parole officer assured the court that Florence was "tired of the 'broad way'" and only wanted to go home—not to her husband, who said he wanted her with him, but to her parents, who declared a willingness to help her reform. The magistrate gave her a suspended sentence and put her on probation.[6]

Florence probably did not go back to Finlay ever again because later that year she married a man named Alonzo Frederick Rutledge, although it is possible that she did not officially marry either of these men. It would not have been possible for her to get a divorce quickly enough to have married Rutledge, and Rutledge took off just two years later in April 1921. There is no record of these marriages anywhere in New York State. Rutledge himself has not left a paper trail, either, so maybe that was not his real name.[7]

So far, Florence had not learned anything from her destructive lifestyle and her brushes with the law. Despite whatever help she might have received from her parents to turn her life around, by 1922, she was living in a Manhattan tenement house on East 32nd Street. In late January of that year, she was arrested yet again in a dime novel–esque scene that easily could have taken place in a vaudeville skit.

Florence was "visiting" an apartment on East 31st Street with a man and three other women, a residence the police called "a disorderly house,"[8] which meant that prostitution was taking place there. Detectives Drake and Sheridan went to the apartment to conduct a raid. Immediately, Florence drew a revolver and pointed it at the policemen, then told the three other women to get dressed and "beat it" while she covered for them. She told Drake, "One false move and there'll be one less cop," whereupon one of the other women (who identified herself as "Jane Doe") panicked: "My God! Don't kill him, he's a cop and we'll get into an awful scrape." Florence told her to keep dressing, that she had him covered. Detective Sheridan quickly left to get reinforcements.[9]

One of the women, who was quite large, went to leave the apartment, but Drake grabbed her to use as a shield, then pulled out his own gun and maneuvered the woman and himself to the middle of the room, toward Flo, who challenged him: "Come on, you coward, from behind that woman. Get her out of the way and it will be you or me." Instead, Drake pushed the fat woman against Flo, causing Flo to fall into a chair. Drake then took her gun away. By that time, the reinforcements had arrived to arrest the four women and the man.

At the station house, Flo gave her name as Florence Rutledge, age twenty-seven, but it was soon discovered that she was the thirty-nine-year-old former Florence Burns. She said she was only trying to get away because she knew her past record would work against her, then improbably claimed that she had no idea the intruders were policemen but thought they were robbers, despite her tough talk about "one less cop." She was charged with assault and a violation of the Sullivan Act (carrying a concealed weapon without a permit). The man was charged with vagrancy and given a $500 fine, and all four women were to be arraigned with "another charge," not stated, but probably prostitution.

On February 15, 1922, the twentieth anniversary of the death of Walter Brooks, Florence pleaded guilty to the Sullivan Act violation and the assault in exchange for the dropping of the other charges. This time, there would be no trial. At her sentencing the following week, once again she invoked the theme of "poor me, I'm being persecuted" by claiming that she had found several good jobs, but the police "hounded her" so much that she lost them. This is why she had to resort to illegal means to support herself.[10]

After only four years since her release from the Auburn Women's Prison, Florence would be going back under a sentence of three years. Early in her second tenure there, she tried to pull a scam on the warden, fifty-one-year-old Col. Edgar S. Jennings, a veteran of the Spanish-American War and World War I. When she heard his voice in the hall, she called to him to come and see her. She then walked to the opposite end of her cell and looked out through the bars, her back to the doorway. As soon as she could hear his steps approaching, she began to scream, but, as she turned around, she was dismayed to see that the warden, who had not been born the day before, had prudently brought the matron to accompany him.[11]

Flo took the failure philosophically: "You mustn't think, warden, that I've anything against you personally. That's my game, you know." Jennings responded that he would not hold it against her, that being a warden was *his* game, and that he hoped she would not hold it against him either.

What was Flo's endgame with this attempted frame of Colonel Jennings, by all reports a well-liked warden? She was obviously intending to set up an accusation of attempted rape, maybe to use it as blackmail against him for prison favors or even to threaten him with removal from office. Or, as the article reporting this cynically suggested, she was merely trying to make sure she didn't lose her skill set while in prison.

By this time, the Burns family had moved to a multiunit building at 642 St. Mark's Avenue in Brooklyn. On June 20, 1923, Fred, who was still working at his job as a broker at the Custom House in Manhattan, was rushed to Sea View Hospital in Richmond. He had a chronic valve disease and chronic nephritis, now complicated by pulmonary edema, all of which combined to cause his death the following day, just shy of his sixty-third birthday.[12] It is not difficult to imagine that Fred's health problems were exacerbated by the very real distress he felt at the disgrace his family's name had suffered as a result of Florence's many high-profile criminal arrests. And, of course, because of her incarceration, Florence was not allowed to attend her father's funeral.

Gladys Burns had eloped to New Jersey with Harry Mettais in 1909, another event—because of the Brooks-Burns case—that was reported in the newspapers, embarrassing the Burnses and also Harry's mother, none of whom had any idea of the marriage until contacted by reporters. The young couple claimed they were waiting for Harry to be able to afford a place for them to live, but in 1910, they were living with the Burnses, so that was obviously something made up for publication.[13]

The marriage did not go well. By 1915, Harry was back living with his mother, and in 1920 he reported himself as single instead of divorced or widowed. It is Fred Burns's probate papers that reveal that Gladys (who spelled her name as Gladyss) had remarried somewhere along the way, now with the surname of Coultas. Both daughters had to sign off as potential legatees in the line of succession, but they would not be getting anything: Fred left it all to his wife.[14]

It's obvious from what Florence revealed in the 1910 trial that there was friction between her and Gladys, but there also seems to have been some between Gladys and her parents. It sometimes happens that when parents focus much of their time, energy, and money on one child because of that child's illness, disability, or bad behavior, the other children feel neglected and undervalued. Gladys might have resented her parents for all they did and tried to do for Florence, especially when it got them nothing but heartache, and that she herself received short shrift from them.

Fred Burns is buried in Brooklyn's Evergreens Cemetery's Tulip Grove Section, the first in what would be the Burns family plot.[15]

Florence was paroled from Auburn Women's Prison in August 1924, having served two and a half years of her three-year sentence.[16] She was forty-two years old and had spent approximately ten and a half of the span of years from 1902 to 1924 in a jail or prison cell.

EPILOGUE

When Florence Burns Wildrick Finlay Rutledge left Auburn Women's Prison in August 1924, she had obviously determined never to return, making a complete break with her past lifestyle. She had had enough of it and, with middle age and then old age facing her, she was forced to confront reality.

In 1924 or 1925, Florence got married for the fourth and last time to a man nine years younger. He was a high school shop teacher named John Vincent Stankevich, completely different from her previous husbands: Stankevich was steady and solidly middle class, with a respectable job.[1]

It was clear, though, that people had still not forgotten the Brooks case and the fact that Florence had probably gotten away with murder. In 1929, Florence was subjected to the angry rants of a woman on the street, who yelled "damned murderess" at her. Soon a crowd gathered to watch as the woman, Mary Mueller, shouted, "How did you feel when you murdered Walter Brooks?" Because of this scene, John Stankevich lost his teaching position at Brooklyn's P.S. 45 and had to find a job with a machine shop.[2] As a result, Flo went to court to swear out a summons against Mueller for "disorderly conduct," but there was no follow-up report on the outcome.

In July 1937, Mrs. Burns died of cardiac renal disease at the age of seventy-five. What is astonishing is that she left everything to Florence Stankevich, who was also her executrix, with "confidence that [she] will look after her sister Gladys Caltoris [sic; probably Coultas]."[3] This indicates two things: first, that Florence had fully reconciled with her mother and, second, that Gladys had some kind of problem (alcoholism?) that made it unwise to leave her any money of her own. It is not known whether Gladys was still married, or divorced, or widowed at this point, but she was in a position of vulnerability and in need of care at the age of fifty-three, an age when she should normally be able to look after herself.

Mrs. Burns's estate was not large—about $5,000 in real property (possibly the building at 642 St. Mark's Avenue) and $1,000 in personal property. Flo and John moved into the apartment on St. Mark's Avenue after that.[4]

In March 1944, a near tragedy occurred in the Stankevich kitchen at 642 St. Mark's Avenue. Two police officers noticed smoke coming from the window and forced their way into the second-story apartment, where they found the kitchen on fire and Florence unconscious on the floor. She was taken to a nearby hospital, where it was undoubtedly determined that she was all right, as there was no follow-up in the newspaper.[5] Was it the result of an illness that caused Florence to faint? Had she slipped back into her habit of swigging gin throughout the day? Or was she merely overcome by the smoke? Although there was quite a bit of damage done to the apartment, Florence and John continued to live there.

What is notable about this article is that by 1944, apparently nobody was making the connection between Florence Stankevich and Florence Burns, as had been done in 1929. Nor was there a connection in August 1949, when a notice of her death described her only as the "loving wife of John."[6]

Florence's cremated remains were buried in the plot with her parents. She was sixty-seven. There are no markers for any of them in the Evergreens Cemetery, just a short walk away from the section where Walter Brooks is buried. Florence's husband John died in 1971, but he is not buried in Evergreens. Nor is Gladys.[7]

So, after all the rebellion and all the self-indulgence and all the self-destruction for most of her life, Florence got it right in the end. After three short, disastrous marriages, her fourth lasted the rest of her life—about twenty-five years. After causing so much distress and humiliation to her family, she finally reconciled with her mother and maybe also her sister. It is not an ending that most people following her post-1902 "career" would have predicted for her, given the increasingly downward trend her life took, culminating in her second prison sentence in 1922—a pleasant surprise, indeed!

What about the other people in Flo's story? On the whole, a disturbing number of people who touched her life in some way did not fare well, dying young or dying within a few years after or otherwise having their lives take disappointing turns.

THE 1902 BROOKS CASE

The Von derBosches

Florence's Uncle Oscar, who had footed the bill for her defense and provided her with a "hideout" during the inquest, remarried at the age of sixty-five, exactly a year and a day after his first wife died in 1922. In 1929, he had a fatal stroke while visiting Florida and is buried in Cortlandt, New York.

Oscar's son, William Oscar "Willie" Von derBosch,[8] who could have answered the question as to when Florence got home on February 14, 1902—if asked—lived with Mrs. Burns, his aunt, until at least 1930 and possibly longer. A year after she died in 1937, he shot himself with a .32-caliber pistol (the same caliber used in the shooting of Walter Brooks) in Westfield, Massachusetts, where he had moved six months earlier. Willie was deemed to be depressed at being alone as he had never married, and at having no money (several pawn tickets were found in his pocket). He was sixty years old.

Mr. and Mrs. Brooks

Mary Brooks lived only five years after the death of her son Walter. On January 12, 1907, she was taken to Cumberland Street Hospital in Brooklyn with a serious heart valve problem, where she died on February 22. She was only fifty years old. Mrs. Brooks is buried in the Evergreens Cemetery with her son Walter, her daughter Gertrude, her mother Hainza Williams, and her brother John Williams. As with the Burns family plot, there are no headstones marking that of the Brooks family.[9]

After his wife's death, Thomas Brooks moved back to their native Petersburgh, Virginia. In 1923, he was involved in an automobile accident and was killed by a piece of glass from the windshield that severed an artery. An early version of safety glass for windshields was available in 1923 but not widely used at that time. Mr. Brooks was seventy years old. He is buried in Petersburgh's Blandford Cemetery.[10]

Foster L. Backus

Florence's attorney in the Brooks case was another person who did not live long afterward. Less than a month after the death of Mary Brooks, Backus died on March 10, 1907, at the age of fifty-eight. There is no mention in the *New York Times* obituary, but the one in the *Tribune* reported that Backus had "suffered a nervous breakdown" while he was representing Florence. It must have been an unbearable burden if he knew the truth as to whether she had shot Walter Brooks, which was another reason he could not put her on the stand to defend herself as he would be guilty of suborning perjury.[11]

Justice Julius M. Mayer

The justice who presided over Florence Burns's hearing and dismissed the case against her became the state attorney general the following year. In 1912, President Taft appointed him to the Federal District Court, and from there he was appointed to the Circuit Court of Appeals by President Harding in 1921. One of Judge Mayer's most famous cases was that of the sinking of the *Lusitania,* which he held to be an act of piracy.

Judge Mayer died suddenly of a heart attack on November 30, 1925, at the age of sixty.[12]

William Travers Jerome

Florence's prosecutor went on to have a stellar career as district attorney, fighting both crime and political corruption until 1909, when he left for private practice. His most well-known case is one that raised the Unwritten Law: the trial of Harry Kendall Thaw for the 1906 murder of the architect Stanford White. Thaw's wife, the famous "Gibson Girl," Evelyn Nesbit, had related to her husband the sordid details of White's alleged rape of her after he had drugged her in his home some years before she and Thaw were married. Thaw, who had been mentally unstable his entire life, was acquitted of the murder, which was committed in front of a roomful of diners, on the grounds of "temporary insanity." His defense attorney, Delphin Delmas, had argued that it was a case of "Dementia Americana":

> And if Thaw is insane, it is with a species of insanity known from the Canadian border to the Gulf. If you expert gentlemen ask me to give it a name, I suggest that you label it Dementia Americana. It is that species of insanity that inspires of every American to believe his home is sacred. It is that species of insanity that persuades an American that whoever violates the sanctity of his home or the purity of his wife or daughter has forfeited the protection of the laws of this state or any other state.[13]

William Travers Jerome died of pneumonia on February 13, 1934, one day before the thirty-second anniversary of the shooting of another Unwritten Law victim, Walter Brooks.[14]

The Bedford Avenue Gang

Life for the members of the Bedford Gang and their followers, as a whole, did not turn out well. Many of them died in their thirties and forties, much earlier than would have been normal for that era.

"Handsome Harry" Casey, the erstwhile leader of the gang and the one who introduced Walter to Florence, got married in 1907 at the age of twenty-five. In October 1922, his wife Margaret died, and Harry remarried eight months later, in June 1923, to Gertrude Harrison, fifteen years younger. They had been married only about two years when, one night in September 1925, Harry came home at dinnertime from his job as an insurance salesman and was so drunk he could barely stand up. His wife helped him up the stairs to his bedroom, which she obviously did not share with him as she did not check on him again until 6:45 the next morning. He was sprawled across the bed, partially dressed but deceased, and in full rigor mortis.

Because Harry had been healthy and not under a physician's care, the medical examiner took charge of the body to conduct an autopsy and to have a toxicology report done for the presence of alcohol. There were no signs of violence. The cause of death was initially listed as "congestion of viscera," which was a code phrase for "we have no idea what happened here." The autopsy, conducted by Dr. Thomas Gonzalez, assistant medical examiner, found nothing unusual except for congestion in the lungs, kidney, liver, stomach, and brain—so the "congestion of viscera" conclusion turned out to be correct! But what really killed Harry Casey was chronic alcoholism. He was forty-three. He had no children with either wife.[15]

The other self-designated "handsome" member of the gang, Edward Cole "Handsome Ed" Watson, Florence's former boyfriend, who had been divorced in 1899, married again in 1903. His new wife's maiden name was Brooks (no relation to either of the Brooks families in this narrative). They had a daughter, Ruth Emily, the following year, who died in 1907. In 1913, Ed's wife served him with divorce papers, alleging that he had been drinking heavily and was also living with a stenographer. He wasted no time in acquiring Wife Number 3, which he did in 1915, a woman whose middle name was Florence.

"Handsome Ed" Watson died in the 1950s. His lifelong career was in advertising, the career of choice, along with insurance or stocks, of so many of the Bedford Avenue Gang.[16]

Theodore Burris, who, along with Harry Casey, was one of Walter Brooks's best friends, made his way to Colorado Springs, Colorado, in May 1911. Given his previous activities, he possibly had some get-rich-quick scheme in mind, maybe concerning mining. But Burris's life of decadence had caught up with him: he was suffering from syphilis, which he had contracted at the approximate age of eighteen to twenty. It was obviously causing him some distress as he had consulted a Colorado Springs doctor in May, but by September, his brain was infected. He was admitted to the hospital on September 13 and died the following day.

Theodore Burris's family had evidently had enough of him. Although they told authorities in Colorado that a family member would be arriving to bring back the body, they sent his brother-in-law's younger brother to arrange for burial in Colorado Springs. He is buried in the Evergreen Cemetery there, almost the same name as that of the Brooklyn burial ground where his friend Walter Brooks is interred, and where he might have been buried himself had his life turned out differently. Burris was thirty-one years old.[17]

William Maxwell "Max" Finck continued plying his confidence games. In 1905, he was arrested on a charge of petit larceny when he was caught selling letters for job recommendations for $15 each to men who were looking for employment with the Union Railway. Finck was passing himself off as a Tammany captain who could arrange to use his influence for the purchaser to get consideration for a job. When the real captain discovered that money was being collected in his name, he pressed charges.[18]

In 1910, Max was in Dannemora State Prison in upstate New York for unknown crimes.[19]

In November 1912, there was a report of a William M. Fink [sic], the superintendent of a mine in Mexico, being held for a $5,000 ransom by rebels in Santa Eulalia. Was this "our" Max? Probably not, but, if so, was it a real kidnapping or a hoax? There was no follow-up as to whether the ransom was paid.[20]

In 1915, Max filed for bankruptcy, so his financial life was not going well—no surprise there.[21] And after this, he drops from the available records. Significantly, he did not fill out the required draft registration card for either World War I or World War II. Of course, with a wooden leg, he would have been exempt from the draft but probably not from registration. The "Old Man's Draft" in 1942 for World War II, for example, required everyone up to age sixty-four to register, even if they would have been too old, so Max—while he might have been safe from the draft—would still have been required to fill out the forms for both wars. His previous felony conviction would not have made him exempt from registering, as Eddie Brooks also registered in 1918 after his release from Sing Sing Prison.

Max Finck's mother, brother, sister, brother-in-law, and brother-in-law's parents all relocated to the West, but Max did not show up there. Based on his life's pattern to 1915, with no signs of turning it around, it's a safe bet that he was in prison during some of this time. It is entirely likely that he was dead by 1918 when he would have been required to fill out the draft card.

Although Samuel Thomas Maddox Jr., did not figure in any specifically named activities of the Bedford Avenue Gang, some of the members claimed that he was one of them. Moreover, he was a close friend of Harry Casey's and a frequent guest at the Caseys' summer estate in the Catskills. The son of a judge whose father had presided over Martin Thorn's trial for the murder of Willie Guldensuppe (see p. 112), Sam Maddox became a lawyer as well, was married by 1902, and had two daughters. In 1911, he had to be forcibly removed from his home and placed in a hospital ward for alcoholics and the mentally ill. A doctor declared that Sam was not alcoholic but had had a "nervous breakdown" from working too hard. When he got out of the hospital, he went to live with his parents and not with his wife and daughters. Although he and his wife did not formally divorce, he never lived with her again. In 1916, Sam died at his parents' home, reportedly of pneumonia, just before his thirty-eighth birthday, and exactly one month before the death of his father, Samuel T. Maddox Sr.[22]

Ruth Dunne was one of the many female followers of the Bedford Avenue Gang and also Walter Brooks's last girlfriend. During and after the hearing, she was tagged as "of Florence Burns case fame" and thoroughly enjoyed her time in the spotlight—when it was positive. Between the two hearings, she visited a young woman whose family lived in New Haven, Connecticut, and the two were—to hear them talk about it—wined and dined and "rushed" by several Yale undergraduates, who escorted them to dances, dinners, and the theater. Ruth bragged about maybe going on the stage or taking a trip to Canada, but "I don't know if we shall go while Yale is in session. We are just enjoying ourselves here." She asserted that she did not know where Florence Burns was, but she sure wasn't in New Haven. "No one city would be big enough to hold us both," she boasted.[23]

However, the day before Ruth was interviewed in New Haven, her parents were frantic with worry because she had been missing from home for two weeks and had not contacted her family. Her mother was afraid she might have committed suicide over the death of Walter Brooks. Finally, Ruth telephoned her uncle (but not her parents), ostensibly from Manhattan, to say that she was staying with a girlfriend who had gotten her a job as a stenographer, where she had been working for the past two weeks.[24] An odd story, surely, especially given the fact that she was most likely in New Haven sporting with the Yalies and not working in Manhattan. If the reason for her absence from home was so benign, why not let her parents know instead of making them worry for two weeks?

Equally odd was that the parents waited for two weeks before informing the police of their daughter's disappearance, especially when suicide was suspected. But, as pointed out tongue in cheek by the *Eagle*, there was no need to fear suicide as Ruth was "of a light hearted disposition and the death of Brooks apparently had no serious effect upon her, despite the stories that it undermined her health."[25]

Ruth was not enjoying publicity so much in September 1902, when a friend of hers, sixteen-year-old Ethel Kahl, was arrested at the request of her widowed mother for being "disobedient and wayward," then placed in a home for "wayward girls" for a month. Ethel had left her home for about a week, reportedly at Ruth Dunne's urging, and was seen in theaters and at Coney Island in the presence of "gilded youths" with money to spend. Asked to reveal the names of the young men and women she had been spending time with, Ethel refused to "peach" on her friends.[26]

The day after Christmas that same year, Ethel Kahl attempted suicide by taking oxalic acid, albeit a very weakened dose, because she had stayed out all night with a friend on Christmas and was afraid to go home and face her mother. Once again, Ruth Dunne was tagged in the article as a friend of Ethel's.[27]

A more serious event occurred for Ruth in October 1902, when she, along with four other women and three men, were arrested for being "disorderly persons" in a "disorderly house." A man who lived in the apartment building had gone to the police to complain that when he greeted his young daughter in the hallway on her return home from a convent school, two of the arrested women made "annoying" and "insulting" (in other words, lewd) remarks when he kissed her. The five women had moved into the apartment about ten days previously and the leaseholders were two sisters, ages nineteen and twenty-one. The other women were seventeen (Ruth and one other) and eighteen. The three men, who did *not* live in the apartment building, were twenty-eight and thirty-one. Although everyone arrested was discharged because the complainant did not appear for the hearing, the mother of the other seventeen-year-old girl insisted that she be arrested for "waywardness" and sent to the House of the Good Shepherd. The mother later relented and decided to give her daughter another chance.[28]

Ruth Dunne eventually outgrew her rebellion and, in 1915, at the age of thirty, she married a twenty-three-year-old machinist named John William Murphy. They followed her sisters, their families, and her mother to California, where Ruth died in 1961 at the age of seventy-seven.[29]

Harry Cohen
Harry Cohen, Walter Brooks's silent partner in the grocery commission company, never married. He died in April 1908 of pulmonary thrombosis at the age of thirty-three. He was single and not working at the time, having been under a doctor's care since October 1907.[30]

William Armit "Fatty" Eyre
William Eyre moved into the St. Mark's Avenue Hotel in Brooklyn, which was across the street from where Florence's family—and, later, Florence and her husband—lived for many years. Along with his bar-glass-eating trick, Eyre may have had a problem with alcohol: in 1905, when he was twenty-two, he was charged with disorderly conduct by the manager of the Consumers Park Brewery in Flatbush for causing a disturbance in the dining room of the establishment. He had to sign a $100 bond to keep the peace for six months.

Eyre got married and worked as a clerk in an office building at the Old Ship pier area in Manhattan. There, on September 16, 1909, at the age of twenty-six, he collapsed and died of what was determined to be chronic endocarditis. Could this have resulted from his old bar habit of eating glass?[31]

Joseph Cribbins
Joe Cribbins, the sixteen-year-old office clerk at Brooks and Wells, who delivered messages from Florence to Walter Brooks, was inducted into the US Army in September 1918, just before turning thirty-two, but he was not sent "over there." Instead, his clerking skills were put to use at Camp Greenleaf, Georgia, where he served until his honorable discharge in December 1918, with the rank of private. Joe never married. He died in 1951 at the age of sixty-five in a facility for terminal cancer patients.[32]

Arthur Cleveland Wible
Arthur Wible, the nineteen-year-old who lied about his age so he could get a conductor's job with the Brooklyn Elevated Railway, turned out to be the source of the most solidly reliable evidence against Florence Burns, placing her near the scene of the crime at a critical time and showing that her own

statement of when she arrived home had been a lie. After his job with the railroad, Wible managed a dairy and then, for most of his life, was a furniture dealer. He married and had three children, the first two of whom died in their first year of life. Arthur himself died in 1950 at age sixty-seven.[33]

Harold Leon Theall

Florence Burns's first "beau," Harry Theall, had been sent to a prep school in Wisconsin to escape her clutches and her stalking. When he finished there, he was admitted to Yale Law School as a special student, but he did not graduate. Like so many young men of his circle, he worked in advertising. He and his first wife, Canadian-born Lillian Langdon, moved to Canada around 1911 with her parents, but Lillian either died there or she and Harry divorced. He returned to New York and married Edith Maude Hancock. On February 9, 1918, he died of pneumonia at age thirty-seven.[34]

Thomas C. Wells

T. C. Wells, Walter Brooks's partner in the Brooks and Wells grocery commission brokerage, became a traveling salesman after Brooks's death and eventually moved to Baltimore. In June 1903, a year after his former partner's death, Wells drowned in a flood in Galveston, Texas (not the famous flood, which was in 1900, but also the result of a hurricane). He was twenty-three and engaged to be married soon.[35]

Dr. John Vincent Sweeney

Dr. Sweeney, who had attended the dying Walter Brooks in the Glen Island Hotel, never married. He died in 1924 at the age of sixty-six, still working as a physician.[36]

George Bader

The genial proprietor of the Bader's Road House at Coney Island had a bad fall from a porch rocker at his hotel in August 1905, incurring a compound fracture of his arm. It was not healing well and gave him a great deal of pain so that it had to be reset in September. But just a few days after that, on September 19, 1905, while his wife was out shopping, Bader committed suicide in his bathroom by sticking a rubber tube onto a gas jet and putting the other end in his mouth. He was fifty years old.[37]

Charles White Wildrick

Florence's first husband, Tad Wildrick, married Caryl Bensel in 1912 and stayed married to her until his death in 1964. They had no children but gladly spoiled their nephews and grandnephews. Often, they would show up at the prep boarding school the boys all attended, which was in the area where Tad and Caryl lived, to take them out to dinner—a special treat. Caryl usually drove and, even when she was in her eighties, did so "like a bat out of hell" on winding back roads! One particular memory stands out for a grandnephew who, with his cousin, had occasion to ride with Tad and Caryl down that "narrow hilly twisting road." His cousin literally had his fingers crossed, and after an especially hairy moment going around a dangerous curve, "Uncle Tad turned around and said jauntily, 'She usually takes that one on two wheels!'"

Tad's remaining family remembers him fondly as a gregarious man ("a very warm pleasant man, obviously easy to like and trust") who loved to have a good time. At a grandnephew's wedding in 1964, not long before his death at the age of ninety-two, Tad danced with the bride and enjoyed himself immensely. Despite his early brushes with the law and his less-than-honorable dealings with friends and family, it is clear that Tad—possibly "scared straight" by his disastrous marriage to Florence Burns—managed to reset his life's course to become a faithful husband and a beloved family member. (One of the grandnephews named his own son after him, even down to the nickname "Tad.") Although he had no official military career of his own, he honored his family's significant involvement in the armed forces by taking leadership roles with the Army-Navy Club and similar organizations. The fast-driving Caryl died five years after her husband, at age ninety-three.[38]

Eldridge Hildreth Brooks III

Eddie Brooks got out of Sing Sing in August 1918 and relocated to New Jersey to live with his mother. In September of that year, he registered for the draft and listed his occupation as employment manager with the Duesenberg Motor Corporation in Elizabeth, New Jersey. Although Duesenberg was primarily a manufacturer of luxury and racing cars, in 1916, the company moved its operations from Minnesota to Elizabeth under a government contract to build airplane engines for the military, which was soon to be involved in World War I—and just in time for Eddie upon his release from Sing Sing.

One year after leaving prison, he married twenty-nine-year-old Edna Mabel (known as Mabel) Atwater, seven years his junior.[39]

In 1920, Eddie applied for his first passport and traveled to Cuba on behalf of his employer, the Sugar Factories Construction Company, where he worked as a manager. Sugar Factories was a Cuban company with its main office in Havana and a branch office on Broadway in New York City. He made another trip to Cuba in 1922, probably to oversee his company's contract for a new factory in San Cristobal.[40]

In 1926, Eddie was one of several investors in a new corporation for the teaching of "beauty culture" in Newark, and for the 1930 census, he listed himself as an advertising executive. By 1942, he and his wife were living in the Hotel Breslin in New York City. He was fifty-eight years old, had no occupation, and, along the way, had acquired a scar behind his right ear.

Eddie and Mabel most likely died in the 1950s. They had no children.[41]

Eddie's sister Miriam had married in 1908, but at some point in the 1920s, she was committed to an institution for the mentally ill, where she remained for the rest of her life.[42]

CODA

The houses where the Brooks and Burns families lived at the time of the murder in 1902 are still standing in Brooklyn. (The Brooks house is at 258 Decatur Street; the Burns house is at 249 Marlborough Road.) Today's subway from Manhattan to Flatbush stops at the same place as the elevated railroad when Arthur Wible dropped off his passenger that February night and nodded to her. From there, it is just a short walk to the quiet, attractive, tree-lined street she hurried to back then, probably hoping that her parents were not yet home from the theater. The little house on Decatur Street, where the Brookses lived and where Walter's funeral was held, is set back from its neighbors, a distinction those long-ago neighbors thought was an apt metaphor for the aloofness of Mr. and Mrs. Brooks.[43]

The lack of headstones or any markers for the two principal families in the Evergreens Cemetery is puzzling, especially for the Brookses, who had previously buried a little daughter long before the tragedy and shame of their son's murder. For the Burnses, it is perhaps understandable as the ignominy Florence brought to their name lasted at least until 1930 before it faded from memory.

The site of the Glen Island Hotel today marks the inspirational, tasteful, and sobering tribute to those who died on September 11, 2001. The names of the fallen are etched on panels surrounding a waterfall, etchings so deep that visitors stick flowers in them. Busloads of tourists arrive all day, every day to take pictures and say prayers.

It is but a short walk from there, as it was in 1902, to the Brooklyn Bridge with its walkway to the other side and its magnificent views of the New York skyline. New today are the many vendors hawking bottled water, soft drinks, and paintings, as well as the presence of far more pedestrians than at the turn of the century—all of them tourists looking for an experience, rather than city dwellers who need to get back to Brooklyn after a day's work or a night out on the town in Manhattan.

In the years after the Brooks-Burns case and the subsequent citywide spotlight on the activities of the Bedford Avenue Gang (or the Hounds), any suspicious crime, even one with no obvious perpetrator, was attributed to it. A Brooklyn father struck his fifteen-year-old daughter and knocked her down to "chastise her" for being out of control and for going around with members of the Bedford Gang. "I don't want another Florence Burns in my family," he told the police court. She had accused him of assault, then withdrew the charge and was sent to the Convent of Mercy until she turned sixteen.[44]

The suspicious and decidedly odd July 1902 murder of the forty-six-year-old wealthy merchant Albert C. Latimer—unsolved to this day but most likely committed by his young wife's lover or admirer—was thought to be the work of "the son of well-to-do Brooklyn parents . . . a member of an organization known as the 'Bedford Avenue Hounds.'" Likewise, when a young man, son of a prominent Brooklyn resident, was found bleeding and unconscious on the street from stab wounds, it was quickly pointed out that the victim had friends in the Bedford Gang and also knew both Walter Brooks and Florence Burns. The "stabbing" turned out to be punctures caused by his falling on an ink eraser in his vest pocket (a small instrument, similar to an Exacto knife, for scraping off ink from paper).[45]

Or was it? Two years later, this same young man, Joseph Cabble, now twenty-four, claimed to have been knocked down and robbed of a gold watch and a stick pin at 1:00 A.M., supposedly by members of the Bedford Gang. The 1902 ink eraser incident was never discussed among his family, and the police always suspected it as false. However, as nothing had been taken from him in 1902, the matter was dropped. A detective reported that in 1903, he came across Cabble staggering about and complaining that his watch had been stolen from him. It was later found to be in his coat pocket.[46] So, Joseph Cabble's problems most likely came from an overindulgence in alcohol and needing an excuse for his family.

Two years after the Brooks murder, many of the old Bedford Gang began frequenting the places they used to visit, after having kept a low profile since 1902. Approximately eleven members, some old and some new, were "resorting to all sort of tricks to get money without working." Now, however, there was a new wrinkle as most of them were carrying revolvers and brandishing them in stickups and extortion threats. Robbery and blackmail were the new crimes, whereas the "b'hoys" had previously relied primarily on elaborate confidence games. Their victims were primarily those men and young girls, like Joseph Cabble, who had drunk too much alcohol and were easily stripped of any money they were carrying. There was even a rumor that murder would not be beyond this new iteration of the Bedford Avenue Gang.[47]

The gang developed a plan to finance a trip to the St. Louis World's Fair in 1904. They would steal a new automobile from a Brooklyn resident, then sell it to a dealer in Manhattan. However, the plot was discovered before they could act on it—most likely through indiscriminate bragging to the wrong people.[48]

Another gang member informed a wealthy man that he wished to marry the man's daughter, knowing full well that the father would object. "If you want to prevent this and also save your daughter's reputation," the youth told him, "you will have to pay me $5,000." The father kicked him out of the house, whereupon the young man was back the next day with a reduced offer of $3,000 to prevent the smearing of the daughter's—and the family's—good name. The father called the gang member's bluff and kicked him out again. The threat was not carried out.[49]

There was also a rumor that former Bedford Gang members were behind a sophisticated mining company swindle in 1904 that suckered in over one hundred Wall Street stock promoters. They would get themselves hired by mining companies by claiming to have access to investors in other large cities, which they would then pretend to contact. Then they wrote to their employer, exulting in a great success and asking for reimbursement of costs. One swindler got hundreds of dollars by falsely providing the name of the former New York State lieutenant governor as a reference.[50]

More distant from the 1902 murder was the suit brought in 1913 against William Sulzer, the governor of New York, by a shopgirl named Mignon Hopkins, who worked at Wannamaker's in Philadelphia. She claimed that she and the governor had been lovers back in 1903, that he had asked her to marry him, and that he had presented her to others as his wife. According to Hopkins, Sulzer told her they had to keep their engagement quiet as he sought to establish his political career. Instead, in 1908, he married another woman, a nurse who had tended him while he was ill. When Hopkins sued him for $30,000 for breach of promise to marry, Sulzer was already embroiled in combat with Tammany Hall, and he—probably rightly—concluded that this was a put-up job by them, given the length of time between his marriage and her complaint. They succeeded in impeaching him later that year, and the breach of promise lawsuit does not seem to have gone anywhere or even been filed. The governor accused Mignon Hopkins of having been a member of the Bedford Avenue Gang, which she vehemently denied, but clearly it was seen as a nefarious connection.[51]

Today, there are hardly any references to the Brooks-Burns case or to Florence's post-1902 career. You will not find any mention of them in a biography of William Travers Jerome or in any compilation of Gilded Age New York events. There are no plaques to the Bedford Avenue Gang at the sites of their usual haunts. By the 1930s, the murder case and those who played a part in it had faded from memory, with the occasional exception of an old-timer's nostalgic musings in a distant era's newspaper.

But, in its time, it served as a cautionary tale of the perils of the young in the New Century. And, for future centuries, it gives a perspective on the effects of rapidly changing technology on manners and mores as experienced by a group of people uniquely unprepared to deal with these changes maturely.

NOTES

The names of these newspapers have been abbreviated:
Brooklyn Daily Eagle = BDE
Daily People = DP
New York Evening World = NYEW
New York Sun = NYS
New York Times = NYT
New York World = NYW

The *Sun* and the *Evening World* can be accessed for free through the Library of Congress at www.chroniclingamerica.loc.gov, and the *Brooklyn Daily Eagle* is free at www.newspapers.com. Others are available on microfilm (through Interlibrary Loan) or through subscription databases.

1. MURDER AT GROUND ZERO

1. "Burns Girl Shaken by the Day's Events," *BDE*, Feb. 23, 1902.
2. Edwin G. Burrows and Mike Wallace, *Gotham: A History of New York City to 1898* (New York: Oxford Univ. Press, 1999), 343; "Schulte Buys Robert Fulton Corner," *NYT*, July 13, 1923 (Fulton land). The 1896 Raines Law was designed to cut down on the rampant Sunday consumption of alcohol (often the only day off that laborers had) in stipulating that the only establishments that could legally sell it that day were hotels with a minimum of ten rooms, as long as food was served with the alcohol. Richard Zacks, *Island of Vice: Theodore Roosevelt's Doomed Quest to Clean Up Sin-Loving New York* (New York: Doubleday, 2010), 245. The mystery here is that the Glen Island had been an established hotel since the 1880s, so it should not have been considered a Raines Law hotel, which usually meant a saloon that had slapped

together some small upstairs cubicles that could serve as "rooms." Possibly the Glen Island did not have the requisite number of rooms in 1896. When Walter and his "wife" were assigned Room 12, it was stated to be in "the old section." "Girl Accused of Killing Her Sweetheart," *NYW*, Feb. 16, 1902 ("no questions asked").

3. "Florence Burns Identified by 'L' Conductor," *NYW*, Feb. 23, 1902 ($2 room); "Murder of Brooks Charged to a Girl," *BDE*, Feb. 16, 1902 ($60 in safe); "Brooks and Woman Alone at Hotel," *NYW*, Mar. 3, 1902 (names of three couples registering at the Glen Island).

4. "Florence Burns Identified."

5. "New Witness in Burns Case," *Boston Post,* Mar. 5, 1902.

6. George Washington's testimony is covered in "Burns Girl Shaken," "Murder of Brooks Charged," and "Florence Burns Identified."

7. "An Examination Begun in Case of Florence Burns," *BDE*, Feb. 22, 1902.

8. "Girl Accused"; "Brooks Shot in a Hotel, Girl Arrested," *BDE*, Feb. 15, 1902.

9. "Murder of Brooks Charged."

10. "Florence Burns Identified."

11. "Girl Accused"; "Murder of Brooks."

2. THE BEDFORD AVENUE GANG

1. "The Gang of Scoundrels Exposed by Brooks Case," *BDE*, Feb. 18, 1902 (colored vests); Edward Wagenknecht, *American Profile: 1900–1909* (Amherst: Univ. of Massachusetts Press, 1982), 15 (rainy-day dresses); Florence was frequently sketched in court wearing an "automobile coat," very much like a duster, which also gives rise to a possibility of her hiding a pregnancy. John F. Kasson, *Amusing the Million: Coney Island at the Turn of the Century* (New York: Hilland Wang, 1978), 6 (rebellion).

2. Florence Burns, "Relates Madcap Career," *Pittsburgh Press,* Nov. 30, 1902. This article originally appeared in Hearst's *New York Journal* and possibly had a byline there as it is written in the first person. However, the *Journal* is unavailable online or via Interlibrary Loan; the only extant copies are at the University of Texas Library.

3. "Evidently Murdered," *Daily People,* Feb. 16, 1902; "Brooks a Virginian," *Baltimore Sun,* Feb. 18, 1902; "Florence Burns in Court," *BDE*, Feb. 18, 1902.

4. Sandra Vermilyea Todd, *Vermilyea Family Genealogy,* http://vermilyeafamily reunion.com/pdf/VBook2011/SixthGen.pdf , 236. See also *Brooklyn Citizen Almanac for 1894,* 432, available as a free e-book download from www.books.google.com. For the surname Von derBosch, there were so many spelling variants that it would be impossible to duplicate them all. This one is the most likely.

5. In the 1940 census, Florence gave her highest academic completion as Grade

Eight. Her business school foray is from "Florence Burns a Recluse," *Denver Post,* Oct. 30, 1902.

6. "Hearing in Burns Case Over Until Tomorrow," *BDE,* Feb. 24, 1902. The name Harry must have been at the top of the charts for boys born in the late 1870s and early 1880s, as there were a lot of them involved in this case. The court and the newspapers began referring to the core group as "the four Harrys": Casey, Cohen, Gimpel, and Theall, three of whom had dated Florence. There was a fifth one (Butler), who had recommended a boardinghouse for Florence when the Brookses were trying to get her out of their house.

7. Gay Talese, "The Last of the Bare-Knuckle Fighters Still Spry at 93," *NYT,* Nov. 23, 1958 (smoking); "Brooks Ordered Suit for Easter," *NYW,* Mar. 20, 1902 (dragged out of Coney Island).

8. Burns, "Relates Madcap Career."

9. "Think Burns Girl Tried Suicide," *New-York Daily Tribune,* Mar. 23, 1902.

10. Unless otherwise noted, the information on the Bedford Gang comes from a series of exposé articles done by the *BDE* over a four-day span: "The Gang of Scoundrels"; "'The Gang' Is Worried by Tale of Its Deeds," Feb. 19, 1902; "How the Gang Swindled, as Told by One of Them," Feb. 20, 1902; "Police May Take a Hand in the Game of the Gang," Feb. 21, 1902; "A Degenerate Gang," *Daily People,* Feb. 20, 1902.

11. Burns, "Relates Madcap Career."

12. Here is a chronological summary of the "career" of Theodore Burris. The newspapers seem to take a perverse pride in his ability to think of new ways to get into trouble, while at the same time managing to avoid conviction for his crimes: "Brooklyn Man in Trouble," *BDE,* Feb. 20, 1901; "Landlord Ran Him Down," *Boston Herald,* Feb. 20, 1901; "Burris Still in Jail," *BDE,* Feb. 21, 1901; "Theodore Burris Indicted," *BDE,* May 16, 1901; "Broker Puts His Son in Jail," *NYT,* June 17, 1901; "Theodore Burris Discharged," *NYT,* June 18, 1901; "Bedford Gang Member in Clutches of Law," *BDE,* Aug. 21, 1902 (after the Brooks-Burns case, he is always connected with the Bedford Avenue Gang even though it existed before 1902); "Burris Held in Court," *NYT,* May 23, 1904; "Burris of Bedford Gang Had the $1,000 Dog Toby," *BDE,* May 23, 1904; "Mr. Burris to the Bar; Assault Case This Time," *BDE,* June 17, 1904; "Lived High in the Jail," *BDE,* June 20, 1904; "Burris Who Feared Jail Got Job from Dr. Babbitt," *BDE,* June 27, 1904; "Took Another's Name Just to Amuse Himself," *BDE,* Oct. 2, 1904; "Jumped from Moving Car; Fought Five Policemen," *BDE,* Sept. 16, 1905; "Ex-Tackle Beats Police," *New-York Daily Tribune,* Sept. 17, 1905; "Theodore Burris Injects Himself into the Situation," *BDE,* Oct. 6, 1906; "Ted Burris Returns to Old Field of Labor," *BDE,* Aug. 29, 1908. Readers will be highly amused—as Burris's family and his victims were *not*—in reading the accounts of those exploits that made the newspapers from 1901 to 1908, knowing that there must have been several that did not get printed.

13. University Registrar, Cornell University, e-mail to author, Dec. 15, 2015; Harvard University Archives, e-mail to author, Dec. 24, 2015.

14. Maud Gleason, "Is the So-Called Kangaroo Walk Injurious?," *Health: A Home Magazine Devoted to Physical Culture and Hygiene,* Jan. 1904, 385–87, www.books .google.com.

15. The Bedford Gang member who anonymously detailed the activities of the gang said this about a comparison: "They are all alike and the Paterson crowd who were rounded up last spring in the Bosschieter case weren't a marker to them" ("The Gang of Scoundrels"). In other words, both groups were drugging and gang-raping women, except that the Bedford boys had not been exposed. There's a good modern-day summary of the Bosschieter case by David J. Krajicek, "Attacked by the Gang," *New York Daily News,* Oct. 25, 2008, http://articles.nydailynews.com/2008–10–25/news /17907341_1_four-men-physical-affection-george-kerr. The *New York Times* covered the Bosschieter case, but the best articles were done by the *Daily People,* New York's socialist newspaper, which emphasized the class angle of the mill girls and the rich boys in Paterson, New Jersey, as well as in the reactions of the townspeople to the fate of the four defendants. The *Daily People* is available through www.Genealogybank .com (a subscription database).

16. Burns, "Relates Madcap Career"; "'Handsome Ed' Weds Again," *BDE,* July 17, 1903.

17. Kasson, *Amusing the Millions,* 41, 59.

18. "J. Clinton Brower Married," *NYT,* Apr. 24, 1901; see also "Bader's Road House," *BDE,* July 4, 1897, for a review, and "Lively Magnum Races," *NYT,* Dec. 6, 1904, for winter sleigh races to the roadhouses.

19. "Casey Slew a Wild Cat with One of His Boots," *BDE,* Aug. 9, 1901.

20. "Has Big Bills," *Pittsburgh Press,* Oct. 29, 1902.

21. "Casey of Bedford Gang in Frank Keeney's Auto," *BDE,* Jan. 19, 1904.

22. "Harry Casey Is the Man Who Shot Young Cawley," *BDE,* Nov. 20, 1903; "He Shot His 'Best Friend,'" *BDE,* Dec. 3, 1903.

3. FLORENCE BURNS AND WALTER BROOKS

1. New York City Archives, death certificate for Gertrude Brooks.

2. "Mrs. Brooks Denounces Girl," *BDE,* Feb. 16, 1902.

3. "Murder of Brooks Charged."

4. "Murder of Brooks Charged"; "Grand Jury Rushing Florence Burns' Case," *BDE,* Feb. 17, 1902; "Mrs. Brooks Denounces."

5. "Brooks Fought with Woman in Brooklyn," *NYW,* Mar. 14, 1902.

6. "Six New Witnesses," *DP*, Mar. 9, 1902; "Walter Brooks to Figure in Civil Suit Tomorrow," *NYW*, Mar. 9, 1902.

7. "Grand Jury Rushing."

8. "Walter Brooks' Mother Says Her Son Was Drugged," *BDE*, May 15, 1902.

9. "25 Years Ago," *Syracuse Herald*, Mar. 23, 1927.

10. "Says Miss Burns Asked About a Pistol," *NYT*, Mar. 9, 1902.

11. "Walter Brooks' Mother Says."

12. Unless otherwise indicated, the information in this section comes from the testimony of Mr. and Mrs. Brooks at the hearing and inquest: "Mrs. Brooks Faints on the Witness Stand," *NYT*, Mar. 16, 1902; "If You Kill My Son, I Will Kill You," *NYW*, Mar. 16, 1902; "'Third Degree' Evidence May Be Ignored," *NYW*, Mar. 19, 1902; "Sensational Climax Likely in Florence Burns Case," *BDE*, Mar. 18, 1902; "Court Causes Surprise in the Burns Case," *NYT*, Mar. 19, 1902; "Walter Brooks' Mother Denies a Former Story," *BDE*, May 19, 1902.

13. "Saw Miss Burns in Hotel, She Says," *NYW*, Mar. 7, 1902; "Blamed Brooks," *DP*, Mar. 8, 1902.

14. "Florence Burns' Plea to Brooks to Marry Her," *NYW*, Feb. 19, 1902.

15. "Florence Burns' Plea"; "Mrs. Brooks Denounces Girl."

16. "Murder of Brooks Charged."

17. "Girl Held for Hotel Murder," *NYS*, Feb. 16, 1902.

18. "Grand Jury Rushing."

19. "Girl Held."

20. "Murder of Brooks Charged."

4. WALTER BROOKS'S LAST WEEK

1. Ruth Dunne's surname was uniformly reported incorrectly as "Dunn," but census documents and her marriage certificate have it as Dunne.

2. "Ruth Dunn a Witness at the Brooks Inquest," *BDE*, May 16, 1902.

3. Unless otherwise indicated, the reports of the day-to-day activities of Walter Brooks during his last week come from the testimony of Joseph Cribbins (office boy), Harry Cohen, and Ruth Dunne: "Jerome Offers His Aid to Free Miss Burns," *NYW*, Feb. 20, 1902; "Murder of Brooks Charged"; "Burns Girl Shaken by the Day's Events," *BDE*, Feb. 23, 1902; "Sensational Evidence Against Burns Girl," *BDE*, Mar. 8, 1902; "Walter Brooks' Mother Denies"; "Believe Mayer Is Likely to Let Burns Girl Go," *BDE*, Mar. 22, 1902; "Trainman and Newsman Saw Burns Girl at 11:15," *BDE*, Feb. 21, 1902; "Ruth Dunn a Witness."

4. "Some Foolish Theories in Brooks Murder Case," *BDE*, Feb. 20, 1902.

5. Matthew Algeo's delightful book is a thorough—and thoroughly entertaining—compendium of the history of the sport through the years. Matthew Algeo, *Pedestrianism: When Watching People Walk Was America's Favorite Spectator Sport* (Chicago: Review Press, 2014).

6. *Chicago Daily News, Almanac and Year Book for 1902* (Chicago: Daily News Co., 1903), www.books.google.com; see also Eleanor Atkinson, Francis B. Atkinson, and Lewis A. Convis, *The World's Chronicle: A History of the World To-day for the Men and Women of To-morrow,* vol. 4 (N.p.: Little Chronicle Publishing Co., 1901), www.books.google.com.

7. Algeo, *Pedestrianism,* 45–66.

5. ARREST

1. New York City Archives, death certificate for Walter S. Brooks. (Walter's middle name was never mentioned, but it is possible that it was—ironically—Slaughter, as this was his maternal grandmother's maiden name. His father's name was Thomas Walter Brooks and sometimes Walter's middle initial is listed as T., but it was officially S.)

2. Unless otherwise indicated, the interactions between Florence and the arresting detectives come from their testimony at the hearing and inquest: "Girl Held for Hotel Murder," *NYS,* Feb. 16, 1902; "Murder of Brooks Charged"; "Sensational Climax Likely," *BDE,* Mar. 18, 1902; "If You Kill My Son."

3. "'Third Degree' Evidence All Stricken Out," *NYW,* Mar. 23, 1902.

4. New York State and US Federal Census records, www.Ancestry.com.

5. "Celluloid Hair Combs," Vintage Celluloid Collectibles, vintage-celluloid-collectibles.com/celluloid-hair-combs.

6. The interaction between Florence and Detective Riordan (sometimes misspelled as "Reardon" because it is pronounced that way) can be found at "Miss Burns and the Pistol," *NYS,* Mar. 9, 1902; "Crushing Blow for Miss Burns," *NYW,* Mar. 9, 1902; "Sensational Evidence Against Burns Girl," *BDE,* Mar. 8, 1902.

7. "Murder of Brooks Charged."

8. "Weible's [*sic*] Story Upset Burns Girl's Case," *NYW,* Feb. 22, 1902.

9. "Tells How Barbour Died," *NYT,* Sept. 16, 1900 (includes an extended personal account by Helen Southgate of the shooting); "Similar Tragedies," *Boston Herald,* Mar. 12, 1902. This article notes the "remarkable . . . similarity of features" in the two cases and relates that Helen Southgate wrote to Florence to encourage her not to give up hope.

10. "Murder of Brooks." In an eerie coincidence, Florence echoes this philosophy eight years later in her trial testimony for extortion: "If I had a million dollars a week,

I would live up to it." Transcript of People of the State of New York against Edward
H. Brooks and Florence W. Wildrick, Court of General Sessions of the County of
New York, Oct. 24, 1910, Case 1236, Criminal Trial Transcripts Collection, Special
Collections, Lloyd Sealy Library, John Jay College, 1910.

6. FLORENCE AND THE TOMBS ANGEL

1. Nearly every article throughout the arrest and hearing of Florence Burns com-
mented in some way on the incredible calmness—to the point of indifference—on the
part of this teenage girl. For a small sampling, see "Calmness Displayed Astonishes
Officials," *Miami (OH) Daily Star,* Feb. 17, 1902; "Mother Tells Accused Girl Brooks Is
Dead," *NYW,* Feb. 17, 1902; "An Examination Begun in Case of Florence Burns," *BDE,*
Feb. 22, 1902.

2. "Murder of Brooks Charged"; "Grand Jury Rushing."

3. "Mother Tells Accused Girl"; "Florence Burns to the Tombs," *NYS,* Feb. 17, 1902.

4. "Mother Tells Accused Girl."

5. "A Tale of the Tombs," New York Correction Historical Society, http://www
.correctionhistory.org/html/chronicl/nycdoc/html/histry/3a.html; Greg Young and
Tom Meyers, *The Bowery Boys: Adventures in Old New York* (Berkeley, CA: Ulysses
Press, 2016), 101.

6. Unless otherwise indicated, the information about Mrs. Foster comes from "Little
Stories of the 'Tombs Angel,'" *NYT,* Mar. 2, 1902; "Seth Low's Rising Star," *BDE,* June
5, 1896; "Afternoon Tea in the Tombs," *NYS,* Nov. 28, 1896; "Among the Seventeen
Dead," *NYS,* Feb. 23, 1902; Zacks, *Island of Vice,* 196.

7. Says Molineux Is Innocent," *New York Tribune,* Feb. 18, 1900; "Mrs. Nack's Own
Story of the Killing of Guldensuppe," *NYW,* Oct. 3, 1897; "Maria's Cell at Sing Sing,"
NYEW, July 19, 1895; "Editorial" (re: Barberi and the Tombs Angel), *Middletown Daily
Argus,* July 19, 1895; "Marie Barberi's Second Trial," *BDE,* Nov. 16, 1896; James D. Liv-
ingston, *Arsenic and Clam Chowder: Murder in Gilded Age New York* (Albany: State
Univ. of New York Press, 2010), 63. Information on the cases whose defendants were
inhabitants of the Tombs and who were the recipients of Mrs. Foster's kindness can
be found in Livingston, *Arsenic and Clam Chowder* (Mary Alice Fleming); Timothy
J. Gilfoyle, *A Pickpocket's Tale: The Underworld of Nineteenth-Century New York* (New
York: Norton, 2006) (George Appo); Paul Collins, *The Murder of the Century: The
Gilded Age Crime That Scandalized a City and Sparked the Tabloid Wars* (New York:
Crown Publishers, 2011) (Augusta Nack); Gerald Gross, *Masterpieces of Murder: An
Edmund Pearson True Crime Reader* (Boston: Little, Brown, 1963), 140–48 (Maria
Barberi); Gross, *Masterpieces of Murder,* 229–33 (Mrs. Nack; this article is a very

short, tongue-in-cheek and somewhat breezy recount of the Guldensuppe case; the Collins book is excellent and a much superior source).

8. "'Miss Burns Wasn't on Train,' He Says," *NYW*, Feb. 25, 1902; "Hearing in Burns Case Over until Tomorrow," *BDE*, Feb. 24, 1902.

9. "Foster L. Backus Dead," *NYT*, Mar. 11, 1907; "Foster L. Backus," *New York Tribune*, Mar. 11, 1907.

10. "Burns Girl Shaken by Day's Events, *BDE*, Feb. 23, 1902.

11. "Detectives Hunt for Burns Family," *NYW*, Feb. 27, 1902; "Parents Gone," *DP*, Feb. 28, 1902; "Jerome Offers His Aid to Free Miss Burns," *NYW*, Feb. 20, 1902.

12. O'Connor's book is a readable compendium of the cases that comprised Jerome's career as New York City's district attorney, as well as a biography of him. But you won't find any mention of the Brooks-Burns case there, probably because it was so early in his tenure as DA, the case did not culminate in a trial, and it was not a victory for him. Richard O'Connor, *Courtroom Warrior: The Combative Career of William Travers Jerome* (Boston: Little, Brown, 1963).

13. See next chapter for a discussion of the concept of the Unwritten Law.

14. "Burns Girl Faces Accusers Today," *NYW*, Feb. 26, 1902; "Burns Family Evades Subpenas [*sic*] from Jerome," *BDE*, Feb. 22, 1902.

15. "Ban of Brooklyn," *DP*, May 22, 1902.

7. THE UNWRITTEN LAW

1. Jackie Wahl, "Murder in Jacques Canyon: Did the Battered Wife Kill Jim Bachus?," *The Golden Age, Journal of the Nez Perce County Historical Society* 14, no. 1 (1994): 15–18.

2. Gross, *Masterpieces of Murder*, 140–48.

3. "In the Case of a Girl," *Tacoma (WA) Times*, Feb. 20, 1909 (Verna Ware); Bill Neal, *Sex, Murder, and the Unwritten Law: Courting Judicial Mayhem, Texas Style* (Lubbock: Texas Tech Univ. Press, 2009), 40–58 (Verna Ware) and 59–83 (Winnie Jo Morris).

4. Lawrence M. Friedman and William E. Havemann, "The Rise and Fall of the Unwritten Law: Sex, Patriarchy, and Vigilante Justice in the American Courts," *Buffalo Law Review* 61, no. 5 (2013): 1000–1002, 1008–9.

5. Friedman and Havemann, "The Rise and Fall," 1041–42.

6. William Grimes, "Francine Hughes Wilson, 69; "Domestic Violence Victim Who Took Action, Dies," *NYT*, Mar. 31, 2017.

7. "Saved Herself by Killing Husband," *NYW*, Mar. 12, 1902; "Woman Acquitted of Murder," *BDE*, July 16, 1902.

8. "Miss Burns' Motive," *DP,* Feb. 25, 1902.

9. "Miss Burns' Motive" ("She is about to become a mother").

10. "'No Jury Would Convict Burns Girl,'" *NYW,* Mar. 3, 1902.

11. "Jerome Falls from Pedestal," *Atlanta Constitution,* Mar. 30, 1902.

8. FLORENCE IN JAIL AND A CITY OBSESSED

1. "Florence Burns in Court" (Florence to a reporter: "Please let me have a newspaper. I want to find myself").

2. "Similar Tragedies," *Boston Herald,* Mar. 12, 1902.

3. "Vaccination Bee in Tombs Prison," *NYW,* Mar. 11, 1902.

4. "Shot Friend While Explaining Brooks' Murder," *BDE,* Mar. 17, 1902.

5. "Weibel's [*sic*] Story Upset Burns Girl's Case," *NYW,* Feb. 22, 1902; "Burns Girl Faces"; "Vital Witness in Burns Case Lost," *NYW,* Feb. 28, 1902; "'Alice's Sister' Wrote to Save Florence Burns," *BDE,* Apr. 7, 1902.

6. "Said She Killed Brooks," *BDE,* Feb. 27, 1902.

7. "Florence Burns in Court."

8. "Florence Burns in Court."

9. "Florence Burns Carried Pistol, Police Say," *NYW,* Feb. 18, 1902.

10. "Florence Burns Carried Pistol."

11. "Florence Burns in Court."

12. "Fifty Bodies in the Blazing Park Avenue Hotel, Says Chief Croker; Many Are Missing; Four Bodies Found," *NYW,* Feb. 22, 1902.

13. "Burns Girl Sobs at Death Hymn," *NYW,* Feb. 24, 1902.

14. "Eight Sailors Storm Victims," *Chicago Tribune,* Feb. 24, 1902 (first adjournment for a woman); "In Honor of Tombs Angel," *NYEW,* Jan. 30, 1904 (memorial plaque).

9. THE COURT OF SPECIAL SESSIONS

1. "Mother Tells Accused Girl Brooks Is Dead," *NYW,* Feb. 17, 1902.

2. "Judge Mayer Dies of Heart Attack," *NYT,* Dec. 1, 1925.

3. "Burns Case Is Badly Tangled," *NYW,* Mar. 2, 1902.

4. At this time, William Travers Jerome was also involved in the investigation of a police department scandal over the murder of a whistle-blower, James McAuliffe, on the orders of the corrupt chief of police, Bill Devery, which occurred just before the Brooks murder. See "Mystery of Glennon Witness' Death Deepens," *NYT,* Feb. 21, 1902. The preliminary was also presided over by Justice Mayer and, in July, Mayer discounted—as

he had in the Burns case—most of the witnesses' testimony. Unlike his decision in the Burns case, however, Mayer declared the police testimony reliable—testimony that was almost certainly self-servingly untrue as the death occurred when the victim was in their custody. This left Jerome with no choice but to decide not to proceed because of a lack of evidence pointing directly at any specific individual. "Mr. Jerome Says He Can't Act in McAuliffe Case," *NYT*, July 22, 1902.

5. "Beauty Show in Brooks Mystery," *NYW*, Mar. 8, 1902.

6. "Florence Burns Identified by 'L' Conductor," *NYW*, Feb. 23, 1902.

7. "Florence Burns Identified by 'L' Conductor" (for poses); "New Mystery in Brooks Murder," *NYW*, Mar. 1, 1902 (for quote).

8. "Believe Mayer Is Likely to Let Burns Girl Go."

9. "Believe Mayer Is Likely to Let Burns Girl Go."

10. "Florence Burns in Court"; "Burns Girl Not with Brooks?," *NYS*, Feb. 19, 1902.

11. "Burns Girl's Alibi to Jerome," *NYS*, Feb. 21, 1902.

12. Articles regarding the Bedford Gang's activities and their exposure can be found in note 10 of chapter 2.

13. *People v. Durrant*, 119 Cal. 54 and 119 Cal. 201 (1897). For an exhaustive examination of the Durrant case and the people involved, see my book: Virginia McConnell, *Sympathy for the Devil: The Emmanuel Baptist Murders of Old San Francisco* (Westport, CT: Praeger Publishers, 2001).

14. "Burns Girl Shaken by the Day's Events," *BDE*, Feb. 23, 1902.

15. "Burns Girl Shaken."

16. "Detectives Hunt for Burns Family," *NYW*, Feb. 27, 1902.

17. "Burns Girl Shaken."

18. "New Mystery in Brooks Murder," *NYW*, Mar. 1, 1902; "Detectives Hunt for Burns Family," *NYW*, Feb. 27, 1902.

19. "Expect That Burns Girl Will Be Held for Trial," *BDE*, Mar.19, 1902; "Ridiculous, Says Mayer," *DP*, Mar. 9, 1902.

20. "Burns Girl Shaken."

21. "Burns Girl Shaken."

22. Wible's name was consistently misspelled as "Weible" and "Weibles." Also, he had lied about his age, possibly to get the conductor's job, saying he was twenty-two, so the newspapers reported him as twenty-two—except that one said he looked about nineteen! "Burns Girl Shaken." Wible was nineteen and Florence was a pretty girl of the same age, so *of course* he would notice her.

23. "Florence Burns Took 11:15 P.M. Train Home," *NYW*, Feb. 21, 1902.

24. "Burns Girl Shaken."

25. "Weible's [*sic*] Story Upset Burns Girl's Case," *NYW*, Feb. 22, 1902; "Trainman and Newsman Saw Burns Girl at 11:15," *BDE*, Feb. 21, 1902.

26. "Miss Burns Wasn't on Train, He Says," *NYW*, Feb. 25, 1902.

27. "More Scandal Coming," *Boston Herald*, Apr. 11, 1902; "Missing Persons in Burns Case Found," *NYW*, Mar. 12, 1902.

28. "To Flush the Sewers in Search for Pistol," *BDE*, Mar. 21, 1902.

29. "Burns Girl Shaken"; "Backus Tries to Show Brooks Was a Suicide," *BDE*, Mar. 1, 1902.

30. Board of Trustees of American Institute of Homeopathy, *Journal of American Institute of Homeopathy* 1 (1909): 337–38, www.books.google.com.

31. "If You Kill My Son, I Will Kill You," *NYW*, Mar. 16, 1902.

32. "If You Kill My Son."

33. "Some Foolish Theories in Brooks Murder Case." In September 2017, the forensic program *Cold Justice* related the successful examination and reopening of a cold case file for the murder of a young man, previously determined to have committed suicide. The ballistics reports showed a nearly impossible position for a successful suicide: in the back of the head in almost the same location as Walter Brooks's wound. The chances of the victim's being able to do this to himself were very low and, in the span of two seconds, a forensic team member was able to demonstrate the most successful methods of shooting oneself: to the temple, in the mouth, under the chin. All other methods run the risk of a less-than-fatal injury. The victim's wife, long suspected of having killed him, eventually pleaded guilty to this crime. *Cold Justice*, Oxygen Channel, episode on the murder of Benjamin Cooper, Sept. 16, 2017; see also Matt Harvey, "Boothsville Woman Gets 15 Years for Voluntary Manslaughter of Husband," www.theet.com, Dec. 22, 2016.

34. "Found Dead in a Hotel," *NYT*, Jan. 10, 1883 (gas); "An Inventor Found Dead," *NYT*, Feb. 11, 1896 (morphine); "Dead in Glen Island Hotel," *NYT*, Apr. 30, 1904 (carbolic acid). Also not a suicide, but a not uncommon situation with a seventy-four-year-old man (deemed "aged") accompanied by a twenty-eight-year-old woman to the Glen Island, found dead of what turned out to be heart disease ("Aged Merchant Found Dead," *NYT*, Feb. 1, 1916).

35. "Some Foolish Theories."

36. "Brooks Ordered Suit for Easter," *NYW*, Mar. 20, 1902.

37. "Believe Mayer Is Likely to Let Burns Girl Go."

38. "If You Kill My Son."

39. "Burns Girl Freed, Decision Cheered, *BDE*, Mar. 23, 1902; "Florence Burns Freed; Not to Be Rearrested," *NYW*, Mar. 23, 1902.

40. "If You Kill My Son."

41. "If You Kill My Son."

42. "Court Causes Surprise in Burns Case," *NYT*, Mar. 19, 1902.

43. "Burns Girl Freed" ("fat baby"); "If You Kill My Son" (Eyre's testimony).

44. "If You Kill My Son" (late edition).

45. "Girl Friend of Miss Burns to Tell of Threat," *NYW,* Mar. 18, 1902; "'Third Degree' Evidence May Be Ignored," *NYW,* Mar. 19, 1902.

46. Office of the Registrar, Lehigh University, e-mail message to author, Mar. 1, 2017; also in the 1900 census, Eyre listed his occupation as clerk and stated that he had not attended school that year.

47. "Denies He Ate Glass," *BDE,* Dec. 24, 1903.

48. "Expect That Burns Girl Will Be Held for Trial," *BDE,* Mar. 19, 1902.

49. "Believe Mayer Is Likely"; "'Third Degree Evidence.'"

50. "Believe Mayer Is Likely"; "'Third Degree Evidence.'"

51. "Believe Mayer Is Likely."

52. Federal census records for the Dunne family, www.Ancestry.com.

53. "Girl Friend of Miss Burns."

54. "Believe Mayer Is Likely."

10. THE VERDICT AND AN INTERMISSION

1. "Believe Mayer Is Likely to Let Burns Girl Go."

2. "Burns Girl Freed, Decision Cheered"; "Florence Burns Freed."

3. "Useless to Try Miss Burns Again," *NYW,* Mar. 25, 1902.

4. "Burns Girl Freed" (hungry); "Florence Burns Freed" (description of Mr. Brooks).

5. "Florence Burns Freed."

6. "Florence Burns Freed."

7. Burns, "Relates Madcap Career."

8. "Burns Girl Freed."

9. "Editorial," *Watertown (NY) Daily Times,* Mar. 21, 1902. Watertown, smugly boasting of its small size as a buffer against crime, is seventy miles north of Syracuse, close to the Canadian border, and even today has a small population of twenty-six thousand, despite the nearby presence of the US Army's Fort Drum. In 1900, Watertown's population was under twenty-five hundred.

10. "The Burns Case and the 'Third Degree,'" *NYW,* Mar. 24, 1902.

11. "Release of Florence Burns," *BDE,* Mar. 24, 1902; emphasis added.

12. "Editorial," *Troy Press,* cited in *Watertown (NY) Daily Times,* Mar. 27, 1902.

13. "Press Comment," *Charleston (SC) Evening Post,* Mar. 26, 1902.

11. THE INQUEST

1. "Nicholas T. Brown Discharged," *NYT*, Oct. 22, 1901.

2. "Brooks Inquest Begun; Burns Girl Not There," *BDE*, May 14, 1902.

3. "Florence Burns at Lake Hopatcong," *NYT*, Mar. 29, 1902.

4. "Walter Brooks' Mother Denies."

5. "Miss Burns Always Carried a Revolver," *NYEW*, May 15, 1902.

6. "Runaway Boy Injured," *Philadelphia (PA) Inquirer*, Oct. 15, 1895.

7. "How the Gang Swindled, as Told by One of Them," *BDE*, Feb. 20, 1902.

8. The entire sorry saga is laid out in these *BDE* articles: "Girl Weds Strange Man, Thought It Was a Joke," Sept. 29, 1901; "Groom's Leg Involved," Oct. 2, 1901; "Marriage Was Legal," Oct. 3, 1901; "F. G. Jackson Wonders If He Is a Married Man," Oct. 6, 1901; New York City Marriage Index, www.Ancestry.com.

9. "How the Gang Swindled."

10. "Walter Brooks' Mother Says"; "Miss Burns Always Carried."

11. "Walter Brooks' Mother Says."

12. Young and Meyers, *The Bowery Boys*, 312–13. See also Burrows and Wallace, *Gotham*, 1148; Lloyd Morris, *Incredible New York: High Life and Low Life from 1850 to 1950* (Syracuse, NY: Syracuse Univ. Press, 1951), 111.

13. "Police Testify to Indict Burns Girl," *NYEW*, May 16, 1902.

14. "Police Testify."

15. "Walter Brooks' Mother Denies."

16. "Walter Brooks' Mother Says"

17. "Burns Girl's Fate Rests with Jury, *NYEW*, May 19, 1902.

18. "Brooks Inquest Begins," *NYT*, May 15, 1902.

19. "Walter Brooks' Mother Denies" (Ruth hired by yellow paper); "Ruth Dunn [*sic*] a Witness at the Brooks Inquest" (her testimony); "Walter Brooks' Mother Says" (Harry Cohen saw muff).

20. "Burns Girl Exonerated by Coroner's Jury," *BDE*, May 20, 1902.

21. "Burns Girl Exonerated."

22. "Brooks Murder Case Ends," *NYT*, May 21, 1902; "Burns Girl Is Freed by Coroner's Jury," *NYEW*, May 21, 1902.

23. "Miss Burns' Motive, *DP*, Feb. 16, 1902.

24. "Miss Burns Wasn't on Train, He Says," *NYW*, Feb. 25, 1902.

25. "Florence Burns Not Ill," *BDE*, Apr. 18, 1902.

26. "Miss Florence Burns Starts for Charleston," *Columbia (SC) State*, May 26, 1902.

12. FLORENCE'S NEW LIFE

1. "Florence Burns a Recluse," *Denver (CO) Post,* Oct. 30, 1902.

2. "Florence Burns a Recluse" (re: housework); Burns, "Relates Madcap Career" (for quote).

3. Burns, "Relates Madcap Career."

4. "Florence Burns Home, Living in Seclusion," *BDE,* Sept. 17, 1902.

5. "Two Hours of Intense Agony," *NYT,* Nov. 12, 1881.

6. Abram Wildrick was the first in an impressive line of West Point graduates: two sons, two grandsons, three great-grandsons, and one great-great-grandson. West Point Association of Graduates, *The Register of Graduates & Former Cadets of the United States Military Academy* (West Point, NY: West Point, 2015); correspondence with the Wildrick family.

7. For a capsule summary of Wildrick's (self-reported) derring-do, see "Florence Burns' Parents Didn't Know of Marriage," *BDE,* Nov. 28, 1902, and "All Hope of Solitaires," *Marion (OH) Daily Star,* Dec. 1, 1902.

8. Interviews and correspondence with the Wildrick family, all of whom refer to him as "Uncle Tad." Several newspaper articles also mention the nickname.

9. "Corum and Coates Appear," *Salt Lake Tribune,* July 2, 1895.

10. "Friend of Many Women," *NYS,* Apr. 27, 1901; "Charley Wildrich [*sic*] a Marvel as a Conqueror of Hearts," *St. Louis Republic,* May 5, 1901.

11. "Friend of Many Women."

12. "Friend of Many Women" (Spanish-American War); "Wildrick Had a Novel Career," *Chicago Inter Ocean,* Apr. 28, 1901 (Montgomery Ward).

13. "Dying Woman Faints in Court," *New-York Tribune,* Apr. 26, 1901; "Friend of Many Women."

14. "And Yet Another," *Marion (OH) Star,* May 1, 1901.

15. "Friend of Many Women."

16. The Mabel Strong story was such a dramatic one that it was covered by newspapers all across the country. She was the faithful woman standing by her "scapegrace" man, who was presented as totally undeserving of such loyalty and love. One article even refers to her as "his victim" when it was very obvious that she was a willing partner. From Tad's arrest through Mabel's death and burial, here is a representative sampling of articles: "Fainted," *Cincinnati Enquirer,* Apr. 26, 1901; "Dying Woman Faints in Court"; "Friend of Many Women"; "Wanted Love to Last Longer Than Her Life," *Philadelphia Inquirer,* Apr. 27, 1901; "Wildrick Had a Novel Career"; "His Debts," *Cincinnati Enquirer,* Apr. 30, 1901; "On Verge of Grave," *Marion (OH) Star,* Apr. 30, 1901; "Wildrick's Victim Dying," *Chicago Inter Ocean,* Apr. 30, 1901; "And Yet Another"; "Charley Wildrich [*sic*] a Marvel"; "Wife Loyal to the Last," *Minneapolis*

Star Tribune, July 16, 1901; "Wildrick's Defender Dead," *NYT,* July 16, 1901; "Miss Strong's Funeral," *Akron (OH) Daily Democrat,* July 18, 1901; "Mabel Strong Dies True to Scapegrace," *Minneapolis Star Tribune,* July 21, 1901.

17. Burns, "Relates Madcap Career."

18. Burns, "Relates Madcap Career" ("playthings of fate"); "Florence Burns Is Applicant for Divorce," *New Castle (PA) Herald,* Apr. 17, 1908 ("I will devote my whole life").

19. "Florence Burns' Parents."

20. "Florence Burns an Ex-Convict's Wife," *NYW,* Nov. 29, 1902.

21. "Bill to Punish Adultery," *NYS,* Dec. 2, 1902.

22. "A Tragic Quartette," *Anaconda (MT) Standard,* Dec. 4, 1902.

23. "Ban for Brooklyn," *DP,* May 22, 1902.

24. "Florence Burns and the Stage," *BDE,* Mar. 26, 1902.

25. H. A. Kemble and William E. S. Fales, *Blue Pencil Magazine,* Feb. 1900, vi, www. books.google.com (re: Irving Pinover); "Florence Burns to Star," *BDE,* Dec. 8, 1902 (vaudeville plans).

26. "Florence's Return Engagement," *BDE,* Dec. 12, 1902.

27. "The Wildricks the Cynosure of All Eyes at Theater," *Great Falls (MT) Tribune,* Dec. 14, 1902.

28. "Florence Burns Facing Rialto Belles Boycott," *BDE,* Dec. 17. 1902.

29. "Florence Burns to Sing; She Has Not Rehearsed," *BDE,* Dec. 15, 1902.

30. Maurice Jacobs (words) and Harry Robinson (music), "Gracie Brown," A. A. Lupien Music Publishing Co., 1902.

31. "Florence Burns' Debut," *Baltimore Sun,* Dec. 16, 1902.

32. "Florrie Wasn't Scared, But She Couldn't Sing," *BDE,* Dec. 16, 1902.

33. "Florence Burns Facing."

34. "Florrie Wasn't Scared."

35. "Florrie Wasn't Scared."

36. "Florrie Wasn't Scared."

37. "Florence Burns Facing."

38. "Hyde & Behman's for the Week Commencing December 15, 1902," Keith-Albee Manager Reports for Sept. 2, 1902–Sept. 3, 1903, from the Keith-Albee Collection, DIY History, Univ. of Iowa Library, https://diyhistory.lib.uiowa.edu/transcribe/4721/150446.

39. Bing Crosby was a member of the Newsboy Quintet when he was young, erenow .com/biographies/bing-crosby-a-pocketful-of-dreams-early-years-1903–1940/26.html.

40. "Florence Burns Facing." For the picturesque and outrageous careers of Howe and Hummel, see Cait Murphy, *Scoundrels in Law: The Trials of Howe & Hummel, Lawyers to the Gangsters, Cops, Starlets, and Rakes Who Made the Gilded Age* (New York: HarperCollins, 2010); and Richard H. Rovere, *Howe & Hummel: Their True and Scandalous History* (New York: Farrar, Straus and Giroux, 1974).

41. "Florence Burns Facing."

42. "Florence Burns in Posse," *BDE*, Dec. 20, 1902.

43. "Florence Burns Jeered," *DP*, Dec. 20, 1902.

44. "At the Theaters," *DP*, Feb. 16, 1903.

45. Wagenknecht, *American Profile*, 261–66.

46. Wagenknecht, *American Profile*, 261–66. Anyone wishing to experience a re-
alistic description of the turn-of-the-century variety show could not do better than
to read the scene in Frank Norris's *McTeague*, where the titular character takes his
fiancée, her mother, and her brother to a show in 1899 San Francisco. Frank Norris,
McTeague: A Story of San Francisco (New York: Signet Classics, 2003), 76–84.

47. For a thorough account of the Gillette-Brown case, see Craig Brandon, *Murder
in the Adirondacks: "An American Tragedy"' Revisited* (Utica, NY: North Country
Books, 1986, with a 100th Anniversary edition in 2006).

48. "White Rats Win," *DP*, June 25, 1903.

49. "Florence Burns Again," *BDE*, July 23, 1903.

50. "Carrie Nation Appears with Florence Burns," *Salt Lake Telegram*, Sept. 14, 1903.

51. "Florence Burns Sues for Absolute Divorce," *BDE*, Apr. 17, 1908.

52. "Florence Burns Sues," *NYT*, Apr. 18, 1908.

53. "Seeks Absolute Divorce from Charles W. Wildrick," *New-York Tribune*, Apr.
18, 1908.

54. "Florence Burns Sues for Absolute Divorce"; "Once Held as Slayer; She Seeks
a Divorce," *Washington (DC) Times*, Apr. 18. 1908.

55. "Alimony and Counsel Fees," *BDE*, Apr. 21, 1908.

56. Transcript of People of the State of New York.

57. "Kept Marriage a Secret," *BDE*, Nov. 12, 1909.

58. Transcript of People of the State of New York.

13. THE BADGER GAME

1. Unless otherwise indicated, the information in this chapter comes from Transcript of People of the State of New York.

2. "Uncle Ready to Fight for Estate," *Amsterdam (NY) Evening Record and Daily
Democrat*, Sept. 8, 1911. The history of the litigation can be found in "Western N.Y.
News," *Rochester Democrat and Chronicle*, Feb. 25, 1887; "Western New York," *Roches-
ter Democrat and Chronicle*, Jan. 21, 1895; "Wayne," *Rochester Democrat and Chronicle*,
Nov. 14, 1895.

3. Probate of the will of Lyman Hurlburt, www.Ancestry.com; "Uncle Ready to Fight."

4. "Meet Tonight," *Little Rock Arkansas Democrat*, Dec. 10, 1900.

5. "Uncle Ready to Fight."

6. New York, Sing Sing Prison Admission Records, 1865–1939, for Edward H. Brooks, www.Ancestry.com.

7. Registers of Enlistments in the US Army, 1798–1914, p. 266, www.Fold3.com.

8. 1900 Federal Census, www.Ancestry.com.

9. Information on the career of Ed Brooks Sr. can be found in the following articles, all from the *Lebanon (PA) Daily News*: "20 Years Ago," Jan. 27, 1906; "Two More Arc Lights," Jan. 7, 1889; "In and About Town," June 20, 1890; "Notice," May 6, 1891; "Work Begun," May 6, 1891; "Electric Light Plant," Sept. 18, 1891; "Fottrell Insulated Wire," July 28, 1891; "Half Interest in the Avon Inn," May 19, 1892; "Resignation Accepted," Sept. 7, 1892; "Mr. E. H. Brooks," Mar. 17, 1893; "Will Leave for the West," Apr. 8, 1893; "Runs a Vessel on Puget Sound," June 9, 1893; "Eldridge H. Brooks" (obituary), Apr. 4, 1898.

10. B. Frank Scholl, *Library of Health: Complete Guide to Prevention and Cure of Disease* (Philadelphia: Historical Publishing, 1927), 650–52.

11. See www.Dictionary.com/browse/badger-game for a definition and some background. Charles Kushner, the father of President Donald Trump's son-in-law Jared, in an especially odious use of the Badger Game, hired a prostitute to seduce his brother-in-law, either in revenge or to silence him and his sister, who were to testify against him in federal court. See Laura Mansnerus, "Major Donor Admits to Hiring Prostitute to Smear Witness," *NYT*, Aug. 19, 2004.

14. ARREST, TRIAL, AND THE LAW OF UNINTENDED CONSEQUENCES

1. Unless otherwise indicated, the information in this chapter comes from Transcript of People of the State of New York.

2. "Florence Burns Again in Hands of Police," *New York Tribune*, Sept. 21, 1910; "Florence Burns in Bold 'Badger' Game, *NYT*, Sept. 21, 1910.

3. The newspaper reports of the case can be found in "Florence Burns Again"; "Florence Burns in Bold"; "Girl Once Tried for Murder Held in Badger Case," *Denver Post*, Sept. 21, 1910; "Charge Badger Game," *Washington Post*, Sept. 21, 1910; "Florence Burns in 'Badger' Plot, Lawyer Charges," *NYW*, Sept. 21, 1910; "Woman Given Long Term," *Indianapolis Star*, Nov. 3, 1910; "Once Belle, Now Criminal," *Elyria (OH) Evening Telegram*, Oct. 29, 1910; "Florence Burns Goes to Long Prison Term," *BDE*, Nov. 2, 1910; "Florence Burns Again," *Tampa Tribune*, Nov. 3, 1910; "Florence's Big Sentence," *Indiana (PA) Evening Gazette*, Nov. 3, 1910.

4. "Mystery in Death of Accuser of Florence Burns, *NYEW*, Sept. 2, 1911.

5. "Uncle Ready to Fight."

6. "Florence Burns's Accuser Found Dead," *NYT*, Sept. 2, 1911.

7. "Mystery in Death."

8. "Mystery in Death."

9. "Florence Burns' Victim Found in Hudson River," *Wilkes-Barre (PA) Evening News*, Sept. 2, 1911.

10. "Uncle Says Nephew Slain for Revenge," *Lincoln (NE) Evening News*, Sept. 2, 1911; "Investigate Death of Man in River, *Trenton (NJ) Evening Times*, Sept. 2, 1911.

11. John E. Wehrum Jr. and Owen C. Marx, "Palmagiano: The Constitutionality of Prison Mail Censorship," *Catholic University Law Review* 21, no. 1 (1971): 216n2, http://scholarship.law.edu/lawreview/vol21/iss1/14.

12. "Uncle Ready to Fight"; "Will of C. W. Hurlburt Filed," *NYT*, Sept. 8, 1911; "Contests Charles Hurlburt's Will, *NYT*, Nov. 14, 1911; "Writ for Badger Woman, *BDE*, Nov. 14, 1911.

13. "Find Hurlburt's Clothing," *Santa Cruz (CA) Evening News*, Sept. 20, 1911.

14. "Lawyer Hurlburt Not Murdered," *Pittsburgh Post-Gazette*, Sept. 3, 1911.

15. "Suicidal Thoughts: When Is It Time to Worry?," www.depressiond.org/suicidal-thoughts-when-is-it-time-to-worry/.

16. "Suicidal Thoughts."

17. "Hurlburt's Will Sustained," *BDE*, Dec. 11, 1911.

18. See www.Findagrave.com.

15. LESSONS NOT LEARNED

1. "Florence Burns Reappears; May Be Bride Again," *Syracuse Herald*, Mar. 21, 1915; www.Findagrave.com for Caryl Bensel.

2. "Whitman Angered at Pardon Appeal," *BDE*, Dec. 21, 1915.

3. "Florence Burns Tries to Shoot Detective in Raid," *NYEW*, Jan 27, 1922.

4. "Burns Woman Is Taken into Custody Again," *Syracuse Herald*, July 13, 1919.

5. "Burns Woman."

6. "Florence Burns Repents," *BDE*, July 12, 1919.

7. "Florence Burns Held After Police Raid," *NYT*, Jan. 27, 1922.

8. The term *disorderly house* was generally used to refer to any residence that was the subject of a complaint made to the police, even for something as benign as a loud party. However, it was understood to refer specifically to houses of prostitution, as well as dwellings dealing in drugs or gambling. Here, because the police were already committed to a raid, and given the nature of what they found there, it's clear that it was a house where prostitution occurred, even if it was not an outright brothel.

9. "Florence Burns Tries"; "Florence Burns Held After"; "Florence Burns Is Held for Gun-Play," *BDE*, Feb. 1, 1922.

10. "Florence Burns Tells Court She Is Guilty," *NYEW*, Feb. 15, 1922; "Florence Burns Guilty," *NYT*, Feb. 16, 1922; "Florence Burns Gets 3-Year Term," *BDE*, Feb. 23, 1922.

11. "4 Women Criminals, Well Known Locally, Serving Terms at Auburn," *BDE*, Mar. 9, 1924.

12. Death certificate for Frederick Burns, New York City Archives.

13. "Kept Marriage a Secret"; State of New Jersey marriage certificates; 1910 Federal Census, www.Ancestry.com.

14. Probate of the Last Will and Testament of Frederick Burns, www.Ancestry.com.

15. Records of The Evergreens Cemetery, Brooklyn, NY.

16. "New York Day by Day, with O. O. McIntyre," *Logansport (IN) Pharos Tribune*, Aug. 14, 1924.

EPILOGUE

1. 1925 New York State Census; 1930 and 1940 Federal Censuses, www.Ancestry.com.

2. "Woman Freed in 1902 Slaying Asks 'Gossip' Be Silenced," *BDE*, Apr. 22, 1929; 1930 Federal Census for John Stankevich's occupation after this incident.

3. "Obituary, Henrietta Burns," *BDE*, July 24, 1937.

4. "Obituary, Henrietta Burns."

5. "Two Cops Save Woman in Blazing Kitchen," *BDE*, Mar. 2, 1944.

6. "Stankevich—Florence," *BDE*, Aug. 29, 1949.

7. The Evergreens Cemetery records (for Burns plot); Social Security Death Index (for John Stankevich). Florence consistently reported her age as younger than she really was, admitting her actual age in only one census. The cemetery records have her as fifty-five when she was really sixty-seven. For the kitchen fire incident in 1944, she reported herself as fifty-three when she was a month shy of sixty-two. Did John know how old she really was? He would have been the one giving the information to the funeral home and the cemetery.

8. Sandra Vermilyea Todd, Vermilyea Family Reunion, http://vermilyeafamilyreunion .com/pdf/VBook2014/VERMILYEA%20GENEALOGY%ADDITIONS%20AND%20 CORRECTIONS.pdf, 2014.

9. Death certificate for Mary Brooks, New York City Archives.

10. Death certificate for Thomas Walter Brooks, www.findagrave.com.

11. "Foster L. Backus," *New York Tribune*, Mar. 11, 1907; "Foster L. Backus Dead," *NYT*, Mar. 11, 1907.

12. "Judge Mayer Dies of Heart Attack," *NYT,* Dec. 1, 1925.

13. O'Connor, *Courtroom Warrior,* 233–34.

14. "Jerome Dies at 74; Long Tammany Foe," *NYT,* Feb. 14, 1934.

15. Marriage Records, New York City Archives; death certificate for Harry Casey, New York City Archives; Medical Examiner's Report on the Death of Harry Casey, New York City Office of the Chief Medical Examiner.

16. "'Handsome Ed' Weds Again," *BDE,* July 17, 1903; "Mrs. Alma Watson Announces Divorce," *BDE,* May 17, 1913; US Draft Registrations Cards, 1917–18, for Edward Cole Watson, www.Ancestry.com.

17. "New Yorker Dies at Springs," *Denver Rocky Mountain News,* Sept. 16, 1911; "Deaths and Funerals," *Colorado Springs Gazette,* Sept. 15, 1911; State of Colorado death certificate for Theodore Burris.

18. "Jobs at $15 Each," *NYT,* Nov. 12, 1905.

19. 1910 Federal Census, www.Ancestry.com.

20. "Hold American for $5,000 Ransom," *NYT,* Nov. 23, 1912.

21. "Bankruptcy Notices," *BDE,* June 8, 1915.

22. "Maddox, Jr., in Hospital," *BDE,* Nov. 21, 1911; "Died," *NYT,* Feb. 13, 1916. For an excellent account of the Guldensuppe case, not only involving Judge Maddox as presiding judge for Martin Thorn's trial, but also the nefarious law firm of Howe & Hummel (mentioned elsewhere in this book), see Collins, *The Murder of the Century.* The reason I use "reportedly" regarding Maddox Jr.'s cause of death is that I am skeptical that it was from pneumonia, although it is entirely possible that it was. But there is no entry for him in any of the New York City death indexes and he is supposed to have died at home in Brooklyn. I sent for his death certificate and was sent the one for his father instead (an easy mistake as the father, who had the same name, died a month later). When I reordered the certificate for the son, accompanied by a letter about the confusion between father and son and giving the son's family-reported date of death, I was sent another certificate for the father! Because of Maddox Jr.'s mental problems, I thought possibly the cause of death might have been suicide.

23. "Talks of Florence Burns," *BDE,* Apr. 13, 1902; "Ruth Dunn [*sic*] at New Haven," *BDE,* Apr. 11, 1902.

24. "Ruth Dunn [*sic*] Finds Herself and Notifies Her Family," *BDE,* Apr. 10, 1902.

25. "Ruth Dunn [*sic*] Finds Herself."

26. "Ruse of a Girl's Mother to Make Sure of Arrest," *BDE,* Sept. 11, 1902.

27. "Ruth Dunn's [*sic*] Chum Took Acid to Die," *NYEW,* Dec. 29, 1902; "Girl Who Tried Suicide Proves to Be Ethel Kahl," *BDE,* Dec. 29, 1902.

28. "Said She Was Ruth Dunn [*sic*]," *BDE,* Oct. 8, 1902; "Ruth Dunn [*sic*] Made Prisoner in Raid," *NYEW,* Oct. 8, 1902; "Ruth Dunn [*sic*] Caught in Raid," *DP,* Oct. 9, 1902.

29. Marriage certificate of Ruth Maria Dunne and John William Murphy, New York City Archives; California Death Index, www.Ancestry.com.

30. New York City Municipal Deaths, www.FamilySearch.org; death certificate for Harry L. Cohen, New York City Archives.

31. "Eyre Signed a Peace Bond," *BDE*, Mar. 13, 1905; death certificate for William A. Eyre, New York City Archives (his age is listed as thirty, but he was actually a month shy of age twenty-seven; he was born in October 1882). The Consumers Park Brewery (building still standing today) was part of a delightful beer garden complex called "a theme park of beer" by Walkabout author Suzanne Spellen, containing a market, benches, restaurant, and foliage. Suzanne Spellen, "Walkabout: Consumers Park Brewery, Part 2," July 10, 2012, www.brownstoner.com/history/walkabout-consumers-park -brewery-part-2/.

32. New York, Abstracts of World War I Military Service (for Joseph E. Cribbins), www.Ancestry.com; US Headstone Applications for Military Veterans (for Joseph E. Cribbins), www.Ancestry.com.

33. Federal Census records; US World War I, Draft Registration Cards, 1917–18 (for Arthur Cleveland Wible); US World War II Draft Registration Cards, 1942 (for Arthur Cleveland Wible), www.Ancestry.com.

34. Federal Census records; death certificate for Harold L. Theall, New York City Archives.

35. "T. C. Wells Drowned in Texas," *NYT*, June 23, 1903.

36. New York City Death Index, www.Ancestry.com.

37. "George D. Bader a Suicide," *NYT*, Sept. 20, 1905.

38. Interviews and correspondences with members of the Wildrick family; "Obituary No. 1," *NYT*, Nov. 10, 1964 (for Capt. Charles W. Wildrick).

39. US World War I Draft Registration Cards, 1917–18 (for Eldridge Hildreth Brooks), www.Ancestry.com; Duesenberg history, www.historicstructures.com/in /indianapolis/duesenberg_auto_company.php.

40. US Passport Applications, 1795–1925 (for Eldridge Hildreth Brooks), www.Ancestry .com.

41. "New Jersey Charters," *NYT*, June 23, 1926; Selective Service Registration Cards, World War II, Fourth Registration (for Eldridge Hildreth Brooks), www.Ancestry.com.

42. Federal Census records.

43. "Mrs. Brooks Denounces Girl," *BDE*, Feb. 16, 1902. Decatur Street was originally composed of houses that were set back modestly from the street and had gardens in the front, but the newer brick homes did not. The Brookses, who had a reputation in the neighborhood of being "exclusive"—which probably meant they did not mingle much—objected to the modern house being built next to theirs because it supposedly came too close to their yard and possibly infringed on their lot line. Today, you can see

the Brooks house set quite a way back from the street, while the one to its left (facing the house) juts out boldly, close to the sidewalk. The Brooks house can't be seen until you are right in front of it.

44. "Her Father Fears 'Bedford Gang,'" *NYEW,* June 19, 1902.

45. "After a Hound," *Watertown (NY) Daily Times,* July 21, 1902 (Latimer); "Man with Stab Wounds Found Lying in Snow," *BDE,* Mar. 6, 1902.

46. "Bedford Gang Suspected of a Highway Robbery," *BDE,* Jan. 27, 1904.

47. "Bedford Gang Revived in Its Old Time Infamy," *BDE,* June 5, 1904.

48. "Bedford Gang Revived."

49. "Bedford Gang Revived."

50. "Mining Co. Promoters Swindled by Wholesale," *BDE,* Mar. 11, 1904.

51. "Murphy Conspiracy Sulzer Calls Suit," *NYT,* July 3, 1913; "Woman Explains Basis of Suit Against Sulzer," *Washington (DC) Herald,* July 12, 1913.

BIBLIOGRAPHY

Algeo, Matthew. *Pedestrianism: When Watching People Walk Was America's Favorite Spectator Sport.* Chicago: Review Press, 2014.

Atkinson, Eleanor, Francis B. Atkinson, and Lewis A. Convis. *The World's Chronicle: A History of the World To-day for the Men and Women of To-morrow.* Vol. 4. N.p.: Little Chronicle Publishing Co., 1901. www.books.google.com.

Brandon, Craig. *Murder in the Adirondacks: "An American Tragedy" Revisited.* Utica, NY: North Country Books, 1986, with a 100th Anniversary edition in 2006.

Burrows, Edwin G., and Mike Wallace. *Gotham: A History of New York City to 1898.* New York: Oxford Univ. Press, 1999.

Chicago Daily News. Almanac and Year Book for 1902. Chicago: Daily News Co., 1903. www.books.google.com.

Collins, Paul. *The Murder of the Century: The Gilded Age Crime That Scandalized a City and Sparked the Tabloid Wars.* New York: Crown Publishers, 2011.

Friedman, Lawrence M., and William E. Havemann. "The Rise and Fall of the Unwritten Law: Sex, Patriarchy, and Vigilante Justice in the American Courts." *Buffalo Law Review* 61, no. 5 (2013): 997–1056.

Gilfoyle, Timothy J. *A Pickpocket's Tale: The Underworld of Nineteenth-Century New York.* New York: Norton, 2006.

Gross, Gerald, ed. *Masterpieces of Murder: An Edmund Pearson True Crime Reader.* Boston: Little, Brown, 1963.

Jones, Ann. *Women Who Kill.* New York: Holt, Rinehart, and Winston, 1980.

Kasson, John F. *Amusing the Million: Coney Island at the Turn of the Century.* New York: Hilland Wang, 1978.

Kemble, H. A., and William E. S. Fales. *Blue Pencil Magazine,* February 1900. www.books.google.com.

Livingston, James D. *Arsenic and Clam Chowder: Murder in Gilded Age New York.* Albany: State Univ. of New York Press, 2010.

McConnell, Virginia. *Sympathy for the Devil: The Emmanuel Baptist Murders of Old San Francisco.* Westport, CT: Praeger Publishers, 2001.

Morris, Lloyd. *Incredible New York: High Life and Low Life from 1850 to 1950.* Syracuse, NY: Syracuse Univ. Press, 1951.

Murphy, Cait. *Scoundrels in Law: The Trials of Howe & Hummel, Lawyers to the Gangsters, Cops, Starlets, and Rakes Who Made the Gilded Age.* New York: Harper-Collins, 2010.

Neal, Bill. *Sex, Murder, and the Unwritten Law: Courting Judicial Mayhem, Texas Style.* Lubbock: Texas Tech Univ. Press, 2009.

Norris, Frank. *McTeague: A Story of San Francisco.* New York: Signet Classics, 2003.

O'Connor, Richard. *Courtroom Warrior: The Combative Career of William Travers Jerome.* Boston: Little, Brown, 1963.

Rovere, Richard H. *Howe & Hummel: Their True and Scandalous History.* New York: Farrar, Straus and Giroux, 1974.

Scholl, B. Frank, PhG, MD., ed. *Library of Health: Complete Guide to Prevention and Cure of Disease.* Philadelphia: Historical Publishing, 1927.

Spellen, Suzanne. "Walkabout: Consumers Park Brewery, Part 2." July 10, 2012. www .brownstoner.com/history/walkabout-consumers-park-brewery-part-2/.

"A Tale of the Tombs." New York Correction History Society. http://www.correction history.org/html/chronicl/nydoc/html/histry3a.html.

Transcript of People of the State of New York against Edward H. Brooks and Florence W. Wildrick. Court of General Sessions of the County of New York, October 24, 1901. Case 1236. Criminal Trial Transcripts Collection, Special Collections, Lloyd Sealy Library, John Jay College.

Wagenknecht, Edward. *American Profile: 1900–1909.* Amherst: Univ. of Massachusetts Press, 1982.

Wahl, Jackie. "Murder in Jacques Canyon: Did the Battered Wife Kill Jim Bachus?" *The Golden Age, Journal of the Nez Perce County Historical Society* 14, no. 1 (1994): 15–18.

Wehrum, John E., Jr., and Owen C. Marx. "Palmigiano: The Constitutionality of Prison Mail Censorship." *Catholic University Law Review* 21, no. 1 (1971): 215–28. http:// scholarship.law.edu/lawreview/vol21/iss1/14.

West Point Association of Graduates. *The Register of Graduates & Former Cadets of the United States Military Academy.* West Point, NY: West Point, 2015.

Young, Greg, and Tom Meyers. *The Bowery Boys: Adventures in Old New York.* Berkeley, CA: Ulysses Press, 2016.

Zacks, Richard. *Island of Vice: Theodore Roosevelt's Doomed Quest to Clean Up Sin-Loving New York.* New York: Doubleday, 2010.

INDEX

Page numbers in italics refer to illustrations.